D0075840

RESILIENCE FOR TODAY

RESILIENCE FOR TODAY

Gaining Strength from Adversity

Edited by Edith Henderson Grotberg

Contemporary Psychology
Chris E. Stout, Series Editor

Westport, Connecticut
London

Library of Congress Cataloging-in-Publication Data

Resilience for today : gaining strength from adversity / edited by Edith Henderson Grotberg.

    p. cm.—(Contemporary psychology)

  Includes bibliographic references and index.

  ISBN 0–275–97984–9 (alk. paper)

  1. Resilience (Personality trait) I. Grotberg, Edith Henderson, 1928– II. Contemporary psychology (Praeger Publishers)

BF698.35.R47R47 2003

155.2'32—dc21   2003051057

British Library Cataloguing in Publication Data is available.

Library of Congress Catalog Card Number: 2003051057

ISBN: 0–275–97984–9

First published in 2003

Praeger Publishers, 88 Post Road West, Westport, CT 06881

An imprint of Greenwood Publishing Group, Inc.

www.praeger.com

Printed in the United States of America

∞™

The paper used in this book complies with the Permanent Paper Standard issued by the National Information Standards Organization (Z39.48–1984).

10 9 8 7 6 5 4 3 2 1

Contents

Series Foreword

As this new millennium dawns, humankind has evolved—some would argue has devolved—exhibiting new and old behaviors that fascinate, infuriate, delight, or fully perplex those of us seeking answers to the question, "Why?" In this series, experts from various disciplines peer through the lens of psychology telling us answers they see for questions of human behavior. Their topics may range from humanity's psychological ills—addictions, abuse, suicide, murder, and terrorism among them—to works focused on positive subjects including intelligence, creativity, athleticism, and resilience. Regardless of the topic, the goal of this series remains constant—to offer innovative ideas, provocative considerations, and useful beginnings to better understand human behavior.

Series Editor
Chris E. Stout, Psy.D., MBA
Northwestern University Medical School
Illinois Chief of Psychological Services

Advisory Board

Bruce E. Bonecutter, Ph.D.
University of Illinois at Chicago
Director, Behavioral Services,
  Elgin Community Mental
  Health Center

Joseph A. Flaherty, M.D.
University of Illinois College of
  Medicine and College of Public
  Health
Chief of Psychiatry, University of
  Illinois Hospital

Introduction: Resilience for Today

Edith Henderson Grotberg

There may be as many disasters today as ever. There may be as many tragedies, killings, riots, snipers, and criminals as ever. But today we learn about them, see them on television, read about them in papers and journals, and are bombarded with news of them. The result is that we experience more stress than ever before with a constant barrage of bad news. Even our private lives have lost much of their privacy as attempts to sell us products or protect us from harm increasingly invade our homes. Maybe there is some privacy in our cars, but that is mainly the privacy created by the car frame, not privacy from the stares or too-frequent unfriendly signals of other drivers. In short, we are living with more stress than is good for our sense of well-being.

We are not helpless, however. We have this human capacity to become resilient, which allows us to deal with the bombardment of events causing so much stress. And in dealing with these events we become stronger, more confident in our abilities, more sensitive to the stress others are experiencing, and even more able to bring about change to minimize or eradicate the sources of stress.

Today, more than ever, certainly as much as ever, we need to promote and use resilience in our daily life, our work life, our personal life, our social and political life, and our family life. In other words, resilience has application to any source of stress or to any experience perceived as an adversity. We are not implying that resilience protects us from these stresses, these risks, these dangers. That is not the role of resilience. We want protections, yes, but resilience involves not only supports, strengths, and skills, but actions to deal with the inevitable adversities we all face in life. To the extent we protect ourselves and each other, we do not need resilience. As a matter of fact, there is considerable concern today that we are overprotecting our children so that they do not become resilient, but rely on others to protect them from adversities. This book is written to provide information and ideas about the role of resilience in today's world. The world keeps changing and we can count on the flexibility of resilience to be effective in change.

Chapter 1, "What Is Resilience? How Do You Promote It? How Do You Use It?" contains the basic ABCs of resilience, and you will want to read it first as a foundation. The other chapters can be read in any order, because they are independent of each other in most ways. However, some are organized by the developmental stage of children and youth and from individual to family to school to community. The final two chapters are general in recognizing the role of resilience in dealing with a range of disasters and tragedies.

Edith Henderson Grotberg is the author of chapter 1. She has conducted international and national research on resilience, applying the findings to workshops, publications, and policy decisions. As editor of this book, she is delighted with the authors who bring a wide range of studies, knowledge, and experience into each chapter.

Chapter 2, "The Yin and Yang of Resilience," describes ways to gradually introduce adversities so that those becoming resilient can build up the skills and the inner strengths, drawing on the surrounding supports as one deals with structured adversities. Rhoda Baruch and Suzanne Stutman, always creative, have zeroed in on the stress and release that accompany dealing with adversities. They provide clear examples of promoting resilience in children and youth through controlled exposure to danger or adversity rather than protecting them from such exposure.

Chapter 3, "Enhancing Family Resilience: A Transgenerational Approach to Positive Change in Dysfunctional Families," presents important information on how to help dysfunctional families restore their ability to function effectively. The connection with resilience strengthens the families as they continue in their rebuilding of relations and are more effective in dealing with family issues and common adversities. Sandra Neil is a pioneer in the blending of resilience with the Satir approach to restoring family functioning.

Chapter 4, "Resilience in Families with Children Who Are Exceptional," examines how families meet the needs of their exceptional child while also sustaining the well-being of the family as a whole. The new emphasis on having families totally involved with the care of their exceptional children is a dramatic change from earlier recommendations to remove the children for the sake of the other members of the family. The stress on the family, then, becomes an important issue to consider in the promotion of resilience. Sharon Ramey, most sensitive to what these families face, has no trouble pointing out the limitations of many services. Stephanie DeLuca contributes stories from her clinical work, and Karen Echols provides information about the role of therapy in the promotion of resilience.

Chapter 5, "Resilience, the Fourth R: The Role of Schools in This Promotion," brings attention to the schools and their role in promoting resilience and preventing behaviors that threaten the well-being of children. Judy Papházy went directly into the schools, working with the administration, the teachers, and the children. This is no preplanned program that required faithful following; rather, it is an ongoing, dynamic process that involves the entire school. Integrating the promotion of resilience into the daily functioning of a school system is seen as more effective than a program that may be imposed and may end when the financial support ends. Resilience is not a separate phenomenon; it is an integral part of the school day. Her accomplishments in her work are dramatic and suggest imitation.

Chapter 6, "Resilience for Those Needing Health Care," focuses on children and youth who need long-term health care and the impact of that need on them and on their families. Bette Keltner describes the resilience already in these children and how health services can promote it in others. Her intent is to help these children and youth become increasingly independent, using their resilience to deal with their many adversities. The tendency to become dependent on others or for others to provide unneeded services is challenged by the effectiveness of promoting resilience to help these children and youth deal with the problems and adversities they face. Bette Keltner goes into the field to gather her information and insights and is a great advocate for children and youth. Leslie Walker, who works directly with youth needing long-term health care, provides clear examples of how resilience enhances their lives.

Chapter 7, "Resilience and Biculturalism: The Latino Experience in the United States," is a major foray into the world of the immigrant, especially immigrant Latino youth. The special problems immigrants face interlace with cultural clashes, discrimination, bullying, poverty, and a host of problems associated with the conditions on which entrance was obtained. Latino youth are caught in all of these issues. They have serious conflicts with their parents, because the youth want to function effectively in the new culture, whereas their parents want to maintain the values and customs of the Latino culture. If the youth reject their Latino culture, they experience unnecessary stress and conflict; but, as they see the strengths and resilience in their Latino culture as well as in their new culture, they become increasingly comfortable with biculturalism. Francisca Infante, an immigrant herself, is steeped in the issues needing to be dealt with and presents a powerful case for the role of resilience in that process. Her colleague, Alexandra Lamond, provides examples from her clinical work of the role of resilience in dealing with the adversities immigrant youth face.

Chapter 8, "Community Resilience: A Social Approach," presents a conceptual framework for recognizing a resilient community and does likewise for recognizing a community that is not resilient. The insights into what differentiates a community that recovers from a disaster and a community that does not recover are striking and creatively described by Elbio Nestor Suarez-Ojeda. He draws on his many official roles, obtaining information provided from others but also from personal experience. Lilian Autler, a researcher for community issues, did the translation from Spanish to English, and as a writer, she polished the chapter. It was a challenge to find a resilient community in the United States, but, one was found—Winchester, Virginia. Edith Henderson Grotberg had made presentations on resilience some months previously and recognized it as a resilience community. She received permission to interview various key members of the community, who provided information on what is involved in building a resilient community. The resilience was there even though the word was new to the community. There is a wonderful "Ah Hah!" reaction when people become aware of what they have been doing. It tends to reinforce the resilient behaviors already in place.

Chapter 9, "In the Wake of Disaster: Building the Resilience Initiative of APA's Public Education Campaign," describes a trajectory of dealing with the aftermath of disasters over the years and arriving at a critical point where the importance of resilience is highlighted. The American Psychological Association has always been concerned about the mental health of people, but one section is primarily concerned with disasters and their aftermath. Russ Newman, Executive Director for Professional Practice, has led the unit in its quest for finding ways to help people recover from disasters. He has succeeded mightily, learning that people do not just want to be able to cope with disaster, but were more interested in being resilient in the face of disaster—not just recovering from, but being prepared to deal with disaster. Luana Bossolo, Director, Public Relations & Special Projects for the unit, was especially effective in bringing staff together for sharing thoughts, for maintaining the continuity of their involvement, and for making her own contributions to the chapter.

Chapter 10, "Resilience and Tragedy," provides information on how people have overcome the effects of innumerable tragedies, becoming stronger, more determined, and more resilient as a result. There is no escaping adversities; they are ever there. But, again, we are not helpless. We have built into us the capacity to become resilient. The fact that many people do not become resilient is a tragedy. They see no end to suffering; they become depressed; they give up; they become aggressive; they become chronically ill. They fear life or are simply flattened by it. They tend to have children who seem equally defeated, unless they find an adult who is a role model for resilience. We are not resilient all the time. And it is more difficult to be resilient in unfamiliar situations. But if the foundation is there, if past experiences—yours and others'—are used as models, resilience can be mobilized to take on the new adversity.

CHAPTER 1

What Is Resilience?
How Do You Promote It?
How Do You Use It?

Edith Henderson Grotberg

Think of an experience you had that made you feel vulnerable, frightened, threatened, at risk of failure, health, or any experience that upset you.

What did you do?

How did you feel?

What did another or others do in response?

How did they feel?

How did things work out, or how are things now?

You may want to respond to these questions on a separate piece of paper and set it aside until you read the entire chapter or even the entire book. Then you will want to come back to it, decide which resilience factors you were using, what resilience behavior you engaged in, and how you would deal with the occurrence differently if it happened now.

What is resilience?

Resilience is the human capacity to deal with, overcome, learn from, or even be transformed by the inevitable adversities of life. No one escapes adversities. It is true that what is perceived as an adversity is very likely in the eye of the beholder. If, for example, a very close friend moves, you may well see this as an adversity. You relied on that friend to help you, to share thoughts and feelings, to help you resolve problems. You feel the loss and are sad. But her moving may be perceived by others as a good thing. They say you were too limited in your social connections and were too dependent on your friend. You needed to be free to make new social connections. And, as it turned out, they were right. You find new friends—more than one; you feel greater freedom of expression. But, having said that, there are some adversities, such as terrorism, that no one mislabels.

In studies here and around the world, people identified the adversities they faced (Grotberg, 1995, 2000). These adversities included those experienced within the family itself and those originating from outside the family. For clarity, they are listed below.

Adversities Experienced within the Family:
Death of a parent or grandparent; divorce or separation; illness of a parent or sibling; poverty; moving; accident causing personal injury; abuse, including sexual abuse; abandonment; suicide; remarriage, homelessness; poor health and hospitalization; fires causing personal injury; forced repatriation of family; disabled family member; parents' loss of job or income.

Adversities Experienced outside the Family:
Robberies; war; fire; earthquake; flood; car accident; adverse economic conditions; illegal refugee status; migrant status; property damage from storms, floods, cold; political detention; famine; abuse by a nonrelative; murders in the neighborhood; unstable government; drought.

Today we would certainly want to add terrorism, as well as drugs, violence, teen pregnancy, bullying, road rage, single-parent families living in poverty, discrimination, racism, and mental health problems. You probably have a list of your own to add. Making such a list would be a useful thing to do because identifying an adversity is usually a first step in learning how to deal with it. So, take a little time to think of adversities you are dealing with now. You might even think about past adversities and how you dealt with them. Write them down so you can come back to them later and see what other, perhaps more resilient, ways could have been used to deal with the adversity.

Now, if this chapter sounds to you like Resilience 101, you're probably right. My defense is that without knowing the basics of resilience, you will be handicapped when you want to promote resilience in yourself and in others, engage in resilience behavior, and assess the outcomes. As you become familiar with the concept of resilience, the tools of resilience, and resilience behavior, you are in a stronger position to benefit from the role resilience plays in dealing with adversities.

If resilience is a human capacity to deal with adversities, where does it come from? Is resilience a quality only a few lucky people have? It is true that about one-third of the people in different parts of the world consistently show resilience; that is, they deal with adversities, overcome them, and were strengthened or transformed by them (Grotberg, 1995, 2000)? Are they special? Is resilience limited to a few lucky ones? The answer is a resounding "No!" Everyone can become resilient. The challenge is to find ways to promote it in individuals, in families, and in communities.

Some of the early research on resilience provided characteristics or factors of resilience that helped identify what was useful and effective in dealing with adversities (Werner & Smith, 1982; Garmezy, 1974; Rutter, 1979). The research generated information that differentiated children who were doing very well, despite living in dysfunctional families with problems of mental illness, drugs, abuse, etc., from those children who were predictably damaged by such an environment. The differentiating characteristics or *factors*, the more commonly used term today, are many. It seemed useful, then, to organize the factors into external supports that promote resilience, inner strengths that develop over time and sustain those who are dealing with adversities, and interpersonal, problem-solving skills that deal with the actual adversity. I found it easier to grasp these factors by organizing them into I HAVE, I AM, and I CAN, as follows (Grotberg, 1995).

I HAVE (External Supports)
1. one or more persons within my family I can trust and who love me without reservation;
2. one or more persons outside my family I can trust without reservation;
3. limits to my behavior;
4. people who encourage me to be independent;
5. good role models;
6. access to health, education, and the social and security services I need; and
7. a stable family and community.

I AM (Inner Strengths)
1. a person most people like;
2. generally calm and good-natured;

3. an achiever who plans for the future;

4. a person who respects myself and others;

5. empathic and caring of others;

6. responsible for my own behavior and accepting of the consequences; and

7. a confident, optimistic, hopeful person, with faith.

I CAN (Interpersonal and Problem-Solving Skills)

1. generate new ideas or new ways to do things;

2. stay with a task until it is finished;

3. see the humor in life and use it to reduce tensions;

4. express thoughts and feelings in communication with others;

5. solve problems in various settings—academic, job-related, personal,
   and social;

6. manage my behavior—feelings, impulses, acting out; and

7. reach out for help when I need it.

These resilience factors can be promoted separately, and that is an important beginning point. However, when dealing with an adversity, the factors are always used in combinations, drawing from each category as needed. Most people already have some of these factors; they just don't have enough or don't know how to use them to deal with adversities. And some people are resilient in one situation and not in another. This difference usually occurs because they are resilient in more familiar, less-threatening situations, but are not resilient in new or dramatically different situations where they feel a loss of control over what is happening. They need help from others in the more threatening or unfamiliar situations. They need to learn to reach out for help.

Promoting Resilience in Children, Youth, and Adults

Resilience can be promoted at any age. And many parents and service providers are becoming more resilient as programs are developed for them and the children or clients they work with. Some of those programs are described by authors of other chapters in this book. However, promoting resilience in any age group is made easier if you think in terms of the building blocks of growth and development. These building blocks correspond to ages and stages of development common to all people and identify and set limits as to which resilience factors can be promoted at different ages. However, many of these building blocks are not well developed in adults, who need to revisit the developmental stages to see what is missing in their ability to deal with adversities.

The building blocks are trust, autonomy, initiative, industry, identity, intimacy, generativity, and integrity (Erikson, 1985). Looking back at the list of resilience factors given above, you can see that the building blocks are included, especially through *identity*. All of the resilience factors can be developed by the time the person reaches this stage of development, and then reinforced or strengthened after that. Generativity, for example, is reached when you can help others by community and/or political involvement, or by helping children and youth develop their skills and talents, or by working with vulnerable youth. In other words, you pass along the resilience factors to others.

It is important, however, to recognize that some resilience factors are more relevant to one stage of growth and development than to another stage. A young child does not need to be concerned about *industry* or *identity*, whereas a school-aged child or youth does. Expectations are different for different ages and developmental status—an obvious fact. So, it seems obvious, then, that the age of a child or youth or adult will indicate the resilience factors already promoted.

But, the truth is that many youth and adults have not been able to develop even the first resilience factor of the first developmental stage: *trust*. The starting point for promoting resilience, then, must be where the child, youth, or adult is according to their stage of development. For youth and adults it is also important to determine what resilience factors have already been developed, however. The youth, for example, may be able to solve academic problems, but not be able to resolve interpersonal problems. The first requires little trust in others; the second requires a lot of trust in others. The adult may be able to treat others with love and respect and empathy, but does not assume responsibility when it comes to meeting deadlines at work or acquiring the skills needed for new job demands.

Trust

Children and youth have difficulty becoming resilient unless they have help from adults. But they don't accept help from just any adult, only those whom they trust, respect, love, or with whom they feel bonded. From the beginning, trust is the key to promoting resilience and becomes the basis for promoting other resilience factors. When children and youth feel trusting, loving relationships, they are more ready to accept limits to their behavior and imitate role models (I HAVE); are more likely to become likable, empathic and caring, optimistic and hopeful (I AM); and can more easily engage in successful interpersonal relationships, solve problems in various settings, and reach out for help (I CAN). They not only trust others, they learn to trust themselves, knowing those they trust will not allow harm to come their way.

Adults who do not trust others often learn to control others or rely only on themselves: if you want something done right, do it yourself, would be a plausible mantra. These adults separate themselves from others, go their own way, and often are highly successful in their chosen work. However, they avoid getting involved emotionally and reject efforts of others to develop any meaningful relationships.

Not only do individuals need to learn to trust others, but also to trust themselves. When they do not trust themselves, they may well become dependent on others, feeling certain others are better than they are, know more, and are the most likely to protect them.

An entry point for those who wish to promote resilience in children and youth is clearly by building a trusting relationship with them. Are you reliable? Are you honest? Do you respect the information they provide you? Will you help them? Children and youth who have been neglected, exploited, or abused do not trust adults, and overcoming that distrust is a challenge to anyone offering help.

For those who wish to promote resilience in adults, they will quickly learn that there is more skepticism in adults; the defenses are higher and stronger in resisting trust. What they can learn is to select a few people they are willing to take the risk of trusting and see what happens. They don't have to share their more personal information just yet, but they can test the person they are taking a chance on and decide when to share more. You can suggest this procedure or use it yourself if you are having trouble trusting. The joys of trusting relationships are worth the risks.

Autonomy

Autonomy is defined as independence and freedom—the ability to make your own decisions. It begins to develop around age two, a time when you realize you are separate from those around you and that people respond to what you say or do. It is this sense of separation that introduces awareness that there are consequences to your behavior; you learn about right and wrong; you feel a sense of guilt when you harm someone or disappoint someone.

Autonomy is basic in promoting new resilience factors and reinforcing some already promoted. As children and youth become autonomous, willingness to accept limits of behavior is reinforced (I HAVE); respect for themselves and others is promoted, empathy and caring are reinforced, and being responsible for their own behavior is promoted (I AM); managing feelings and impulses is promoted (I CAN). The autonomy and trust resilience factors can be integrated so they become part of the overall promotion of your resilience.

Many children and youth do not become autonomous. Sometimes they live in homes where fear of punishment and physical harm make any expression of autonomy dangerous. Sometimes they made mistakes that brought responses of such derision and ridicule they wouldn't try again. Many adults had these same experiences as children and never tried to become autonomous, always deferring to someone else, someone more powerful, someone more assertive. Self-confidence is shattered. These people are often easy prey for leaders who have unhealthy goals in mind.

An entry point for promoting resilience in these children, youth, and adults is to make clear to them it's okay to make mistakes; they can learn from their mistakes. You can tell or have them read stories of the failures everyone experiences. Many famous people have powerful stories to tell about their failures before becoming successful. You can assure them that mistakes are nothing to be ashamed of, and you can encourage them to take the risk of making mistakes. You will be there whether they fail or succeed.

Initiative

Initiative is the ability and willingness to take action. It begins developing around the ages of four and five, when you started to think and do things on your own. You probably started all kinds of projects or activities that you did not or could not finish. But whether or not you succeeded was not the point. It was the willingness to try that was important to building initiative. Creative ideas in art and science, new inventions, and problem solving in every area of life require initiative. Creativity asserts itself very early in life.

Initiative is needed to promote related resilience factors. When initiative is promoted, it reinforces trusting relationships, recognizing limits of behavior, and accepting encouragement to be autonomous (I HAVE); it reinforces generally being calm and good-natured, empathic and caring, responsible for one's behavior, and being an optimistic, confident, hopeful person (I AM); and it contributes further to generating new ideas or ways to do things, expressing thoughts and feelings, problem solving, managing feelings and behavior, and reaching out for help (I CAN). The number of resilience factors you can draw on has grown.

Many children and youth do not develop initiative. They are often scolded for making a mess with their unfinished projects. They are made to feel guilty for bothering people. They experienced too much rejection from those they asked for help, and thus they felt unworthy of help. No one cared; no one wanted to help. Eventually, they stopped wanting or trying to take the initiative in anything. Adults who do not take the initiative have the same fear of making mistakes. A researcher is unsure of her writing skills, so she finds excuses for not meeting deadlines rather than taking the initiative in seeking help. A police officer sees the need to make changes in the way safety is being carried out, but will not take the initiative in sharing this at meetings, fearing he or she is wrong and might even be ridiculed.

An entry point for promoting initiative is to encourage children and youth to decide what they would enjoy doing. You can talk about ways they can make plans, help them identify the problems or obstacles they may encounter; help them identify alternative ways to put their plan into action; help them take the risk of action, assessing outcomes, and making any needed changes. You will be there for them and help them overcome obstacles and learn from their mistakes as well as their successes. You can counsel adults, of course, with more appropriate language, but with the same intent. Help them see that failure can be a great learning experience. It opens them up to new ideas of how to be successful.

Industry

Industry is defined as working diligently at a task and is usually developed during the school years while mastering skills, both academic and social. Being successful is very important for academic achievement, interpersonal relationships, and self-image. You want to be seen as a competent person by your teachers, to be accepted as a friendly person in the social scene, and to feel a sense of pride in yourself. The same desires are in adults, but instead of the teacher, it is the boss or colleagues who must see you as competent, friendly, and showing self-respect. Adults are fully capable of promoting their own resilience, but they need help from at least one person to give them the necessary resilience tools to succeed.

Industry is a powerful building block and is enhanced through its connection with other resilience factors. From the I HAVE category, good role models and encouragement to be independent are important. From the I AM category, being an achiever who plans for the future and who is responsible for his or her own behavior are helpful. From the I CAN category, staying with a task until it is finished, problem solving, and reaching out for help when needed, reinforce or add to the resilience factors that are being promoted. What is different, however, is learning how to differentiate not only what resilience factors to use in any given situation, but also how to use them. For example, you would use different factors in school from those you use at home or, perhaps more accurately, use the factors in different ways. You may, for example, show empathy at home by hugging your brother or sister or mother, but you can't do that when you show empathy for a teacher. You may use argument with family members as decisions are being made, but you are cautious about arguing with the principal. You can share your fears and anxieties in the home setting, but you don't like to show these feelings while in public. You may show some anger at home, and it is tolerated, but if you show anger in the work setting, you may find yourself looking for another job.

Many children and youth do not develop industry. They were unable to succeed in mastering the academic and social skills needed, and they developed feelings of inferiority. They become extremely sensitive about their limitations. They may well have been teased, bullied, or excluded from a group because of their failures. Their feelings of failure and frustration may cause them to drop out of school or become troublemakers. Adults who have not developed this stage of industry are often those who dropped out of school because of failure there, including social failure. They were often bullied or rejected as geeks. They lost their desire to master skills, were reluctant to deal with any more failures, and decided to get away. Many adults who had such experiences have difficulty opening themselves to similar, more sophisticated ways of being rejected.

An entry point for promoting industry is to focus on mastering interpersonal and problem-solving skills by drawing on earlier building blocks. For example, you can encourage people to draw on their autonomy and independence to help them do their work, complete tasks, ask questions when something is not clear, assume responsibility for their work, and feel proud of their achievements. You can talk with them about developing cooperation by looking around them to see with whom they can work comfortably. Cooperation also suggests they can resolve conflicts in decision making and in taking actions. You can point out that problem-solving skills include being willing to take the initiative, but also being able to deal with inevitable conflicts. You can help them improve their communication skills, practice being assertive, and learn to listen. Companies often have specialists come in to teach employees many of these skills—both technical and interpersonal.

Identity

Identity is developed during the teen years. The major questions you usually ask during these years are as follows:

1. Who am I?
2. How do I compare with other teens?
3. What are my new relationships with my parents (and other authority figures)?
4. What have I accomplished?
5. Where do I go from here?

When you answer these questions to your satisfaction, you show skills in monitoring your own behavior, comparing your behavior with accepted standards, being helpful and supportive of others, using your fantasy and initiative to make dreams come true, and recognizing the role of idealism in thinking and planning. In other words, not only should all your resilience factors be developed, you should be enjoying them.

Many teens cannot answer these questions to their satisfaction and become self-doubting and unsure of who they really are. They feel that no one understands them, including themselves. They may be totally confused about how to behave and about their role in life. These feelings of insecurity may bring on frustration, anger, and a sense of hopelessness. And, increasingly, many of these teens become aggressive or, indeed, depressed. Many adults continue to have these same problems and spend countless hours and large amounts of money trying to find out who they are. Perhaps they need to realize they are constantly changing as a result of experiences, new insights, and new adversities.

The building block of identity completes the five basic building blocks of resilience. It incorporates the resilience factors important to each stage of development, and it integrates all the resilience factors for use in dealing with the adversities of life.

An entry point for promoting identity can be to help the development of good interpersonal and problem-solving skills. You can do this by discussing the interpersonal skills individuals have and those they need. Social skills include making friends who challenge them in constructive ways, learning how to listen, and learning how to express anger, disappointment, disagreement, and empathy. You may have to start with a vocabulary for emotions. Too few teens or, in fact, adults can label feelings they have or tell someone else exactly how they feel. Some don't know how to be a good friend, and they need help in what is involved—loyalty, sharing, helping, trusting.

Many teens need help in coming to terms with their tendency to get involved in overly stimulating activities. Most teens like excitement, new experiences, and risk-taking behavior. However, it can become self-destructive, and you need to help them understand the potential dangers. You can suggest that they seek out friends to engage in activities that are exciting and fun, but not self-destructive. These friendships can help them avoid boredom while improving their social skills. Adults who are not sure of who they are or enjoy remaining "teenagers" continue to engage in risky behavior.

You can help teens maintain family ties, but with some changes in the relationships. You can talk with them about their need for more privacy, their desire to have their ideas taken more seriously, and their desire to help negotiate some of the rules of behavior. Help them find ways to discuss these new needs with their families. You can use these guidelines for promoting resilience in teens, and even suggest the guidelines to parents:

1. Balance autonomy with available, but not imposed, help.
2. Modulate consequences for mistakes with love and empathy so that the youth can fail without feeling too much stress or fear of loss of approval and love.
3. Communicate about and negotiate some limits to growing independence; discuss new expectations and new challenges.
4. Encourage youth to accept responsibility for consequences of behavior, while communicating confidence and optimism about the hoped for and desired outcome.
5. Encourage and model flexibility in selecting different resilience factors as an adverse situation changes; e.g., seek help instead of continuing alone in a very difficult situation. Show empathy instead of continuing with anger and fear. Share feelings with a friend instead of continuing to suffer alone.

A summary of suggestions for promoting resilience in youth include the following:

1. Build trust.
2. Focus on the individual, not the problem.
3. Keep the accent on the positive.
4. Set high expectations and provide the support youth need to meet them.

Put resilience to the test by doing the following:

1. Provide opportunities for meaningful work and community involvement.
2. Pull in the parents.
3. Create a sense of community.

You can also help both teens and adults work on long-range planning. They need to plan not only for tomorrow, but for the long term. You can ask them to consider their options and identify who could help them with their long-range planning. Encourage them to antic-ipate the adversities they will probably face—lack of money, not meeting qualifications, having the wrong courses for certain subjects they want to take—and adjust their plans to address those adversi-ties. Adults at similar points in their lives can benefit from similar kinds of help.

The temperament of each person determines, to some extent, which resilience factors are most comfortably used, which are diffi-cult to promote, and what actions are taken. Temperament is basi-cally the speed with which a person reacts to stimulus. In other words, do you respond very quickly, almost without thinking, when something happens? Or do you respond very slowly, not easily being moved to action? The difference is important, because if you react quickly, you will need to promote setting limits and managing your own behavior with greater vigilance than the person who is very slow to react and, indeed, needs to learn to react more quickly, especially in a crisis situation. Your temperament is part of you and will not change. However, you can learn to recognize that you tend to react too quickly and need to learn how to manage your responses so you don't act on them prematurely. If you are slow to react, you may want to practice ways to respond to threatening sit-uations so that you are not overpowered by the speed of what is happening.

Promoting Your Own Resilience

Enough about helping others become resilient! Recall the expression, "Look at the beam in your own eye before you focus on the mote in someone else's eye." For resilience, this means before you take on promoting resilience in others, you need to look at your own resilience factors: Which resilience factors do you already have, which ones are not consistent with your temperament or personality, and which ones need to be promoted? A unique feature of resilience is that you can promote the factors independently of experiences of adversity. You can even engage in a game of "what if?" This means you can pretend an adversity or tragedy has occurred, and you can imagine what you would do to deal with it and which resilience factors you would use. Making sure you are familiar with the factors and getting them ready for use gives you an advantage when the inevitable adversities occur. The following sections provide some suggestions for specific ways you can promote each factor in yourself.

I HAVE One or More People I Can Trust

There is someone in my family I know I can turn to and trust during adversity. But I will not take that person for granted. I will keep the relationship fresh and reinforce it by spending time with that person. I will also begin thinking about someone else in the family with whom I can build a trusting relationship, because the one I trust most now may move, become ill, or grow too old to help me. Who else can fill the bill?

Who do I now have outside the family I can trust completely? Do they live close by? Are they available to talk to and share thoughts and feelings with? Can they give me the support I need in most situations or only in some? Who else can I build such a trusting relationship with, and how will I go about building it? I have to give trust in order to receive it. I'll take the risk and begin some casual conversation with the person I've selected, and see how the person responds. If the response is friendly enough to talk about something more personal, I'll suggest lunch or playing a game together. I'll try telling the person something even more personal and ask that it not be repeated so I can see if my confidence is respected. I find I can usually trust people who do what they say they will do, keeping their word.

However, I also need to be sure I trust myself to deal with adversities. If I am afraid to take any risks for fear of failure or making a fool of myself, I need to practice taking small risks where the consequences are not damaging. Then, I need to practice taking larger risks, having some safety net, like a friend, nearby.

I HAVE Limits to My Behavior

Do I know how far I can go in asking for or expecting help from someone? Do I know how far I can go in becoming dependent on someone else to deal with the experiences of adversity I have? I may need to practice thinking about and setting limits for my own behavior as I seek supports. To use rules effectively in experiences of adversity, I'll need to think about their value and their limits. Breaking rules can often lead to unwanted outcomes. I'll use my intelligence to decide what the rules are for and what and how I can use them—or, at least, respect them—as I express my freedom. Sometimes rules are unreasonable and arbitrarily set, and challenging them may be necessary as I deal with an adversity.

I HAVE People Who Encourage Me to Be Independent

Do the people I look to for support do things for me, or do they encourage me to try to solve my problems myself? I must not become overly dependent on others, so I need to practice thinking through how far I can take care of things myself. Then I can decide how much support I need. Am I able to tell by people's reactions—body language, tone of voice, and behavior—whether or not I am depending too much on them to deal with adversities? If someone expects more independence from me than I can handle, I need to find the words to let them know I need help.

I HAVE Good Role Models

Are the role models I am using still the ones I want or need? Do they guide me as I get older and have new or different kinds of experiences of adversity? Where do I find new role models? In the news? In books? On screen? In history? Among my friends? Can a relative be a role model? Perhaps I should read about how someone else behaved in the adverse situation I am now in. That, plus talking to someone I respect as a role model, should be helpful as I deal with my own adversity.

I HAVE Access to Health, Education, and the Social and Security Services I Need

Are the health services I need, and will need, available? Perhaps I should find some additional resources. Is my favorite doctor moving or retiring? Do I feel as safe as I used to, or do I need to find some greater security for my house and workplace? Do I know where to find the stores, libraries, educational centers, or other services I need or will need? For example, do I know how to select a doctor? Can I find a police officer, a firefighter, an emergency vehicle, and a hospital, even when I am under severe stress? If I am injured or ill, do I know how to describe what happened, how it happened, and what I think I need? I will take an inventory and plan ahead as my needs change. I will build a directory of services I think I may need and practice what I will say when I need them.

I HAVE a Stable Family and Community

As people move, as children leave, as relatives die, I can build new relationships so that I create a family. Because I am part of a community, I can become more active in it, establishing relationships and contributing to its growth and stability. Can I donate my time at a youth center? Could the hospital use my services? Can I help tutor students and be a mentor? I should contribute to the community so that I can help not only when things are safe, but more so, when the community faces adversities.

I AM a Person Most People Like

Am I friendly enough? Do I make new friends easily? Do I show my acceptance of people I meet? Do I need to change any of the ways I communicate my liking of others? To practice, I will smile at people I work with and give a greeting, praise someone I interact with when they do a good job, and bring some humor to the lunch table or to a working group. Not only does this kind of likable behavior make everyone feel better, it is a pretty good guarantee that people are more willing to help in times of adversity!

I AM Generally Calm and Good-Natured

Has my temperament changed a bit without my noticing? Am I more irritable than I used to be? Am I less patient with people? Can I find better ways to protect myself from being upset with others? To practice, I will calm down before I go into a meeting or some other social or work setting where tensions may be high. And I will try to create an atmosphere of calmness in a stressful situation. I know that I have trouble dealing with adversities when I am short-tempered or tend to get angry easily. People may actually turn away from me when I need help. I can also think better when I am calmer.

I AM an Achiever Who Plans for the Future

Do I think in terms of the future? Do I still make good plans that are consistent with where I want to be in the future? When thinking about the future, I should think about the kinds of adversities I may face. If money dries up, do I have a substitute plan? If my house burns down, do I have someplace else to go? If I am in an accident, do I know what to do? The future planned for is not just setting goals, it is also being prepared to deal with adversities that may interfere with achieving those goals.

I AM a Person Who Respects Myself and Others

When I respect myself, I do not allow people to take advantage of me or humiliate me without a clear protest on my part and a clarification of what I expect in terms of respect. If I am mistreated physically or emotionally by someone, as in an act of violence, I need to remember that no matter what happens, I will respect myself. No one will take my self-respect away from me. I also need to respect others, even those who do terrible things and are the cause of great adversities. I know that is not easy, especially if they have done harm to me or to someone I love. I need to remember each human being has rights if for nothing more than humane treatment when captured or apprehended.

I AM Empathic and Caring of Others

Do I show that I empathize with a person's suffering and pain? Do I do nice things for people to show I care? Do I give them the help they need and express my concern? Am I, in short, a compassionate person? If I have trouble in these areas, I should practice by first finding empathic people in books or movies and thinking about the ways in which they show empathy. Then I can emulate them, in small ways at first, and gauge the response I receive.

I AM Responsible for My Own Behavior and Accept the Consequences

Do I find it hard to assume responsibility and easier to blame someone else? What have I done lately for which I was at fault but did not assume the responsibility? Do I need to reexamine my behavior more carefully so that I make more accurate assessments of responsibility? I may find it difficult to admit my responsibility, but that is better than having people lose trust and confidence in me because I am, in fact, irresponsible. In times of adversity, I especially need to be responsible for what I do, just as I trust other people will be responsible for what they do.

I AM a Confident, Optimistic, Hopeful Person

Do I still feel that things will work out all right if I do my best to deal with them? Do I visualize positive outcomes? Even when situations are bleak, do I still have the faith that there will be a resolution I can live with? I know that being optimistic and hopeful make chances of dealing successfully with an adversity much more likely. Can I renew my faith by participating more often in the things I believe in (prayer, church services, spiritual retreats)?

I CAN Generate New Ideas or New Ways to Do Things

Do I still get pleasure out of suggesting new ways to do things and solve problems? Am I willing to take risks by testing some new ideas? Do I need to reexamine how much I use the same methods for problem solving—do I tend to go to the same people or look for the same solutions? Perhaps I should read more books in areas of interest to me and expand my knowledge and thinking about what needs to be done in a subject that interests me. I know that being creative and coming up with new ways to think can help when dealing with adversities, many of which tend to have many surprises.

I CAN Stay with a Task until It Is Finished

Do I still have persistence, or do I give up more quickly than I used to? Perhaps I should practice making a commitment to a project and following it through to the end so that I can remember how good that makes me feel. Persistence in dealing with an adversity is certainly necessary if I am going to overcome it.

I CAN See the Humor in Life and Use It to Reduce Tensions

Do I see the humor in events around me? Do I share jokes and make people laugh? Nothing breaks tensions like humor, and when I am dealing with an adversity that involves more than me, I find humor frees energy to deal with the adversity. When a child who was very tense with anger was told a joke, she said, "Don't make me laugh; I want to stay mad!" I should find jokes to use when adversities require those of us dealing with them to lighten up.

I CAN Express Thoughts and Feelings in Communication with Others

Am I able to express my thoughts and feelings without too much embarrassment or hesitation? Do I need to enlarge my vocabulary for describing emotions? Can I pick up the emotional tone of someone I am listening to? Can I help the person clarify his or her thoughts and feelings during the conversation? I will practice what I am going to say to someone who has upset me so that I am calm and have the right words. I can build a vocabulary of words that describe my feelings so that when I express them to someone, they really convey what I am feeling. These interpersonal skills are important to daily life and critical during and after an experience of adversity. Such sharing helps restore a sense of well-being.

I CAN Solve Problems in Various Settings

Am I skilled at helping others solve their problems, without intruding on their privacy? Can I solve my own problems? Are there some skills I am lacking? Do I need to learn some new techniques? Am I good at resolving interpersonal conflicts? What are some of the latest techniques being used? Am I up-to-date? It would help if I practiced dealing with real or imaginary adversities.

I CAN Manage My Behavior

What techniques am I using to manage my feelings? Do I rely on control or even repression of my feelings? Am I able to manage my feelings without acting out? What helps me express my thoughts and feelings without doing something impulsive and dangerous? How do I slow my reactions down? Perhaps I can practice counting to 10 before acting on a feeling or practice writing down all my feelings before I confront somebody about something I'm angry about. Do I need to practice reading body language? Can I tell by facial expressions and other body movements what mood a person is in? Am I in the habit of using it as a gauge to know when to approach people and when to leave them alone? I will think about real or imagined adversities and decide how I would behave for the best results.

I CAN Reach Out for Help When I Need It

Can I ask for help without feeling as though I am weak? Can I practice by asking for help with minor things (moving furniture or planning and cooking a dinner party) and gauging people's reactions until I can predict how they'll respond? If one attempt to reach out doesn't work, have I thought of other approaches? Have I tried using the phone book, calling someone for information, or asking someone who had a similar adversity? I may be taking a risk by reaching out for help, but they can really only say yes or no. What's so bad about that? If the answer is no, then go on to someone or some place else. Big deal.

Resilience in Action

Resilience becomes active when adversity is experienced and needs to be dealt with. The sequence for responding to potential adversity is prepare for, live through, and learn from. However, many adversities come unexpectedly, and there is no time to prepare for them. In fact, an adversity such as a flood or a tornado may have to be dealt with as it is occurring, and the focus will be to do whatever can be done to minimize damage.

Preparing for Adversity

If you have time to prepare for the adversity, you will want to ask these questions.

1. What is going to happen? Describe on paper or in your mind exactly what the adversity consists of or looks like. You'll be doing a certain amount of guess-work here, but talking to other people who have been through such an adversity is very helpful.

2. Who will be affected by the upcoming adversity and how? If more than one person is involved, the views of each are important to incorporate in your description. Will more than one person be affected? Will someone you love be affected? Few adversities are limited to one person or even to one place. They tend to impact many people and places.

3. What are the obstacles that need to be overcome to deal with the upcoming adversity? This will require some imagination. You and others will need to think through various scenarios, suggest decisions that might be made in response, and then play those decisions out in your minds. You can write down the possible consequences of each decision.

4. Who needs to know what? Do you need to consider reaching out for help at this point? Do you need to alert other members of the family, the school, or the community about the upcoming adversity?

5. Who can provide help? A critical part of dealing with an adversity is in the I HAVE resilience factor. During your preparation phase,

it is very important to know what supports are available to you and to others who will be affected.

6. What inner strengths do you and others need to draw on as the adversity is faced? The I AM resilience factors are the ones that provide confidence and a sense of responsibility for how the adversity will be handled. It is helpful to recognize in the other people involved what their inner strengths are that will help everyone get through the experience. If you don't know what their strengths are, ask them.

7. What skills do you and others need to use? The I CAN resilience factors provide actual how-to skills. When more than one person is involved in the upcoming adversity, you'll want to determine the problem-solving and interpersonal skills of each person. Again, ask them what they see as their strengths in these how-to skills.

8. What dynamics of resilience factors will be useful in dealing with the adversity? Draw resilience factors from I HAVE, I AM, and I CAN categories because resilience behavior always involves some factors from each category. The dynamic interaction of resilience factors in resilience behavior must be flexible enough to change as the adversity changes over time.

Living through Adversity

A major problem of living through adversity is that it begins to have a life of its own. You may increasingly find yourself reacting to what is happening rather than being proactive, that is, trying to have some degree of control over what is happening. You will need to become a monitor of the process as you live through the experience. Here are some questions you can ask that will help keep you focused as you monitor what is happening:

1. Where are things today? Do an assessment of the status of the adversity. Is any part of it over? Is something new emerging? What can you forget about now in order to focus on some new part of the adversity?

2. How are the people involved handling the situation? Who needs to be comforted? Who needs to be encouraged to believe you will all get through the experience? Does anyone need to calm down and rethink what is happening? Who needs to reassess what is happening, what they can do, and what can be expected to happen as a result?

3. What new actions need to be planned and taken? Does someone else need to be notified? Do some new plans need to be made? Can

anything be done to help break the tension you are under? The major advantage of being in the adversity is that usually you must do something . . . and action uses up some of that anxiety energy so you aren't quite so stressed. Taking action also helps keep you from feeling completely helpless—a feeling that can be damaging to your sense of who you are. A challenge to your belief that you are a capable person threatens you at a very fundamental level. Use that as a motivation to do something.

4. What resilience factors will you need to draw on as you live through the adversity? Will the supports you need change as the adversity continues? What are they? Who are they? Where are they? (I HAVE factors.) What is going on inside you as this adversity continues? Do you still have confidence that you can handle this? Do you find you can show empathy and caring as the situation seems to get worse? Do you show respect for yourself and others when you encounter someone who should but does not help you? Are you pleasant when you ask for help or point out something that is terribly wrong and needs correction? (I AM factors.) Can you share your feelings as this experience continues so that you do not bottle them up too much? Can you ask for help without feeling humiliated? Can you process all the information you have as you live through the adversity so that the problem can be resolved? (I CAN factors.)

Learning from Adversity

You will not want to underestimate the role of hindsight in adversities. You learn from your mistakes as well as from your successes. Here are some questions that can guide your thinking about what you learned.

1. What did you learn about the resilience factors? Are you using them for the best results?

2. What did you learn about your friends? Did you seek their help and were they there for you?

3. What did you learn about support services? Did you know where to go to get the services you needed?

4. What did you learn about yourself? Are you stronger, more confident, a better person than before the adversity? Do you have some new insights about yourself, your emotions, and your interpersonal relationships?

As you think about past experiences of adversity you dealt with, you might find it useful to recall them in terms of preparing for, living through, and learning from them. Having a clear process of thinking can provide a greater sense of control and empowerment.

Entry Points for Promoting Resilience

You are certainly able to promote resilience in yourself or in others by taking each resilience factor separately, using them in dynamic interaction, and assessing the results in terms of how successful you were in dealing with the adversity. That process is effective and increasingly becomes automatic in response to adversities.

But you can promote resilience in yourself or in others if you can identify an entry point at which to begin the process. That point might well be when you see some behavior or engage in some behavior yourself that seems out of control and destructive. That point might be when you see acts of violence. Such acts show lack of the resilience factor I CAN manage my behavior—feelings, impulses, acting out—and the resilience factor I AM a person who respects myself and others.

One school system in a neighborhood with many dysfunctional families, a lot of poverty, crime, and drive-by shootings, wanted to help the children in middle school have the support of the school to help them develop their inner strength, acquire skills in problem solving, and interpersonal relationships, so that they could deal more positively with the environment they lived in. The entry point chosen was the emotion anger.

The process for accomplishing this was by

1. accepting an invitation from the school's guidance counselor,
2. presenting the RETHINK program to the entire staff,
3. conducting a RETHINK class for faculty interested in bringing these skills and concepts to the children in their classes,
4. supporting staff efforts informally,
5. maintaining a regular presence at the school,
6. reaching out to parents,
7. reaching out directly to the children, and
8. teaching the RETHINK skills—extending this learning so older students can provide service to younger children.

Anger is an important emotion because it is a red light telling you something needs to be changed. You are angry when people take advantage of you, frighten you, threaten you, cheat you, disrespect you, engage in acts of violence against you—you get the idea. You have every right to feel anger; it is what you do with it that becomes critical to resilient, empowering outcomes or to destructive outcomes. And too many of the children in this school system were angry and were acting out by bullying, fighting, stealing, skipping school, failing, or joining gangs. They knew too much about violence.

The leader of the program to learn to deal with anger in more constructive, effective ways is Paula Mintzies, Ph.D., who gave permission to share some of the program information. She introduced the program, RETHINK (IMHI, 1991), which was developed to deal with anger, using an act for each letter that added up to dealing with someone who makes you angry or who is angry with you. Briefly, *R* stands for *recognizing* you are angry; *E* stands for *empathy* for someone who is angry with you or with whom you are angry; *T* stands for *thinking* of another way to assess what has happened, which may not, in fact, induce an angry response; *H* stands for *hear* what the person you are angry with or who is angry with you is saying, so you know what is going on to elicit the anger; *I* stands for making *statements* of your feelings and how you see the problem and *integrating* respect with your feelings of anger as you deal with it; *N* stands for *notice* what calms you down and taking that action, as well as what calms the other person or persons down; and *K* stands for *keep* the focus on the immediate situation of anger without bringing up all the old grievances.

The program continued for one school year, 2001–2002, with sixth graders meeting with Dr. Mintzies once a week. At the end of the year, participants were asked to write about how they used the RETHINK skills in dealing with events rousing anger in themselves or rousing anger in someone else. Here are three reports from students, two from girls and one from a boy:

Girl's Report:
I think it is important to use the skills of recognizing your anger because if you don't realize that you have any anger, then it becomes a bigger problem. I think it is important that we use the skills of RETHINK because it can really help you. It also teaches you a couple of things. Here is an example: When I didn't come to school for a couple of days, my best friend was upset that I was not in school. I called her many times, but she didn't return any of my calls. I felt she was neglecting me.

Then I talked to myself and tried to figure out if she was mad or maybe she was busy. Then I decided to stop calling and wait till she returned my calls. She finally returned my calls and we finally talked. Then we found out, it was just a misunderstanding! We became best friends again.

The lesson I learned is: Never give up because sometimes it may just be a misunderstanding.

Boy's Report

The skill of Thinking is an important skill. When you think, it can help tell you what not to say in a bad situation, such as when there is a threat. Thinking can help you keep out of trouble. Thinking is also important because it helps you think of ways to prevent a bad situation from happening again. When you are in a bad situation and you really are thinking, you think of the consequences of the situation.

The skill of thinking also helps when you are in school taking a test. You have to believe that you can pass the test. When you think of the negatives such as "I can't take this test—I am not going to pass anyway," that is not thinking positively. This is why I think the skill of thinking is important.

The information and the skills that we are learning are helping me manage my anger because I use it when I am at home, school, in the public. It has been helping me not get into trouble.

I think it is important to learn these skills because it keeps us out of trouble, and it will help you when you are in the real world. It will help our world become a better place in the future.

Girl's Report

I think it is important to use the RETHINK skills, like noticing, and thinking when I am feeling angry. Because I might try to take my angry feelings out on someone else and get angry with them when my problem is not even involving them. I can get angry too fast. I have learned that I have to stay in a nice silent place and calm down and then begin to think about the situation. After I am calm I can ask myself if I was right or wrong and RETHINK! Then I can apologize to who ever I was mad at and who ever it was I might have taken out my angry feelings on.

I think RETHINK will help other students my age, younger students and even students who are older than me. I think that most people keep angry feelings inside them, about something that may have happened in the past, present, or something that will happen in the future. If they just recognize that you shouldn't keep so much anger inside, then they will not have as many things on their mind. Every time they do that, they will be able to start over again!

One incredible outcome of this program was the sixth grade students teaching these anger management skills to kindergartners, using all the right language!

Job Stress

The United States has the distinction of having a workforce with the highest rate of production and the most time spent on the job. It should not be surprising that job stress is a major problem to at least one-fourth of employees in the country. More than half believe they experience more job stress now than was experienced a generation ago. Health complaints are more strongly associated with stress at work than with financial or family problems. The adversities faced on the job include: heavy workload and/or long hours; infrequent breaks; routine tasks with little inherent meaning; non-use of skills; little sense of control; lack of participation in decision making; poor communication, lack of family-friendly policies; poor social environment and lack of support or help from coworkers and supervisors; conflicting or uncertain job expectations or too much responsibility; job insecurity and lack of opportunity for growth, advancement, or promotion; and unpleasant or dangerous physical conditions, difficulty in concentrating, short temper, upset stomach, job dissatisfaction, and low morale.

Too much stress over time can lead to serious health problems, including cardiovascular disease and psychological disorders, such as depression and burnout. Some studies report evidence of a relationship between high levels of work-related stress to suicide, cancer, ulcers, and impaired immune function. Workers under stress account for about 50 percent more in expenditures for health care than do others.

Career Resilience

Career resilience is a relatively new concept that has emerged from the growing interest in employee welfare as well as a recognition of the dramatic changes in career requirements. Career resilience incorporates the resilience factors and behaviors: the availability of resources (I HAVE); the inner strengths of autonomy, initiative, optimism, and persistence (I AM); and the problem-solving and interpersonal skills (I CAN) needed to address career-related issues. When you use these resilience factors in relation to your work, you are better able to deal with adversities that will inevitably emerge. You are not in a dependent position, relying on others to deal with your adversities. You are part of the solution.

Career resilience can benefit from taking three steps: self-assessment, the acquisition of competitive skills, and being informed about job openings.

Step One

Do a self-assessment to determine your skills, interests, values, and temperament. If you know, for example, you have a tendency to become impatient with unhappy, critical customers, you certainly do not want to put your energies into a job that requires you to deal with them. If you have certain ethical or moral beliefs that you feel strongly about, you know you don't want to work for a company that doesn't share those beliefs. If learning new things is important to you, you don't want to work in a place that is unable to add to your knowledge.

A general ignorance of who we are, what we feel, and how others perceive us continues to be a problem for many people. They are unaware of how their style of work affects others or how their interpersonal relationships influence how people react to them. Some people simply lack an awareness of which work-related skills or interests have the potential to excite and challenge them. There are all kinds of tests you can take to find out what your skills and interests are; the human resources division of most companies and organizations offer these tests. They are worth taking, even if they have limits. One person, for example, kept learning from the tests that she should be a lawyer. She wasn't interested in the law at all. She was interested in empowering people for daily living; not winning lawsuits. Step one clearly involves resilience factors from each of the categories: help, confidence, skills.

Step Two

Acquire competitive skills that the constant changes in different fields demand. To do that, you need to be aware of the direction a company is taking, what future skills might be needed, and what's happening in the economic market specifically related to your own career. You may want to stay with the company where you now work and contribute to its growth, so you need to be informed. Many companies provide training in how to plan for the future. They have learned that preparing someone who is already within the company culture saves much time compared with training someone new.

Step Three

Keep yourself informed about job openings. The majority of companies today announce job openings within their organization, and sometimes they even provide information about jobs outside the company. Some companies provide funds for training employees in writing resumes and learning interviewing skills. Web sites are used for posting openings available, accessible to anyone with a computer, and, of course, there is always the newspaper with its employment section.

Resilience and Aging

With almost a guarantee you will live a quarter century longer than your parents, certainly your grandparents, you have a real challenge. What do you do with those added years? The culture still focuses on youth and provides all sorts of standards and behaviors appropriate for that age; middle age is accepted, and there is certainly a culture developing for that age group beyond raising children and working. But, for those beyond their 50s, there are not clear expectations, nor is there a culture that enhances and enriches their lives. It is only recently that society is addressing this lack.

Resilience can play a great role in the enjoyment and sense of purpose in your later years. For the continued promotion and use of resilience throughout the course of your life, you should reexamine your life asking yourself these questions:

Do I want to continue where I am?

What changes interest me?

Am I qualified for something else?

Reconsider old dreams you once had or new dreams you're just beginning to form. Do you want to work overseas for a while? Teach somebody something? Take violin lessons or learn some new technology skills? Think back—have you ever said, "I've always wanted to do that?" Well, maybe now is the time.

You can find older friends or mentors whose successful aging can inspire your own changes. Talk to them about what they enjoy in life and how they made the inevitable changes that were required. Do they start new things? Have they, for example, moved to a new and more interesting place? Has their energy level changed? How do they deal with that?

You can respect the fact that new health problems will develop over time, new diets may be needed, new use of your energy may be required. Health services are available, and you probably already know how to go prepared with a list of questions, including what are the side effects that accompany so many drugs.

You need to be willing to let go of relationships, responsibilities, and old grudges and hurts that sap energy from your life rather than contribute to it. Revenge is sweet, but if you can't do anything about it, let it go. Perhaps some of your friends expect more from you than you are willing to give—in fact, they may be exploiting you. You can set some limits to expectations or drop the relationship.

You can use your maturity and the strengths it provides to take on political, educational, and social issues—the adversities outside your more immediate concerns. Within this larger framework you can develop new networks to share ideas, plans, and strategies, and then compare results. You can be part of a formidable action group.

One way to do this is by seeking out younger people in need with the goal of becoming a mentor. You have years of experiences, with the knowledge they bring, to share with insecure people facing the adversities of life. Help them. You can help by seeking new career options for yourself: you can return to school, explore volunteer opportunities, or create new businesses or services. Help for yourself and others go hand in hand.

There are a few straightforward behaviors for maintaining high levels of functioning as you age: understanding how you react to stress, getting sufficient sleep, doing things one at a time, and being sure to draw on past experiences. Three specific actions that address ways to maintain high levels of functioning are selection; optimization; and compensation. The pianist Arthur Rubinstein is an example. He said he could maintain high levels of functioning as a world-class pianist by selecting fewer pieces (but those he liked best and was best at playing), optimizing his skills by practicing more often, and compensating for his losses by using variations and contrasts in speed to give the impression of faster playing. He was 80 years old when he said this—clearly, the adversities of aging can be resolved by using some tricks! But, no matter what your age, the use of resilience factors right now will prepare you for later.

References

Erikson, E. H. (1985). *Childhood and society.* New York: Norton.

Garmezy, N. (1991). Resiliency and vulnerability to adverse developmental outcomes associated with poverty. *American Behavioral Scientist, 34* (4), 416–430.

Grotberg, E. H. (1995). A guide to promoting resilience in children: Strengthening the human spirit. The Hague, The Netherlands: The Bernard

van Leer Foundation. Can be downloaded or printed from www.resilnet.
uiuc.edu

Grotberg, E. H. (2000). International resilience research project. In A. L. Comunian & U. Gielen (Eds.), *International perspectives on human development* (pp. 379–399). Vienna, Austria: Pabst Science Publishers.

IMHI. (1991). *The RETHINK method.* Champaign, IL: Research Press.

Rutter, M. (1979). Protective factors in children's responses to stress and disadvantage. *Annals of the Academy of Medicine, Singapore, 8,* 324–338.

Werner, E., & Smith, R. S. 1982. *Vulnerable but invincible: A study of resilient children.* New York: McGraw-Hill.

CHAPTER 2

THE YIN AND YANG
OF RESILIENCE

Rhoda Baruch and Suzanne Stutman

Give lots of yin and a dash of yang! That's the prescription we have arrived at for fostering resilience. At the Institute for Mental Health Initiatives we have been pondering the question for about 15 years— How can we foster resilience? We have convened conferences for experts from around the world, posing this question to them. We have conducted searches of the literature on resilience, based on research, on clinical experience, and on autobiographies and accounts of survivors of various ordeals. We have woven together themes from these varied sources, and that's what we have come up with: when yin and yang are combined, we have a good chance for building the strengths needed to overcome adversity and to succeed against the odds. Either component in the absence of the other is insufficient, and may even be harmful. So what are the yin and the yang of resilience?

The yin refers to the love, the devotion, the care of at least one person in a child's life. As Uri Bronfenbrenner put it, "Every kid needs one adult who is crazy about him" (Bronfenbrenner, 1986). And unfortunately, for filling the prescription of the yin of resilience we cannot assume that every kid automatically has that. Some parents mean to love their children, but they are too oppressed with their own depression to even look the child straight in the eye, or they may be too focused on their own personal needs as is the case of an addiction to a drug. Perhaps they are too overwhelmed by the stresses and demands of their difficult circumstances. When a mother feels betrayed, abandoned, used by the child's father, she may see in the child too much of the man with whom she is so angry. Some programs help a parent to get back on their feet and become that loving adult. In other instances, a surrogate parent, an adoring grandparent, an uncle or neighbor may help fulfill the need. As the child gets older, mentors, either natural or provided by an institution, may be made available. We will describe more of these mentoring programs later in this chapter.

The yang part of the prescription may seem paradoxical at first. Every child needs small exposures to adversity, challenges appropriate to his age and capacity for mastery. It was the eminent British epidemiologist Michael Rutter who first posed this notion of "controlled exposure to adversity." Perhaps he was thinking of the medical analogy with inoculation, where some toxin is injected so that the body builds immunity (Rutter, 1987). That may not be the best analogy for this important component of resilience. The work of the Wolins gives us another perspective on how exposure to adversity can help build resilience. They have treated children of alcoholics, and have demonstrated how thinking about the challenges one has overcome can be strengthening. Such reframing can provide a cornerstone for a sense of personal pride and self-worth (Wolin & Wolin,1994). The ways in which resilience is fostered by exposure to small doses of adversity is not yet fully understood. However, many programs, most influenced by the Outward Bound Wilderness Challenge Model, have been proliferating in this country since 1960. In this chapter we will refer to recent research on the effectiveness of these wilderness experiences on children's growth and development.

The Road to Resilience

Every person has the potential to face, overcome, and even grow through adversity. What does it take for that to happen? As we think about resilience and how we might foster it, there are many important elements that contribute to enhancing resilience. We have selected two seemingly paradoxical elements and focus on the yin and the yang. The first element, the yin, refers to every child's need for at least one person who is crazy about him. That person can be a natural mentor or parent or a supportive, nonparental or arranged mentor who helps build resilience in a child.

Mentoring: One Person to Change the Odds

Thank you speeches given by award recipients, such as inductees into halls of fame or those who receive an Oscar, often include a statement of deep appreciation for a special someone in their lives. Frequently, a recipient has overcome significant odds, and proudly speaks about the struggle and the help received and the person the recipient credits with being responsible for his/her success. Often the person receiving a prestigious award will credit one individual who played a particularly significant role early in his life when he was most at risk and needed some guidance; the one person who changed the odds for her; the high school teacher who gave him the part in the school play; the coach who helped bring out her talent when others could not; the teacher who encouraged him when they and others had all but given up; the boss who was supportive when she was most vulnerable. Often the stories the recipients tell are replete with against-the-odds resilience, or "ordinary magic" (Masten, 2001): ordinary because the resilience emerged through the course of normal development; magic because it transformed their lives. Sometimes it is a parent who is that special supportive person.

In his autobiography, *It's Not about the Bike* (Armstrong, 2000), world-class bicycle racer Lance Armstrong credits his mother with putting him and keeping him on the early path to greatness. After establishing himself on the international racing circuit and winning the prestigious and challenging Tour de France twice, in 1998 Armstrong was diagnosed with life-threatening cancer. A major part of his autobiography describes his subsequent battle with cancer and his efforts, thereafter, to return to bicycle-racing greatness. Since his recovery, Armstrong has won five consecutive Tour de France bicycle races. Armstrong's story is truly one of heroic conquest. But his story is about more than one man's victory over a terrible illness. It is also about how he was able to overcome adversity in his youth and achieve success in the first place. In his book, Armstrong discloses that he had what he calls a turbulent youth. He never knew his biological father and tells of how his stepfather whipped him and ultimately betrayed his mom. The hardship of Armstrong's childhood caused one writer to remark that Armstrong's early success as a triathlete emerged from his need to create physical pain to smother his emotional pain (Lipsyte, 2002). After that marriage disintegrated, Armstrong and his mother grew closer, with his mom becoming, in his words, his "best friend and personal ally." Of her he writes:

My mother had given me more than any teacher or father figure had.
And she had done it over some long hard years, years that must have
looked as empty to her as those Brown Texas fields. When it came to
never quitting, to not caring how it looked, to gritting your teeth and
pushing to the finish I could only hope to have the stamina and forti-
tude of my mother, a single woman with a young son and a small
salary—and there was no reward for her at the end of the day, either,
no trophy or first place check. For her there was just the knowledge
that honest effort was a transforming experience and that her love was
redemptive. (Armstrong, 2000)

It is fascinating that Armstrong uses the word *redemptive* to
describe his mother's dedication. The dictionary defines *redeem* as "to
set free, rescue" (*American Heritage Dictionary*, 1982). The notion that
the dedication of a parent or a teacher to a youngster has the potential for rescue seems intuitive, but it is really a synonym for fostering
resilience in the child.

Referring again to Uri Brofenbrenner's concept of each child needing someone to cherish him or her, we wonder how does that rescue
happen? In Armstrong's case, his mother didn't ride his bike for him.
And what if there is no parent-mentor in a child's life? Or what if the
parent can't do it? Many parents struggle with their own emotional
disorders, with illness or poverty, or addictions of one type or
another. What about a supportive relationship with some sort of surrogate parents, such as other family members, or teachers, or clergy,
or even volunteer mentors, such as Big Brothers or Sisters? Can these
kinds of relationships make a difference, offer redemption or rescue?
A supportive nonparental adult in each child's life is an important element in resilience building. While Armstrong attributes much of his
success to one parent—in fact, a single parent much of the time—
many young people attribute their successful navigation of adolescence to the influence of significant nonparental adults such as
teachers, extended family members, or neighbors. See Anderson's
study (1991), Lefkowitz' study (1986), and Smink's study (1990) (as
cited in Zimmerman & Bingenheimer, 2002).

Nonparental Mentors

Frank's story comes to mind here. Frank is now a grandfather. He
is a loving and beloved member of his family. He had made enough
money at his work to be able to travel and enjoy a game of golf. He
was well read and could engage in lively discussions. It was surpris-

ing to find out that Frank had grown up in an orphanage and had never had a day of schooling after his 16th birthday, when he was released from the orphanage. How did he do it? How did he make music in his life with so little given to him? He credited the librarian at the orphanage where he was raised. She not only gave him books to read, but also seemed genuinely interested in his comments when he returned the books. His ideas were important to her, and they engaged in long conversations together. Frank developed a love of reading, but more important he developed a sense of his own worth as a person. He knew he was both lovable and had interesting ideas. Fortified in this way, later he could surmount the obstacles he encountered.

Wendy's life story also has an important nonparental adult in a central and influential role in her development. Wendy's parents had been alcohol abusers, and she witnessed brawls and suffered neglect when her parents were drinking. Yet, she grew to be a competent parent and a successful professional. What had made the difference? Or better yet, who? "Aunt Fanny," was her immediate reply. Aunt Fanny was not a relative at all, but a neighbor in the same apartment building where she grew up. When discord or neglect reached too high a level at home, Wendy would slip away and knock on her neighbor's door. Aunt Fanny was always delighted to see Wendy and would invite her in for an activity, saying, "You're just in time. Let's wash up and bake some cookies!" Wendy was made to feel she was someone special, and her sense of worth was fed as well as her stomach!

A librarian or a neighbor can tip the odds in favor of success and make the difference in a young life. As we know, adolescence is full of risks; including the emergence of problem behaviors such as alcohol or marijuana use, delinquent behavior, and the possibility of negative attitudes toward school, to name a few. Researchers have found support for the view that a nonparent natural mentor (such as a teacher or extended family member) may play a vital role in the life of an adolescent (Zimmerman & Bingenheimer, 2002). They have found that youths with nonparent natural mentors have a higher level of school attachment and efficacy than similar youth who do not have a mentor. The mentored youth also show lower levels of marijuana use and nonviolent delinquency (Zimmerman & Bingenheimer, 2002). In addition, such youths were less severely affected by negative school attitudes or behaviors of their peers. Even more, research suggests that apart from promoting positive school attitudes and discouraging problem behaviors directly, natural mentors may encourage young people to seek out more wholesome peers and to avoid delinquent peers (Zimmerman & Bingenheimer, 2002).

Here is another true story of a young teen who beat the odds with the support of a special mentoring program. When Precious' father died in an auto accident, something inside the 11-year-old girl almost died, too. Precious' father, who did not live with the family, was more than the most important male in her life. He was her refuge from a chaotic home dominated by her mother's abusive boyfriend. Without the emotional mooring of her father's love and support, Precious felt adrift in a raging sea of grief, fear, anger, and self-doubt.

But Precious was lucky. Her school participated in Project AVID, a program designed to help modestly performing inner-city children prepare for and get into college. AVID, which stands for Advancement via Individual Determination, places C-average students who do not have behavioral problems in a program that combines teacher professional development and parental involvement with intensive academic support for students.

As a Project AVID student, Precious participated in a rigorous course of study; learned practical study skills such as note taking and time management; received tutoring from college students; learned about business, cultural, and educational opportunities through guest lectures and field trips; found a peer group that shared her vision of a productive future; and found mentors who supported her throughout her teen years. Precious credits the mentors and the program with giving her "self-esteem and an understanding of the world," not to mention with enabling her to gain admittance to Howard University, where she is now a student.

Precious' success is typical of the Project AVID participant. According to the American Youth Policy Forum, 93.8 percent of all Project AVID students enroll in college, a rate 75 percent higher than is typical for their socioeconomic group. Indeed, students who have participated in the program for at least two years enroll in college at rates equal to or higher than their middle class peers (American Youth Policy Forum, 1999).

Research Findings on Mentors

Much research has been done into the effects of mentoring, and, overall, findings support the effectiveness of youth-mentoring programs regardless of whether the program takes place alone or in conjunction with other services; whether the program reflects relatively general as opposed to more focused goals; and regardless of a youth's age, gender, race/ethnicity, and family structure (DuBois, Holloway, Valentine, & Cooper, 2002). Even more, research shows that natural (i.e., parent, aunt, teacher) and arranged voluntary mentoring can produce the same benefits[1] (DuBois et al., 2002). Voluntary mentoring has been found to be most effective when there is ongoing training for mentors and structured activities for mentors and youth. Also, frequency of contact, finding ways for support and involvement of parents, and monitoring of the volunteer program itself all contribute to enhancing resilience in children (DuBois et al., 2002). These arranged mentors must be carefully screened. Also, and logically, the stronger the relationship between the voluntary mentor and the youth, the greater the benefit to the youth. Importantly, DuBois et al. found that mentoring works best as a preventive intervention for youth when the risk involves environmental factors such as low family socioeconomic status or general disadvantage, rather than when the risk involves individual characteristics, such as academic failure. They cite Freedman (1992) for the proposition that

> [m]entoring is an inherently interpersonal endeavor. As a result, it may be especially susceptible to obstacles and difficulties that can arise when youth targeted for intervention are already demonstrating significant personal problems (as cited in DuBois et al., 2002).

Resilience is more likely to develop with a mentor or an adult parent surrogate when the relationship begins early in a child's life and makes him feel special and worthy. The effectiveness of a mentoring relationship is related to its duration. Those youths who were in relationships that lasted a year or longer reported improvements in academics, and psychosocial and behavioral outcomes, whereas youths whose relationships terminated earlier achieved fewer positive effects (Grossman & Rhodes, 2002).

The Importance of Mentors

Charles Schultz, the originator of the famous comic strip *Peanuts*, once asked readers to name the last 5 Heisman trophy winners, the

---

1. In their study, DuBois et al. (2002) report that the overall magnitude of the effects of mentoring was small, but observe that there needs to be more consideration of specific factors influencing effectiveness.

last 5 Miss Americas, 10 people who had won the Nobel or Pulitzer prize, and so on. Most respondents couldn't get very far. The results were different when Schultz asked for the names of people who'd made readers feel valued or had helped them through difficult times. The names slip easily off their tongues. These people are so significant that throughout life they are frequently referred to and held in great esteem.

Those who've triumphed despite the odds frequently place teachers, counselors, coaches, clergy, librarians, or other service providers high on their personal lists of award winners. The guidance, tutelage, and faith these adults provide at critical points in a young person's life buttress the will to succeed. They help children build the skills, develop the strengths, and rally the resources they need to stay strong when adversity threatens to overwhelm.

The importance of nonparental adults in the development of adolescents, even when families are intact and the parents are competent is demonstrated. These studies differentiate between *natural* mentors, adults who are in the youth's life, such as an aunt or uncle, or when a volunteer mentor enters a child's life through an organized channel such as the Big Brothers program. Each can play a significant role. A mentor can either build an emotional tie with the teenager or they can serve as role models or sources of information.

Making a Difference

Adolescents are hungry for role models both from within the family and outside their own families. They are developing an increased capacity for empathy, intimacy, and problem solving, all of which contribute to resilience. They are testing their own sense of competence as never before. With the right guidance, they can learn to draw on the inner qualities and outer resources that constitute resilience.

The research on the Big Brothers and Big Sisters of America mentoring programs was completed in 1995 by Public/Private Ventures (P/PV). This three-year study concluded that "caring relationships between adults and youth can be created and supported by programs and can yield a wide range of tangible benefits" (Tierney, Baldwin-Grossman, & Resch, 2000). Like the research cited earlier in this chapter, they found that these mentoring programs act as a deterrent to initiating drug and alcohol use and have an overall positive impact on academic performance (Tierney et al., 2000). Of particular interest, in the P/PV experimental research all participants in both the control groups as well as the treatment groups were from high-risk families; the minority participants, however, were found to be positively effected by the mentoring program more than other participants.

Compared with the controls, these children

- were 70 percent less likely to initiate drug use,
- were one-third less likely to hit someone,
- skipped fewer classes and half as many days of school,
- felt more competent about doing schoolwork,
- showed modest gains in their grade point average, with the strongest gains among the Little Sisters, and
- improved their relationships with both their parents and their peers. (Tierney et al., 2000)

The profile of the mentors appeared to be different from the youth that they supported. Mentors were generally college-educated, non-minority, with yearly incomes ranging from $25,000 to $40,000. Thus, even though there were clear race and class differences between the mentors and the youth, their relationships nevertheless proved successful. Why? What were the components in the mentoring program that led to success (Davis, 1999)?

Two overall elements strengthened the mentoring relationship and led to successful outcomes. They were the one-to-one relationship and the supportive infrastructure. In the one-to-one relationships, mentors and students met frequently and with concentrated time (70 percent met three times a month on an average of three to four hours per meeting). Additionally, in a separate study conducted by the P/PV in May, 1995 (Tierney et al., 2000), the quality of the relationships were considered. The study found that the mentor considered himself/herself a friend, and that enjoying each other and having fun was important. The mentor was aware of the youth's developing needs and was conscious of providing opportunities that the youth would not ordinarily have available to him/her. "While most developmental volunteers ultimately hoped to help their youth improve in school and be more responsible, they centered their involvement and expectations on developing a reliable, trusting relationship, and expanded the scope of their efforts only as the relationship strengthened" (Tierney et al., 2000). Staying in tune with the youth's preferences and capabilities, being present for the youth while listening empathically, and including the youth in decisions, were all characteristics of successful mentor relationships (Davis, 1999).

Some mentors were not able to form solid relationships. These mentors were found to have more of a judgmental attitude, they attempted to change the youth values "for the better," they didn't include the youth in decision making, and they were rigid in their approach to the youth. "Adults in these relationships set the goals, the pace, and/or the ground rules for the relationship. These volunteers were reluctant to adjust their expectations of the youth or their expectations of how quickly the youth's behavior could change." Mostly, these mentors lectured to the youth about doing well in school and seemed to stress what was wrong with the youth themselves rather than what was right about the child (Tierney et al., 2000).

What characterizes a good mentoring program? A supportive infrastructure is very important. The Big Brothers and Big Sisters Program had the following characteristics that proved to be the necessary ingredients for a successful mentoring program:

1. A screening process that eliminates people who seem likely to be unable to keep time commitments and who might pose a safety risk to the youth.

2. Training in communication skills, limit-setting skills, building relationships, and how to interact with the youth.

3. Matching both procedures and characteristics of the volunteer mentor with the youth and their family.

4. Assigning a professional case manager to each match who supervises and is available on a regular basis or when problems arise, to the youth, family/guardian, and to the mentor. The case manager also facilitates a peer support group for the mentor.

Overall, the philosophy and the ultimate success of the Big Brothers and Big Sisters mentoring program is in harmony with the Bronfenbrenner statement, "Every child needs one adult who is crazy about him." This program emphasizes a nonjudgmental, positive, caring acceptance of the youth's ability and strengths. These one-to-one relationships are crucial building blocks in fostering resilience.

As teens move into their college years, frequently there are programs that train them to become the mentors themselves. In programs where "college undergraduate mentors worked with adjudicated delinquents, recidivism was reduced by 34 percent. This resulted in a saving of $5,027 in criminal justice costs and $7,299 in victim costs per youth receiving the program." As we have emphasized above, the importance of training for mentors in order to produce benefits is crucial (Davidson & Redner, 1990; Davis, 1999).

Beyond Love: The Dose of Adversity

The other part of the prescription for fostering resilience—the yang component—involves small exposures to adversity appropriate to the age of the child. The challenges are age appropriate in two senses: (1) they provide an opportunity for mastery of a source of anxiety that is specific to the psychosocial stage of development; and (2) the challenge is brief enough as well as of low enough intensity that the child is not overwhelmed. Although anxiety will be aroused, mastery of the challenge is assured.

The mastery of anxiety was emphasized by Kierkegaard in *The Concept of Dread* (cited by May, 1950). He wrote:

> I would say that learning to know anxiety is an adventure which every man has to affront if he would not go to perdition either by not having known anxiety or sinking under it. He therefore who has learned rightly to be anxious has learned the most important thing.

Such mastery of anxiety can be pleasurable, as Rollo May described in *The Meaning of Anxiety* (1950). He reminded us of the feeling of diving into deep water and then changing direction as we return to the surface as an excitement that comes with mastery of that moment of anxiety. Similarly, for an infant whose fears center around separation, a game of peek-a-boo almost always elicits a big laugh and signs of delight. The game of hide and seek illustrates the way somewhat older children work through and overcome the challenge of separation. Fiction for toddlers, in the form of nursery rhymes, fairy tales, and animated cartoons provides vicarious experiences of anxiety and its mastery.

Research has shown that children who face a trauma, such as hospitalization, do better if they have spent nights away from their parents, either at grandparents or at friend's sleepover parties, at Scout overnights, or at camp (Rutter, 1987). Dealing with some manageable level of hardships in a sense "steel" the child and help build resilience.

Participation in spelling bees, dramatic school plays, music or dance recitals, speeches and debates, as well as sports competitions can help children with overcoming the central issues of the school years, when a sense of industry or a sense of inferiority can be the prevailing outcome (Erickson, 1950). Most children anticipating any of these challenges experience some stress, but managing and overcoming the concern make these events both pleasurable and growth producing. Resilience is fostered with each victory, which does not mean winning the competition, but rather gaining mastery of one's own anxiety, fears, and apprehensions. When a child copes with some manageable level of adversity and ends up feeling a bit more competent and stronger, he/she is becoming more resilient. The child is learning to think of himself or herself as someone who can handle a challenge.

Adventure education has developed as a philosophy closely allied to what we are referring to here as the yang of resilience. Among its proponents are Miles and Priest, who published *Adventure Education* in 1990. They write of the purposeful planning and implementation of educational processes that involve risk in some way. Risk may be physical, social, or spiritual. The aim is to learn from risk taking not to be damaged or destroyed by risk. They speak of the benefits as personal growth and progress toward self-realization.

The Post-Adolescent, Pre-Adult Age Group

Later in the course of development, in the period that some writers are beginning to describe as *PAPAS*, for the post-adolescent, pre-adult period, special anxieties arise. In the past 20 years, wilderness orientation programs have expanded across the country used by colleges, secondary schools, and now graduate education. These programs are usually modeled after Outward Bound, first established in the United States in Colorado in 1961.

Outward Bound was originally introduced in Wales in 1941 to train merchant seamen to withstand the rigors of wartime life (Burton, 1981). The term Outward Bound is nautical in origin, used to describe the moment a ship left its moorings and committed itself and its crew to the open sea (Achuff as cited by Moore & Russell, 2002). The phrase Outward Bound does very well to serve as a metaphor for a young person as she leaves home and embarks on her own way at a new school.

The primary goals of such programs may be to provide fun and build a positive connection to the new school, but additional goals are ones we recognize as related to fostering resilience for this age group. Rick Curtis (1999) of the Outdoor Action Program at Princeton University summarizes these personal growth goals as

- to increase self-confidence,
- to increase self-esteem,
- to assume responsibility for themselves and their choices,
- to enhance communication skills,
- to enhance decision making,

- to adjust and mature, and
- to increase personal initiatives.

Central to the anxiety of this stage of development is the task of transition to a new environment and to new expectations. The goal of better understanding one's own strengths and weaknesses in coping with this anxiety is often well addressed by some of these wilderness orientation programs.

Among the social skills that Curtis lists as goals of these wilderness programs are

- to develop group problem-solving skills, and
- to establish friendships with classmates and with older students.

Curtis finds that the potential for personal growth and development through small-group wilderness programs has been demonstrated (Curtis, 1992). Furthermore, when faculty is involved in a shared wilderness experience a unique out-of-classroom relationship can be established for students. Following such shared activities, students feel less intimidated in recruiting help from faculty or older students. The ability to recruit help as needed is another resilience skill we recognize (Wolin & Wolin, 1994).

College Outdoor Education Programs

A recent compilation of college-orientation programs include more than 40 programs that have Outdoor Wilderness components, with backpacking, or canoeing, or ropes, or rock climbing as part of the experience. These programs help the new college student rise to the challenge. Overcoming difficulties help foster the resilience that college students need to cope successfully with a new setting, new rules, new demands, new stresses. Thus, colleges throughout the United States now provide these outdoor challenges.

Each college emphasizes somewhat different objectives. We are indebted to Jennifer Davis-Berman of the Department of Anthropology, Sociology, and Social Work at the University of Dayton and Dene Berman of Lifespan Counseling Associates for compiling an extensive summary of wilderness new student orientation programs at American colleges and universities (Davis-Berman & Berman, 1995). Antioch College, for example, offers incoming students a two-week canoeing trip in Ontario with three stated goals: to learn about canoeing and wilderness, to learn about Antioch, but also to "aid in self-discovery."

Bloomsbery College uses backpacking to encourage students to "push their limits, develop friendships, build self-esteem, and facilitate their transition to college." The University of California at San Diego sponsors sea kayaking as well as backpacking orientation trips for new students, and their stated mission is to prepare students for their new environment, to help students evaluate themselves, and to make new friends. Davidson College adds rafting to the list of orientation programs and expects these activities to facilitate the transition to college. A small Quaker college, Earlham College in Richmond, Indiana, states its objective, "to challenge students physically, socially, and psychologically." Hamilton College, a small private institution, offers six different canoe trips, four backpacking trips, cycling, or combination trips. They state their goals for these offerings as facilitating adjustment to college, dealing effectively with stress, and working on goal setting. Hartwich College in Oneonta, New York, describes its program goals as "pushing past the comfort zone" and expects the camping, climbing, canoeing, and rope work to ease the transition and adjustment to college. Bates College, a small liberal arts institution located in Lewiston, Maine, offers newly enrolled students the option of attending the Annual Entering Student Outdoor Program (AESOP), which consists of over 30 different multiday trips designed specifically for new students. These trips, which are led by upperclassmen, are designed for new students to meet peers and help in the adjustment of college life before the onset of classes. AESOP occurs before the traditional first-year orientation begins and includes activities that cater to a wide range of ability level, such as backpacking, hiking, trail maintenance on the Appalachian Trail, mountain biking, kayaking, rock climbing, and canoeing. A public institution, Towson State University in Maryland encourages its students to challenge themselves physically and emotionally and to work toward self-understanding and understanding of others in their orientation programs.

Brown University's Outdoor Leadership (BOLT) Program employs a slightly different approach to wilderness experience. They recognize that sophomores face a particularly difficult year of transition from the camaraderie of the first year to increasing expectations and need for independence in the following several years. Hence, this university provides wilderness programs during the course of the sophomore year. Students during these experiences accept the challenges and take the opportunity to reflect and reassess themselves as part of their personal development.

As increasing numbers of foreign students join advanced professional graduate school programs, we can presume they feel challenged and full of apprehension. These turbulent feelings can be addressed before they enter the academic program by participating in wilderness orientation. Among the graduate schools and professional schools that now provide wilderness programs are Cornell Medical School, Harvard Medical School, and the Stanford Business School.

The challenges posed by the outdoor educational programs, managed frequently by development of interdependence as well as personal strengths, are equated with the challenges of the college. Such orientation programs provide a metaphor and help students build self-esteem as they learn to trust their judgment and decision-making skills.

The Wilderness Experience

In *Walking the Bible*, Bruce Feiler (2001) describes his desert experience that he undertook for very different reasons from the college orientation programs we are writing about here. He set out to try to get closer spiritually to the Bible. Yet from his adventure, we may appreciate something of the deprivation and adversity, but also the gratification and growth, that can take place in that setting.

After long hikes and many days without his usual food, he describes eating the bread he and his companions prepared there:

> Ofer (his guide) pulled the pita from the embers and set it on the soil. At this point it was impossible to distinguish the ashes from the bread; both were the color of dusk. He took a stick and began beating it like a dirty rug . . . he pulled off a piece, breathing steam, and handed it to me. I tossed it around my fingers for a few seconds, then put it in my mouth. There was a small coating of sand around the crust, but I no longer cared. And that's when I realized how far I had come in the desert. I no longer craved the apple, the cookie, or the chocolate from my earliest days. I no longed needed cheese, or okra, or tuna. I didn't even need honey. Bread was flavor enough.

What was it like to sleep in the desert? Feiler describes how he squirmed on his mattress with a mix of unease and anticipation. He writes:

> The wind, which had been gaining steadily, was now whipping past me with greater speed. It was blowing with a force unimaginable even a few minutes earlier. I began to estimate its strength—forty miles per

hour, fifty. The wind was cooler than before, and its force had a chilling effect that began at the lower part of my back and spread across to the tip of my fingers. I felt completely exposed, as if my skin were being pulled from my body.

After enduring a night like that, though, Feiler witnessed a dawn such as he had never experienced before. He felt he saw the exact moment when one day ends and another begins. And he felt that he, too, had made a transition along with the place. He said that all the ideas he had been contemplating, including his own identity, came together in a flash. That moment would always be an anchor for him, he writes.

The insight the author of *Walking the Bible* gains from his desert experience, he summarizes as follows:

> Because the place is demanding, it builds character; because it's destructive, it builds interdependence; because it's isolating, it builds community.

The goals of many of the college wilderness orientation programs are precisely the gains that Feiler achieved in his desert adventure.

How Well Do These Programs Work?

Studies that have sought to assess the effects of these wilderness programs appear mainly in unpublished doctoral dissertations and, in some cases, in senior theses. One of the latter was done by Brian Wardwell, who conducted his study as a senior in the Psychology Department at Princeton in 1999 (Wardwell, 1999). He found a particular form of anxiety on the part of entering freshmen was allayed by the wilderness orientation experience. The anxiety around the question, "How will I fit in?" was measured with his social fit score, which increased after the experience. Before the wilderness trip, freshmen feared they would not fit in socially as well as the typical student. Upon return from the challenges of their experience, they tended to think they would feel more comfortable fitting in with other students. We infer that their resilience had been fostered.

The field of research on the effectiveness of wilderness experiences is expanding rapidly. In 2002, Moore and Russell of the University of Idaho Wilderness Research Center reviewed and annotated 247 pieces of research-based literature (Moore & Russell, 2002). Their survey includes programs that use wilderness for therapy, rehabilitation, as well as for personal growth and for educational and leadership development. The programs are varied in their structure, duration, purpose, population, and results. One finding is that stress management is often enhanced by these programs.

Interesting findings are reported by Todd Sawyer Paxton in his doctoral dissertation. In 1999, he presented *Self-Efficacy and Outdoor Programs: A Quantitative and Qualitative Analysis* (Paxton, 1998). He investigated the question of whether the gains achieved in outdoor challenge programs transferred to the daily lives of the participants. Were these gains lasting?

Paxton studied participants in the 21-day-long Voyageur Outward Bound programs. The course, as described by Voyageur, includes a solo experience of two- or three-day duration, providing a "unique opportunity to rest, reflect, and practice self-reliance. With sufficient food and equipment, you spend time alone at an assigned campsite." The participant remains within hearing distance of other group members, and their instructors check on them at least once a day.

The self-efficacy gained by participants in this program did transfer into their daily lives, Paxton found. He also reported that the self-efficacy continued to increase one year after completion of their adventure course.

Another study, this one reported by Don Reid Cross (as cited by Moore & Russell, 2002), also in 1999, involved students in an alternative high school on the Colorado Front Range. After completing a climbing program, the experimental group felt less alienated and had a stronger sense of personal control than the control group.

Hollenhorsh, Frank, and Watson write in "The Capacity to Be Alone: Wilderness Solitude and Growth of the Self" (as cited in Moore & Russell, 2002) about the ability to be alone but not lonely and to learn to view isolation as an opportunity for personal growth and development. They recognize that loneliness is one of the most powerful of human fears. In the absence of external goals, stimulation, and feedback, the optimal experience occurs when a participant can control his attention and find his own rewards, perhaps in the beautiful vistas of nature.

Norris and Weinman reported the psychological changes in a group of 18- to 24-year-old trainees who participated in a long sail training adventure across the Atlantic (Norris & Weinman, 1996). They found no adverse effects, but rather a gain in self-esteem, in coping, and a reduction in psychological stress.

In a technical report, Russell and Hendee in 1997 described their experience with at-risk youth between the ages of 16 and 24 in four

different Job Corps Centers, who were participants in seven-day-long
Wilderness Discovery Programs (Russell & Hendee, 1997). These
rigorous backpacking trips involved sleeping six nights on the trail
using tarps, with no flashlights or watches to foster natural rhythms,
and eating mainly vegetarian diets low in sugar and caffeine. After 45
such trips with different participants, they reported that the
Wilderness Discovery (WD) had an impact in that those who went
on the trips had a higher retention rate in the Job Corps than those
who didn't have the WD experience. In 1993 there were 35 percent
fewer early terminations, and in 1994 the number was 23 percent
fewer early terminations. Young people who stay in the program can
earn a General Education Diploma certificate (Russell & Hendee,
1997).

When participants are troubled youth, however, no clear patterns
of improvement emerge. In those cases subjecting people to adversity
in the form of wilderness experiences alone has no magic or proven
value. The combination of carefully controlled exposure to adversity
and increased rewarding experiences seem to be the components of
the more successful outdoor adventure programs, such as Paxton's
Voyageur Outward Bound School study, which found that enduring
gains for the participants were achieved. A more detailed examination
of that adventure program may inform us of what it takes and how it
works to foster resilience.

"You can't imagine how good it feels to overcome a challenge and
find yourself smack-dab in the middle of beautiful unspoiled wilderness!" That is the testimony of a participant in the Voyageur Outward
Bound Program. This school was started in 1964 in the northern
Minnesota lake country and is now part of a worldwide network of
Outward Bound Schools. Voyageur courses take place in the mountains and the deserts, on rivers, lakes, and an inland sea. Travel is by
foot or ski, by canoe, kayak, or dogsled. According to their Web site
(2002) from which most of this description was taken, "Our courses
deliver adventure, skills and success." They seek to inspire students
and leave them empowered by what they see of themselves in the
wilderness. They say, "We know that you are stronger than you know
and that you can do it."

Outward Bound, according to their literature, is not easy, a summer
camp, a vacation, a guided trip, a survival school, only for wilderness
experts, boring, comfortable, or a free lunch. Outward Bound is a
challenge, asking participants to participate in hard living with less,
pushing limits, living and sleeping outdoors. It promotes teamwork,

confidence, strength, self-reliance, and compassion. A typical course may include river travel, alpine backpacking and a peak ascent, which involves traveling over steep slopes of loose rock, rugged boulder fields, snowpack, or long complex routes. Balancing all these difficulties is the pleasure of exposure to magnificent natural vistas and rare animals. Also, the support of leaders and the group camaraderie may provide the nurturing needed to build the inner strength that accrues to participants.

Alan Ewert points out that these programs "swim against the tide" of our society's preoccupation with safety (Ewert, 1989). These are the benefits and costs that must be understood. It is possible that a good wilderness experience involves its own yin and yang. A recent study (Neill & Dias, 2001) of 49 young adult participants in an Outward Bound program in Australia examined the relation of adventure education and resilience. They looked at what they called the "double-edged sword," by which they meant they wondered whether the gains in resilience were more attributable to the social support of the adventure or the exposure to adversity. This master's thesis was the first piece of research found in which a measure of resilience, a 15-item resilience scale, was used before and after a 22-day Outward Bound program. The gains in resilience were substantial, compared with a control group. The primary goal of this study was to see whether resilience could be enhanced, and this was dramatically demonstrated. However, they also used measures of perceived social support, and they report that this variable accounts for 24 percent of the variance in the gain in resilience scores. It is a fascinating finding suggesting that adventure programs that bring people to encounter the edges of their physical and psychological possibilities do enhance the resilience in participants, but part of the effect may be attributed to the quality of the social support during the challenge.

Conclusions

The prescription of much yin and a little yang for fostering resilience is a general one that probably has merit. How much adversity, in what forms, combined with the right amount of yin, still requires research. We suggest that this is a fertile and important field of endeavor.

The dose of adversity need not be a physical challenge. A summer program for academically gifted high school students held at Boston

University presents students with very difficult mathematical problems and with the expectation that they spend many hours each day tackling one special problem. The mentors in this program are carefully trained to observe and allow each student to wrestle with the seemingly intractable problem and not to interfere unless there is a danger that the student is becoming overwhelmed and ready to give up. In that process of mentoring, a clue may be given at the right moment, but no student is denied the chance to experience stress and to overcome it and feel the victory of eventually solving the problem. That sort of balancing of challenge and caring mentoring might provide us with a kind of model for the yin and yang of fostering resilience that we, as a society, should struggle to achieve for every youngster.

Societal institutions from Big Brothers to Outward Bound can be useful as we give young people the opportunities to develop the strengths and the skills that comprise resilience. They will then be able to bounce back better when they encounter the inevitable vicissitudes that life has in store for them. Success against the odds is the goal of fostering resilience.

References

Achuff, C. (2001). *An exploratory qualitative investigation of specific components viewed as most effective by adjudicated youth in a therapeutic wilderness program originally from the Pacific Crest Outward Bound School.* Unpublished thesis, Georgia College and State University, Atlanta.

American Heritage Dictionary (2nd ed.). (1982). Boston, MA: Houghton Mifflin.

American Youth Policy Forum. (1999). *More things that do make a difference for youth: A compendium of evaluations of youth programs and practices, Vol. II.* Washington, DC: American Youth Policy Forum.

Anderson, E. (1991). Neighborhood effects on teenage pregnancy. In C. Jencks & P. E. Peterson (Eds.), *The urban underclass* (pp. 375–398). Washington, DC: Brookings Institution.

Armstrong, L. (with Jenkins, S.) (2000). *It's not about the bike: My journey back to life.* New York: Penguin Putman.

Bronfenbrenner, U. (1986). Ecology of the family as a context for human development: Research perspectives. *Developmental Psychology, 22,* 723–742.

Burton, L. (1981). A critical analysis and review of the research on Outward Bound and related programs (Doctoral dissertation, Rutgers, The State University of New Jersey, 1981). *Dissertation Abstracts International,* 0542.

Center for Mental Health Services. National Institute of Health. (1999). *Resilience: Status of research and research-based programs.* (http://www .mentalhealth.org/schoolviolence/5-28Resilience.asp). Washington, D.C.: N. Davis.

Cross, D. (1999). The effects of an outdoor adventure program on perception of alienation and feelings of personal control among at-risk adolescents. (Doctoral dissertation, University of Colorado, 1999). *Dissertation Abstracts International, 59*(8-A), 2900.

Curtis, R. (1992). Training college outdoor program leaders. In *Proceedings of the International Conference of the Association of Experiential Education. Celebrating Our Future.* pp. 99–106.

Curtis, R. (1999, November). *Wilderness orientation programs for the new millennium.* Presentation at the 27th International Association for Experiential Education Conference, Rochester, New York.

Davidson, W., & Redner, R. (1990). *Alternative treatments for troubled youth: The case of diversion from the justice system.* New York: Plenum Press.

Davis-Berman, J., & Berman, D. (1995). *Wilderness new student orientation programs: American colleges and universities.* Retrieved July 14, 2002, from Princeton University Web site: http://www.princeton.edu/~oa/ft /berman.html

DuBois, D., Holloway, B., Valentine, J., & Cooper, H. (2002). Effectiveness of mentoring programs: A meta-analytic review. *American Journal of Community Psychology, 30,* 157–197.

Erickson, E. (1950). *Childhood and society.* New York: W.W. Norton, Co.

Ewert, A. (1989). *Outdoor adventure pursuits: Foundations, models and theories.* Scottsdale, AZ: Publishing Horizons.

Feiler, B. (2001). *Walking the Bible.* New York: Harper Collins Publishers.

Freedman, M. (1992). *The kindness of strangers: Reflections on the mentoring movement.* Philadelphia, PA: Public/Private Ventures.

Grossman, J., & Rhodes, J. (2002). The test of time: Predictors and effects of duration in youth mentoring relationships. *American Journal of Community Psychology, 30,* 199–219.

Hollenhorsh, S., Frank, E., & Watson, A. (1993). *The capacity to be alone: Wilderness solitude and growth of the self.* Paper presented at the meeting of the fifth World Wilderness Congress, Tromse, Norway.

Lefkowitz, B. (1986). *Tough change: Growing up on your own in America.* New York: Free Press.

Lipsyte, R. (2002, July 28). Back talk: Individual stars also become dynasties unto themselves. *New York Times,* pp. 8, 11.

Masten, A. (2001). Ordinary magic: Resilience processes in development. *American Psychologist, 56,* 227–238.

May, R. (1950). *The meaning of anxiety.* New York: Roland Press.

Miles, J., & Priest, S. (1990). *Adventure education.* State College, PA: Venture Publishing.

Moore, T., & Russell, K. (2002). *Studies of the use of wilderness for personal growth, therapy, education and leadership development: An annotation and evaluation.* Moscow: University of Idaho, Wilderness Research Center.

Neill J., & Dias, K. (2001). Adventure education and resilience: The double edged sword. *Journal of Adventure Education and Outdoor Learning, 2,* 35–42.

Norris, R., & Weinman, J. (1996). A psychological change following a long sail training voyage. *Journal of Personality and Individual Differences, 21,* 189–194.

Outward Bound Schools. Retrieved August 8, 2002, from http://www.vobs.com

Paxton, T. (1998). *Self-efficacy and outdoor adventure programs: A quantitative and qualitative analysis.* Unpublished doctoral dissertation, University of Minnesota, Minneapolis.

Russell, K., & Hendee, J. (1997). *Testing wilderness discovery: A wilderness experience program for youth-at-risk in the Federal Job Corps.* (Technical Report No. 24). Moscow, ID: University of Idaho, College of Forestry, Wildlife and Range Sciences.

Rutter, M. (1987). Psychosocial resilience and protective mechanisms. *American Journal of Orthopyschiatry, 57,* 316–331.

Sminck, J. (1990). *Mentoring programs for at-risk youth: A dropout prevention research report.* Clemson, SC: National Dropout Prevention Center.

Tierney, J., Baldwin-Grossman, J., & Resch, N. (2000). *Making a difference: An impact study of Big Brothers Big Sisters.* Philadelphia, PA: Public/Private Ventures.

Wardwell, B. (1999). *The effects of the outdoor action frosh tripan freshman's adaptation to Princeton University.* Unpublished thesis, Princeton University, Princeton, New Jersey.

Wolin, S. J., & Wolin, S. (1994). *The resilient self: How survivors of troubled families rise above adversity.* New York: Villard Books.

Zimmerman, M., & Bingenheimer, J. (2002). Natural mentors and adolescent resiliency: A study with urban youth. *American Journal of Community Psychology, 30,* 221–243.

CHAPTER 3

Enhancing Family Resilience: A Transgenerational Approach to Positive Change in Dysfunctional Families

Sandra E. S. Neil

Introduction

Resilience in individuals has been defined by Grotberg (1995, 1999, 2000, 2001, 2002) in the following way: "Resilience is the human capacity to face, overcome, and even be transformed by the experiences of adversity." Said another way, resilience is the ability to bounce back and progress after serious stress, threat, or trauma in life.

Family therapists are concerned with the operations of a family system, in addition to the individuals that populate that system. A resilient family is a family that can continue to grow in the face of problems and remain congruent in their coping methods in the face of crisis. Family therapists with a strong eclectic background, such as Virginia Satir, Bert Hellinger, and Anne Ancelin Schutzenberger, have applied a variety of traditional psychological and psychodynamic paradigms to couples, groups, and families, including newer forms of the family, to facilitate the growth of resilience in the family. Readers wishing more information might read *The Family Chessboard* (Neil & Silverberg, 1995), which not only contains a more detailed description of how families can be helped to become more resilient, but provides a variety of case reports and graphic illustrations, clinical insights, and examples.

The Worldview of Optimism and Pessimism

Constantine (1986) indicates that families are makers of meaning. As a basic unit of society, it provides individuals with a sense of identity

and belonging. It also encourages the production of shared constructs and ways of viewing the world. It is not surprising to find
that, clinically, one of the most unsettling aspects of divorce is the
damage to meaning for the individuals involved and the challenge of
the constructs by which the world is viewed and lives are lived.

Existentially, human beings can contemplate their own mortality
and use intellectual constructs as windows. Each family has its own
unique way of perceiving the world, or worldview. Some families see
the world outside the family as nurturing, a positive place with compassionate people who are supportive of the family worldview, ready
to help if asked. Other families view the world outside their home as
threatening, wherein people cannot be trusted because they are presumed to be hostile to the family worldview.

These two sociopolitical views are in opposition. When applied to
family systems, the romantic view (as presented by the philosopher
Rousseau) leads to an optimistic set of family beliefs, with cooperation
as the mode of interaction. The Hobbsian, dog-eat-dog view is more
pessimistic, seeing the world outside the family as threatening, but
also leads to mistrust of the motives of immediate family members, as
the mode of interaction is seen as competition. Often, family members
are seen as malicious and focused on either causing or avoiding pain.

Clinically, families that suffer from dysfunction tend toward an
innate pessimism, seeing the world as a threatening place. There is
either an overt mistrust of self and others or a covert mistrust that
hides behind a superficial pretence at cooperation. This may be an
overly formalized family arrangement or an artificially peaceful
arrangement where there is an agreement never to disagree.

Sometimes these become self-fulfilling prophecies. For example, if
the family is open and optimistic and believes that they can receive
help when needed, an individual family member might have a higher
probability of asking for help when it is needed, confident that any
rejections need not be taken personally. Rejections would result in the
family member continuing to ask for help until a source is found. The
more people in a family that ask, the more likely the person is to find
help, fulfilling the expectation that indeed the world is helpful and
caring. Members of these families with open, growth-centered views
of interactions have a perspective that tends to prevent a depressive
pessimism and is likely to be linked to health (Alloy & Abramson,
1979; Abramson & Alloy, 1981). The corollary is also that if a closed
family sees the world outside as threatening, dangerous, and not to be
trusted, an individual family member might approach another person

for help, but with an underlying caution in case of rejection. If rejected the first time, though, the family member will likely interpret the rejection as a personal affront and react defensively. It will become a proof of the family proposition that people cannot be relied upon. In such cases, a family member may in the future again expect a negative reply and procrastinate in asking until much later, which then increases the probability of a negative reply. After the first rejection, the family member will have a higher probability of giving up because the initial rejection has matched the family's expectation of the world. Finally, in the family that views both family members and the outside world as people and places not to be trusted, a family member might not even ask people outside the family for help. Such a person will first ask other family members, only to be rejected as each family member in turn reacts defensively.

These examples demonstrate how expectations affect behavior and reinforce themselves in self-fulfilling prophecies. They also demonstrate that one's worldview may have to be taken into consideration when looking at both resilience and families. The worldview that each family brings to therapy determines, to a great degree, how to work and how the therapy will proceed. Extremely dysfunctional families may never trust the therapist and form a therapeutic alliance because their worldview predisposes them to look for behaviors on the part of the therapist that render him or her untrustworthy. Family therapists, however, attempt to influence values, words, constructs, and meaning that the family brings to therapy because these symbols of reality, in the presenting family, function in such a way that they produce symptoms in one or more of the family members.

In my view, resilience in a family is not a static concept. It is an active mechanism and a process that takes place, which allows for a higher level of functioning in a family. The resilient family experiences real hope and excitement when faced with the prospect of change and operates as an open family system, welcoming the inevitability of ongoing change and consistently seeking cooperative, helpful relationships as effective ways to live in the world.

The Family as a Dynamic System

If the family is seen as a dynamic system, then each person belonging to the family is constantly changing, growing, developing, and aging (Neil & Silverberg, 1995). Each family member seeks out ways of meeting needs. Each member of the family is changing, often at a different rate, as are the interactions. The structure of the family is poised for change as a family moves along a developmental continuum from birth to death.

How Do People Become Resilient?

Professor Edith Grotberg and colleagues (Grotberg, 2000) were involved in the International Resilience Research Project, which consisted of interviews with 1,225 parents and their children from 27 sites in 22 countries around the world. Her main conclusions are relevant to this chapter.

- Every resilient person was helped to become resilient.
- Temperament determines how an individual reacts to stimuli.
- The promotion of resilience is influenced by the temperament of each person.
- Socioeconomic environment does not determine resilience.
- No single resilience factor indicates resilience. Rather, it is the dynamic interaction of a number of resilience factors (from the *I HAVE*, *I AM*, *I CAN* paradigm) that indicates resilience.
- Cultural variations are a factor in determining the different dynamics for promoting resilience.
- The age and gender of a child is related to resilience.

Grotberg and others have defined resilience in terms of an I HAVE, I CAN, I Will paradigm. In a sense, resilience then includes external supports, the I HAVE in Grotberg's sense; internal strengths, the I AM in Grotberg's sense; and problem-solving skills, the I CAN in Grotberg's sense. In any systems-oriented family therapy model, if one looks at the family structure, one sees that families are in dynamic interaction. They are circular. A family member is seen as acting and reacting in a chain. Family systems theorists point out that in families, interactions occur in a complex, circular, cybernetic manner, rather than in a cause-and-effect, linear, Cartesian style (Bowen, 1978). When one family member does or says something, it is a stimulus to which another family member responds. This stimulus evokes additional responses in other family members. A family therapist can trace this sequence of interactions. Virginia Satir referred to an active family system as a "can of worms" (Satir, 1983).

In this sense, then, resilience is in the eyes of the beholder, and it is interactive. It very much depends on the context and the situation in which it has to be exerted. As well, other concepts of relevance are that families can be placed on a continuum between open and closed systems. Under stress and over time families can move closer to one pole of the continuum than another, becoming more or less open or closed.

Open Compared with Closed Systems

A closed family system has rigid rules for functioning. It is dominated by power and encourages dependency and obedience. This deprivation and conformity is enforced by fear, rejection, humiliation, punishment, or guilt. Adversity is feared as problems are seen as overpowering. This results in restriction of choices, control of feelings, and aggression or submissiveness in response to stress. In contrast, an open family system has flexible rules for functioning. It fosters equality of value, autonomy, appropriate reliance on self and others, and acceptance of differences. Adversity is accepted with both trepidation and equanimity, because problems are seen to be challenges that are part of the growth process. This results in a diversity of choices, awareness of feelings, and confidence in the ability to meet difficulties in response to stress.

Some of the rigid rules of closed, dysfunctional families include

1. agreeing to never disagree;
2. coercing and exercising power as the ascendant method of discipline;
3. not allowing the five freedoms (as discussed later in this chapter);
4. controlling and dominating of one family member over others in the family;
5. seeking perfectionism that has "shoulds, oughts, and musts," with the impossibility of pleasing self and others;
6. blaming, with one generation blaming another;
7. enforcing a no-talk rule, where communication is limited;
8. myth making, including family secrets, lies, and loyalty ties;
9. agreeing never to disagree, or to pretend to be in agreement all the time (incompletion); and
10. feeling that parents and children feel they cannot rely on each other (unreliability).

It is important for the therapist to facilitate movement of a family toward a more open system. By being alert to the ways in which the

family reacts to stressors, a therapist can plan more effective interventions. The following are some of the questions that a therapist
might think about in trying to assess the existing resilience of a family or to plan interventions that move toward a more resilient family
system.

1. How open is this system?
2. How closed was the family system prior to this current stressor?
3. What effect is the present crisis having on the family?
4. Is it becoming more open or closed?
5. Has some particular event in the past, such as death, illness, divorce,
   or other loss, caused the system to become more open or closed?

It has been my experience that a humanistic, systems-oriented,
experiential approach to families not only promotes the natural continued growth in a family, but also promotes resilience by allowing a
family to update its own worldview, moving from the pessimistic
toward the optimistic, the negative to the positive, from competition
and fear toward cooperation and love.

Virginia Satir's Experiential Humanistic Model for the Family

The organic growth model of Virginal Satir (also called the seed
model) emphasizes the importance of process and feelings over cog-
nition and content. There are several key theoretical concepts that
are important in the Satir model. Peace in the family starts with creating harmony within the self. Virginia Satir (1916–1988) was a
major pioneer in family therapy. For close to 50 years she helped people toward becoming more fully human. She believed in the healing
of the human spirit through learning to make contact with others and
ourselves in a meaningful way. She was a renowned author, lecturer,
and teacher who trained many generations of therapists. Satir developed the therapeutic use of sculpturing, survival stances, metaphors,
integration of parts, communication, and family reconstruction. She
was warm and intuitive in her understanding of people. Virginia's
goal was to develop a consciousness toward peace inside and outside
of ourselves, individual health, and social and personal responsibility.
   Her methods combined concepts of communication theory with
humanistic notions of self-esteem and a dynamic understanding of
how increasing awareness of patterns learned in the family of origin
can lead to change. Satir's approach is experiential, involving families

in exercises and activities during the session. Satir's training workshops have impacted a large national audience, in her time, more than any other family therapy model (Kolevzon & Green, 1985).

I have been personally involved with this process along with her and in my own work. I believe that the effectiveness is due to the combined use of traditional individual psychoanalytically oriented therapy models and Satir's psychodynamically informed family therapy approach. In addition, her model stimulates an innate universal healthy growth process. It taps into the resilience of the person automatically, and it supports the implementation of familiar and comfortable methods for a wide variety of therapists and clients. It is especially practical for private practice, where practitioners have the need to treat individuals and families. Satir's approach is very adaptable.

Key Theoretical Concepts in Satir's Therapy

Relationship between Partners

In family systems theory, the relationship between marital partners is of the most importance. If it is a wounded system, symptoms will develop in a spouse or a child who has been referred to as the identified patient. People with low self-esteem often choose each other as marriage partners because they can more easily blend boundaries and merge into one, not seeing how they are different. After the marriage, when they begin to notice the previously hidden differences, they are neither able to negotiate the differences nor support each other's self-esteem. As married persons, they have difficulty making independent choices or expressing individual wishes. When children come onto the scene and begin to express their own choices and wishes, each parent in turn sees the child as a potential ally, asking them to side against the other parent. If children do this, they may lose the other parent (the psychology of the enemy). The parents live for the children and the children are seen as extensions of the parents and follow the rules of the family. Children in this scenario often develop low self-esteem and conflicted male-female relationships, with a subsequent repeat of dysfunction across the generations.

To develop their own resilience, children require validation of growth by parents. If the parents cannot perform this task, then another adult will be sought. If no adults are available, another child such as a friend or sibling will be sought. When children are encouraged to ask questions and receive considerate answers, their self-esteem is increased. When parents model a satisfying female-male relationship and acknowledge their children as masterful human beings, children acquire self-esteem.

⸍   Triangulation—The Psychology of the Enemy versus Compassion in a Family

When a two-person relationship, a dyad, is calm, it is stable. However, when a stressor enters, anxiety arises, and another person is imported to form a three-person triadic relationship, a triangle. This is the smallest relationship system that is stable (Bowen, 1978). The third person, however, is also usually just as vulnerable as the first two. When tensions become too great in this triangle, others are recruited to form interlocking triangles. Usually, a triangle is made up of two people who are close and a less-close outsider. Under moderate stress, two sides of the triangle are comfortable and one is conflicted. If the triangulation pattern is repeated in a family, family members take on fixed roles in response to each other rather than differentiating as separate people. Satir believed that a basic unit of identity is the harmonious triad of mother, father, and child and that when the system is out of balance, we begin to have problems in families (Satir, 1988).

This leads to incongruent, defensive coping methods and communications. At this point, if the therapist can turn the psychology of the enemy into the psychology of compassion, the resilience of the system can be used. It becomes a turning point, where family members who have cut off meaningful communication can actually develop more satisfactory relationships with other family members, even if those others do not change externally.

In her book, *The New Peoplemaking*, Virginia Satir used the metaphor of a mobile as a way of explaining the principle of balance in family systems (Satir, 1988). She said, "In a mobile, all the pieces, no matter what shape or size, can be grouped together in balance by shortening or lengthening their strings, rearranging the distance between pieces, or changing their weight. So it is with a family. None of the family members is identical to any other; each is different and at a different level of growth. As in a mobile you cannot arrange one member without thinking of the others."

Self-Esteem

Self-esteem, therefore, is a key theoretical concept in the Satir Model. Self-worth is the value that each person assigns to self at any given time. As a metaphor, Satir (1988) likened self-esteem to a pot that sat on the front porch of her family home when she was growing up. At times, the pot was full of good things; at times it was full of nasty things. Sometimes it had very little in it. However, it was never nonexistent. She thought that the amount of self-esteem was a key factor in what happened between people and within them. Though the concepts are not identical, in clinical settings resilience seems to have a high correlation to self-esteem. People with high esteem can directly share their thoughts and feelings and do not have to hide them. Though esteem is innate, its levels felt at any given time can be influenced by other people, such as employers, colleagues, as well as family members. The ability to maintain high self worth in the face of a perceived threat is a learned behavior, and it is important in relation to the I AM of resilience. To foster resilience, Satir devised an exercise entitled, Midwifing Self-Esteem.

Choice and Responsibility

Satir believed that a mature person makes choices, owns them, and takes responsibility for outcomes. For Satir, one of the developmental goals of life, and hence for therapy, was for a person to become his or her own choice maker. This concept relates to resilience. Resilient people deal with situations as they are, rather than how they are expected or desired to be. Resilient people further have the ability to send and receive accurate communications and to check out meanings of confusing communications with other people. Satir referred to the time in a person's life when they can accomplish this as the *third birth*. In this metaphor, the first birth was the union of egg and sperm. The second birth was the entering of a new individual into the world. And the third birth is the time in which each one of us becomes his or her own personal decision maker. The third birth was a time when a mature person could express themselves directly to others, was aware of his or her internal self, that is, what they felt and thought at any given moment, and treated other people as both unique and different to self, worthy of exploration and learning.

Communications Theory

Another important theoretical concept in Satir's work is communications theory. Communication is central to Satir's clinical work. Each one of us responds to a communication in relation to a self (1), a self plus other (1 + 1), and a specific context. The context is composed of that within which the communication occurs: the topic, the place, the atmosphere, and the cultural context of the world. Satir also thought that communication had two levels, the denotative level (the content) and the metacommunicative level (the message about the message). The content is usually expressed verbally, whereas metacommunication is generally expressed nonverbally, although sometimes it is also verbalized. Nonverbal behavior, such as gestures, posture, tone of voice, and facial expression send metacommunications involuntarily. Communicative dysfunctions arise when the verbal message and the nonverbal metacommunications fail to correspond. These incongruities cause children to have to choose the correct meaning, and I have noticed that children believe the metacommunication when the adult may have intended just the opposite. This model of incongruent communication leads children to experience uncertainty in trusting, question their own autonomy, and recoil from developing initiative: the very building blocks of resilience.

At The Satir Centre of Australia for the Family, we try to teach families that congruence in communication is a necessary factor in the development of resilience in the family. Satir believed in the importance of trying to stop overgeneralizations in families using *always* and *every* and using either/or dichotomies, such as right/wrong or enemy/friend, at the lower ends of interpersonal functioning. Hence, she projected that a society that was run on compassion, rather than on the psychology of the enemy, would communicate much better and be filled with far more congruent people.

Patterns of Communication

In the Satir model, communication is either congruent or incongruent. Congruent communications occur when the inside feelings are the same as the outward expressions. Incongruent communication consists of placating, blaming, becoming super-reasonable (computing), or becoming irrelevant (distracting) in the face of perceived self-worth questions. In *The New Peoplemaking* (Satir, 1988), Satir noted that these four incongruent communication stances are often used when people feel threatened and feel the need to protect their self-esteem by not sharing true reactions. Such patterns block real contact between people, and Satir described physical positions, which she called *stances*, that represent each of the dysfunctional styles of communication.

The understanding of this relationship of congruence to health and growth, and by extension to resilience, is an important part of the legacy Virginia Satir left. These observations and the explications of these, the five universal patterns of human communication, are the core methods behind Virginia Satir's extraordinary ability to connect and to facilitate connection. Satir left a collection of teachable, learnable skills about how human communication works.

Stances

Congruence

In congruent communication, words, feelings, and behaviors are all clear and well matched with each other. The words might be, "Let me tell you what I'm thinking and feeling, and you tell me what's going on with you. Let's stay in touch with the situation we're in." The feeling state might be trepidation at times, with courage, strength, and later, peacefulness. The result might be that all reality counts (Neil & Neil, 2001).

Placating

It was Virginia Satir's observation that about half the people she encountered would, when under emotional stress, sell themselves out to please the other person; the immediate response would be, "My own opinion—ideas, wants, needs—cannot be as important as yours are, because I am not worth it." When a person placates in response to stress, this self-effacement means that the person seeks acceptance from others and to be able to depend on them. The main aim of this method of looking after one's self is to avoid rejection, and when people become stuck in that mechanism of coping, they often self-efface for years in their life. The range of possibility for this response extends from sickeningly sweet, patronizing "agreement" to suicide.

Blaming

The next most common response is to blame the other person instead, attempting to gain a sense of importance at the expense of the other. When a person blames others, this results from the seeking of power or mastery. In that sense, because of the unconscious fear of lack of internal power, the person often seeks control, dominance, perfectionism, and sometimes, at the extreme, they will be arrogant or vindictive in search for power. The main reason for this is to avoid helplessness. Although the external message is, "I am worth it and you are not," the inner fear is, "I think I am not quite measuring up." The blamer disagrees with others, blaming other when things fail to work out as planned. Pointing one's finger, with the other hand on the hip, is the physical stance of the blamer. The blamer's body says that the blamer is in charge, and words may be, "It's all your fault!," but the inner feelings of the blamer are covert fears of being unsuccessful and lonely. Although this stance bears the seeds of self-care, its alienating nature mitigates against connection with the other. Carried to extremes, this behavior goes beyond disagreeableness and on to persecution and homicide.

Being Super-Reasonable

A response that is often more frequent among the intellectually gifted is to drain the dialogue of all feeling and focus on the task instead. The computer-like super-reasonable person uses logical words like a computer instead of feeling words like a human. The stance might be depicted as sitting rigidly with hands folded across the chest, or standing straight like a soldier, often looking superior. The body of the super-reasonable person says that he or she is cool, calm, and collected. But inside that person feels vulnerable. In this feelingless response, the context becomes more important than the human beings involved. Many people in our culture equate this with an adult response and do not understand the serious danger presented to the physical aspect of the self that may result from chronic use of this response to self-worth questions. In Virginia's homespun words, "there is a gland for every feeling and a juice for every gland; dry up the feelings and you dry up those juices" (V. Satir, personal communication, 1971). If this occurs over enough years, one's physical self begins to suffer the consequences of the diminishment of those various "juices." Ultimately, this response may also be quite dangerous for the larger society as the excessive dependence on logic sanctions the rationalized behavior of terrorists and all those who believe that ends justify means.

Being Irrelevant

A certain percentage of any population will, when feeling low in self-worth, begin to behave in a manner that is irrelevant to the subject and persons at hand, as well as to their own feelings. This irrelevance is accomplished by distracting behavior, with a hope of avoiding being noticed at all, rather than risking notice and being found wanting. The distracter's physical position is angular and off balance, but inside they feel and think that nobody cares. Being distracting or irrelevant results in a kind of resignation; a seeking of calmness or inertia is a way of avoiding all conflict or coercion. Quite often this will have enormous implications for a family, because energy becomes potential and not kinetic. Plans are made, but never realized. One can be creative or have fun, but not get results. In the farthest extremes of this behavior lies psychosis, wherein an alternative reality is felt to be safer than actual reality.

In family therapy, previously unconscious patterns of communication are explicated. Since such patterns, when dysfunctional, block real contact between people, Satir wanted to translate these covert stances into overt choices. She used the physical positionings of the stances to represent each of the dysfunctional styles of communication. In a family therapy session, these stances are often depicted by the family members themselves to enhance their ability to feel their true feelings at the time. The placator agrees with whatever the speaker says, even though the placator does not actually like what the speaker has proposed. Instead, the placator feels worthless if the speaker blames, and the physical position taken by the placator is to kneel on one knee, with a hand reaching out for help. Historically, this communication stance has often been used by people of low social status, such as women and minorities, but is not their exclusive domain. It has its origin in overvalued illusions of powerlessness.

These four incongruent stances (blaming, placating, being super-reasonable, and being irrelevant) are based on survival—ways of surviving under stress—rather than growth. They are based in the biological responses of fight, flight, or freeze, and so actually have positive aspects in relation to their continued use. For example, the placator has the ability to care for others, and the blamer has the ability to be self-caring. Often in the transformation from placating to congruent communication, the former placator will learn to care for self as well as the other. And the blamer will learn to care for others as well as self. The blamer will become far more reasonable and caring about the other. The super-reasonable can use their intelligence, adding knowledge of the feeling states of self and others. The distracter learns to replace confusion with creativity. Contained within each is the undeveloped kernel of resilience.

Transformation

In the Satir model, the process by which incongruent stances are changed into congruent ones is called transformation. An example of a family reconstruction was published in *A Journey through Three Continents and Four Generations: A Family Reconstruction* (Neil & Neil, 2001). This is an additive process by which previously disowned parts of the self can now be used. In this way, a dynamic balance is achieved (Corrales, 1989). Internally, all parts of a congruent person are working together, with feelings, images, words, and sounds all in support of the external senses. A person who is congruent is truly resilient in that they are aware and in touch with all the facets of themselves and others and give accurate information as well as take in realistic perceptions of people in the external world. The rules of the family are examined in detail. Rules are the stated and covert beliefs, values, and attitudes within which a family system structure is functioning. We examine the flexibility or rigidity of rules, whether or not they change according to the situation at hand. Satir discovered that rules regarding the tolerance of differences, giving and receiving affection, the keeping of secrets, and the sharing of thoughts and feelings were important. She paid particular attention to the rules dictating how anger and other negative feelings are communicated. She also assessed the self-worth of each family member by observing the nonverbal communications with other members, and listening to what they say to each other. Satir often said that the problem is not the problem: coping with the problem is the problem. Something becomes an issue requiring coping when a family member feels vulnerable, ashamed, or worthless as a result of it. When self-worth is thus at stake, the person may begin to blame, placate, distract, or become super-reasonable. They may drink, take drugs, get violent, attempt suicide, or carry out some other defensive behavior in a desperate attempt to defend the self and keep others from knowing about these feelings. Satir would continuously assess the communication stances of family members used most often with whom and under what conditions.

Congruent people have learned to share their feelings of helplessness and vulnerability. They can laugh at themselves and accept their humanity. They do not hide true reactions. Within a family context, they are resilient in the face of vulnerability.

Satir Tools and Methods for Transformation

Satir and her colleagues have described numerous methods that are referred to as *tools*, which are used when working with families to transform incongruent coping so that family members can become more fully human. These are listed in detail elsewhere (Satir, 1976, 1983; Satir & Baldwin, 1983; Satir, 1988; Satir et al., 1991).

For the sake of illustration, I will describe a few of them that have special relevance to the development of resilience in families.

Sculpting

In the Satir model, sculpting is a tool for making an external picture (sculpture) of an internal process such as a feeling, experience, or perception. For example, someone wanting to represent his/her interpretation of an event becomes the sculptor. They will ask other people to assume a specific body position and expression that reflects the sculptor's perception. This allows the sculptor to remove himself/herself from the immediacy of the therapeutic moment to obtain a more objective view and opens the possibility for new awareness.

Family Reconstruction

The Satir method of family reconstruction is a unique technique that is considered representative of her philosophy on the theory of change within families. The star of the reconstruction, the central character, patient, or client, is guided to discover the origins of distorted learnings that have been carried forward into current life from the family of origin. Possibilities for transforming incongruent coping stances are introduced, and the star is helped to begin to make balanced choices and decisions, based on transformed stances and rules.

Family reconstruction begins with the star preparing a list with names of family members, which includes three generations (grandparent, parent, and present generation), along with five or six adjectives, describing each member's perceived personality. In addition, the star will have prepared a chronological account of family events (who was there, what was happening, the setting, the time, and the place) from birth of the first grandparent to the present time. Satir, as the guide, would then use this chronology during the reconstruction and prepare a family map. The therapist develops a trusting relationship with the star by talking about what the star has prepared. The therapist then determines which scenes in the family history will be enacted in a group setting. Three scenes that are always included in every reconstruction are (1) the history of each of the star's parents, (2) the story of the relationship of the star's parents from the meeting to the present, and (3) the birth of the children to the star's parents, especially the star. Other scenes are included on an individual basis. Being able to see the three-generational family through adult eyes and to update family rules, results in new awarenesses.

With these new awarenesses, various coping processes of the star, the parts of that person are portrayed by group members. Disowned parts are transformed and reclaimed and incongruent coping is transformed and again owned by the star, resulting in more congruent coping choices in the star's current life.

Ropes as Therapeutic Tools

Ropes can be used as a metaphor for illustrating the complexity of relationships, interaction, or connections. In this method, long sections of rope, cord, or twine, each representing a relationship of one family member with another, are tied to the waist of each member until each has as many ropes as there are family members. The other ends of the ropes are tied to the other family members. All the family members become aware of how they are connected and how tightness or looseness occurs in the rope as individual members pull away or draw closer. The ropes, as a symbol for relationships, can become entangled. Family members often do not realize that there is no way in which they can be attentive to every family member at the same time and that they also need to move or change in their family relationships. These ropes can bring out the same feelings in participants as those they experience in their daily life when they are not attached by ropes. The therapist can then ask family members how they are able to reduce the tension on the ropes in order to untangle them. When they can verbalize how they might be able to do this, the resulting awareness can be applied in real life.

Observations of Similarities and Differences

By making it evident that members can see themselves and each other differently, in a different context, often Satir would give an opportunity to the members of the family to break stereotypes. She emphasized each member as an individual, unique, and specific person, and identified similarities and differences that existed in each person. However, because each person has his/her own combination of qualities, each is unique and related. The father and the mother are each asked, "Which of your children looks most like you and which looks like your partner?" Each child was asked, "Which of your parents do you think you are most like? How do you think you are different from your father, and how do you think you are different from your mother?" The husband was asked, "How do you see yourself as different from your wife?" The wife is asked, "How do you see yourself as different from your husband?" This method reveals the ease or difficulty with which family members see themselves as separate and distinct from parents and siblings. Boundary issues are clarified, and a growth model way of seeing things promotes healthy choices by referring to the notion that security in the family comes from seeing change as inevitable, with security resulting from trust, cooperation, and the ability to rely on a cooperative style of coping.

How Was This Experience?

A lovely ending to every therapy session was a question that Virginia would ask: "How was this experience for you?" This offered the opportunity for family members to express what the experience was like for each of them. It was unstructured in time, and the feedback can only reflect any differences that resulted from the family members perceiving each other at the beginning of the interview and later, at the end. Each member was asked, in any order, "What was this like for you, to have this time with your family members?" The therapist then would close the session with whatever remarks he or she chose that were appropriate and thank each one individually for coming.

The Stages of Therapy

According to Satir, there are three stages to therapy (Satir & Baldwin, 1983). These stages are

1. making contact,
2. chaos, and
3. integration and transformation.

The stages are presented at each interview and in therapy with the family as a whole. At the beginning of therapy, Satir would focus her full attention on that person. She would validate their uniqueness in some way, including something unique about each person in the family. This basic process of connecting with each person and listening to him or her attentively raises their esteem and fosters hope. In the first stage, throughout the therapy Satir was nonjudgmental and accepted what family members revealed. Therapists always legitimized feelings, and this, in particular, is important. She modeled communication skills for the family, and family members were encouraged to observe and report what they saw. She assessed the family and at the same time would develop a sense of trust with them, trust being one of the pivot points of resilience. Rather than focusing on the problem itself, she would ask each person about his or her hopes and expectations for therapy, not spending too much time with any one member. Usually, Satir would begin to intervene in the first phase and may have conducted a family sculpture. Family sculpture was used in such a way that family members were asked to show the relationship to one or other members of the family using body positions and gestures to represent degrees of closeness and communication patterns. When movement was added, a family sculpture became a stress ballet. She would ask open-ended questions about feelings, but never pushed families beyond the level of their defense and bypassed anger, aiming to develop positive contact in the initial stage of therapy.

In the second stage of therapy, chaos and disorder were the characteristic features of family members risking the unknown by sharing their hurt and pain and underlying angry feelings, often becoming vulnerable.

Satir would often support the person's fear of potential loss of love, which they faced in revealing the self. She would combine toughness with empathy and pushed only after the therapeutic alliance was well established. She supported all other family members and drew on many skills. This stage was often unpredictable because family members open up and work on issues in random order. Sometimes people still feel stuck and hopeless at this stage.

In the last stage of therapy, she would often use metaphors, reframing humor, and her very specific use of touch is very important in that. Often, by the end of this stage, she would sometimes use ropes as therapeutic tools. The third stage of therapy was characterized by integration or closure on this issue that arose in the preceding stage. There was a willingness to change and hope on the part of family members. Often this stage was emotionally more restful than the others, and members worked together until the family was ready for termination.

Encouraging Resilience in Dysfunctional Families

Resilience in the family results from factors analogous to those that promote resilience in the individual.

Consider how attachment theory sees the matter (Bowlby, 1988). We know that patterns of insecure attachment occur in adult life because we have internal working models that are reactivated in times of threat, crisis, illness, or fatigue. Relational ability derives from whether or not a person experiences an attachment as secure or insecure. Secure attachment results from and enables constancy and stability. Insecure attachments result from functional uncertainty and lack of security in early life. Bowlby wrote that events and situations of childhood that cause emotional hunger and emotional insecurity are

1. threats not to love a child,
2. threats to abandon a child,
3. threats to commit suicide,
4. a belief that one or both parents may never have wanted a child,
5. a child being the family scapegoat,
6. induction of guilt,
7. overattachment or overconcern, discouraging separateness,
8. a belief that the child's putative father is not the real father,
9. being likened to a disliked or hated relative,
10. physical abuse, and
11. sexual abuse.

Insecurely attached people say to themselves, "Cling as hard as you can to people: they are likely to abandon you so hang on to them; hurt them if they show signs of going away, then they may be less likely to do so" (Bowlby, 1988).

Securely attached people tend to believe that people are basically reliable and that relationships are basically supportive, encouraging, and helpful to the individuals. Systems-oriented family therapy is one way that a family system can be helped to feel a mature, secure attachment. Virginia Satir's fundamental therapeutic beliefs give an insight into how the Satir growth model is not only compatible with, but brings about, fundamental positive changes in families that increase resilience.

Satir's Therapeutic Beliefs That Encourage Resilience
1. All people are manifestations of the Life Force.
2. People are unique.
3. Change is possible; even if external change is limited, internal change is possible.
4. Parents do the best they know at any given time.
5. We all have the internal resources we need in order to cope successfully and to grow.

6. We have choices, especially in terms of responding to stress instead of reacting to situations.

7. Therapy needs to focus on health, strength, and new possibilities instead of pathology.

8. Therapy is used to access and to provide alternative choices and resources.

9. Hope is a significant component or ingredient for change.

10. People connect on the basis of sameness and grow on the basis of being different.

11. A major goal of therapy is to become one's own choice maker.

12. Most people choose familiarity over comfort, especially during times of stress.

13. The problem is not the problem; coping is the problem.

14. Feelings are universal and belong to us; we are in charge of them.

15. Survival is a basic need.

16. People learn survival/coping in the family of origin.

17. People are basically good; they need to find their own treasure to connect and validate their own self-worth.

18. Parents often repeat the familiar patterns from their growing up learnings even if the patterns are dysfunctional.

19. We cannot change past events, only the impact they have on us; we can transform what is no longer useful.

20. Appreciating and accepting the past increases our ability to manage our present; the past does not have to contaminate the present.

21. The goal in moving toward wholeness is to accept the parental figures as people and meet them at their level of personhood rather than only in their roles.

22. Coping is the manifestation of the level of self-worth; the higher one's self-worth, the more wholesome the coping.

23. Human processes are universal and therefore applicable in different settings, cultures, and circumstances.

24. Process is the avenue of change; content forms the context in which change can take place.

25. Congruence and high self-esteem are major goals in the Satir model.

26. Healthy human relationships are built on equality of value.

27. All behavior is purposeful; we need to separate the behavior from the person and the intent from the outcome.

28. There are multiple interacting factors to an outcome.

Resilience in a family can be said to be present when each member of the family experiences the five freedoms.

The Five Freedoms

1. To see and hear what is here, instead of what should be, was, or will be.

2. To say what one feels and thinks, instead of what one should.

3. To feel what one feels, instead of what one ought.

4. To ask for what one wants, instead of always waiting for permission.

5. To take risks on one's own behalf, instead of choosing to be only secure and not rocking the boat.

The therapeutic effort, then, is to help people move internally and externally from being bound to past dysfunctional patterns and learnings. Satir's emphasis was on teaching and learning how to cope with life's experiences more effectively and less destructively. She called this a process of making people more fully human. Leaning to cope more productively makes possible the realization of the message in one of her many therapeutic poems (Satir, 1976).

I want to love you without clutching,
appreciate you without judging,
join you without invading,
invite you without demanding,
leave you without guilt,
criticize you without blaming, and
help you without insulting.
If I can have the same from you, then we can surely meet and enrich
each other.

Two Examples of Therapeutic Work Related to Resilience

Bert Hellinger—Family Constellations

Resilience can be seen to be a natural consequence of balanced functioning in the family. When love is freely available in the family, then security and confidence result. The recent work of Bert Hellinger (1998, 1999) provides a fresh viewpoint in the application of concepts applicable to notions of resilience in families. He works with individuals in groups, working around a concept called family constellations. The approach seeks to enable the therapist to contact the unconscious of the incongruent person by simply allowing them to repattern some of their cut-off relationships in the family constellation.

A family constellation depicts an individual client's physical and emotional positioning, and a repositioning of substitute family members in relation to each other. Used usually with a therapeutic group, it addresses family of origin issues and has its roots in several therapy schools, including systemic, humanistic, strategic, and others. The approach has been applied to a variety of problems, including reduced capacity for resilience. Hellinger's use of constellations, which "re-members" (Hellinger, 1998, p.165) people into their families, is useful when working with newer forms of family—such as blended families, step-families, single-gender families raising children with special needs, one-parent families, and families who have undergone severe disruption or trauma (abortion, death of children or parents, sexual abuse, and war experiences). It can also be used within the context of organizational consultations.

Theoretical concepts of this approach are outlined below, taken from Hellinger's book (1998), *Love's Hidden Symmetry*, and its sequels. Processes can lead to either smooth family functioning or an unbalancing of the family equilibrium. This results in symptom development such as depression. The concepts can be used to restore order in families and to recreate family resilience. Hellinger indicates several concepts, which include the following:

1. The concept that we have the right to belong to a system of love, the family clan, which is connected by a deep bond of love.

Inability to be resilient occurs when a person born or brought into the system by marriage becomes excluded. All exclusions disrupt the family, unbalancing it. Members of subsequent generations may become depressed as they unconsciously try to rectify these imbalances.

2. The concept that we have one special place, a hierarchical order.

Family groups organize themselves according to a specific hierarchical order following a chronology hierarchy within an immediate family and a generational hierarchy in relation to a wider family system. In a new family, the first-born child, alive or deceased, occupies the first place, the second the second place, and so forth. If there have been previous partners, the first spouse takes the first position followed by the second spouse, and within the intergenerational context, the order is reversed. When a new family is founded, the previous generation allows the new family to take precedence. This hierarchical order, if violated, results in a reduced ability to be resilient. When the orderliness is honored, family members will experience a sense of joy, harmony, completeness, and contentment.

3. Systemic Equilibrium: The Group Conscience

Hellinger assumes that within families there is a group conscience that is governed by principles of fairness and loyalty, in the form of unconscious moral obligations or rules. If rule violation has occurred, the system will press for retribution, and members of the system become depressed by the imbalance.

4. The Violation of Rules: Symptom Development

Lack of resilience results from the violation of natural rules because of the exclusion of a family member or from an imbalance of giving and taking.

4a. Exclusions

Exclusions are often due to family secrets such as adopted or illegitimate children, unresolved conflicts involving parents and children leading to permanent communication breakdown, traumatic loss such as premature death or suicide, or events that are perceived as shameful and guilt provoking, such as crime. Exclusions can be a conscious attempt to expel someone from a system who no longer deserves the right to be part of the system, such as a violent person or a person excluded as a result of divorce or death. There can also be an unconscious attempt to forget, because the memories associated with the person may evoke overwhelming feelings. Sometimes, when an exclusion has taken place, a member of the youngest generation may try to rectify the exclusion by following the excluded person in a symbolic way, for example, by developing similar behavior characteristics, thus bringing the excluded person back into the system. Lack of resilience may indicate the possibility of an exclusion that has not been rectified.

4b. Imbalance in Giving and Taking

The second type of violation of rules is the skewed balance between giving and receiving. Hellinger assumes an inherent order of giving and taking, which follows the time-dependent lines. Hellinger held the view that love flows smoothly when all members of a family follow a hierarchy, which must meet three criteria: time, weight, and function (Hellinger, 1998). For example, with respect to time, "Children come

after their parents and the younger always follows the older. The relationship between mother and father exists before they become parents; there are adults without children, but no children without
biological parents. Love succeeds when parents care well for their
young children, but not the other way around. Thus the relationship
between husband and wife takes priority in the family . . . The older
siblings give to the younger, the younger take from the older. The el-
dest gives more and the youngest takes more" (1998, p. 107).

Hellinger indicated that three common patterns of giving and taking between parents and children are injurious to love in the transgenerational family (1998).

1. Children refuse to take their parents as they are. "Parents
   enter parenthood through the events of conception and
   birth, and these acts alone make them the child's parents.
   Children are absolutely powerless to change anything
   about who their parents are. So when they say, in effect, 'I
   don't like this about you, so you are not my father.' Or, 'You
   didn't give me what I needed, so you can't be my mother,'
   this is an absurd distortion of reality. Children experience
   inner solidity and a clear sense of identity when they
   accept parents as they are. Exclusion of one or both of
   their parents from their hearts causes children to become
   passive and feel empty. This is a common cause of depression. Even when children have been hurt by their parents,
   they need to accept that their parents did the best they
   could, even if it was not good enough. Then they are free
   to set about the difficult task of making the best out of
   what may be a bad situation" (Hellinger, 1998, p. 95).

2. Parents give and children take that which is harmful.
   "Among things that parents must not give to their children, and the children must not take, are debts, illnesses,
   obligations, burdens of circumstance, injustices suffered or
   committed, and any privileges gained by personal achievement. These are things that parents have earned or suffered through personal effort or circumstance. They
   haven't been inherited, and so they remain the parent's
   responsibility. Parents must protect their children from
   negative effects of such things, and children must trust
   their parents to deal with whatever fate has meted out to
   them. When parents give what is harmful or when children
   take it (what is harmful) the natural flow of love is injured"
   (Hellinger, 1998, p. 100).

3. Parents take from children and children give to their parents. "When the parents haven't received or taken enough from their own parents, they expect their needs to be met by their current partner or by their children, and the children feel responsible for meeting them. Parents then take like children and the children give as if they were parents, instead of the natural order of flowing from older to younger." (Hellinger, 1998, p. 102)

By acknowledging the love that exists despite the forced cut-offs that misfortune causes, families can again include, symbolically or literally, previously excluded members. Families can then plan for a future that is influenced by the present, not by the past. Therapy helps families acknowledge and reconnect with their inherent resilience.

Anne Ancelin Schutzenberger—Transgenerational Links and the Ancestor Syndrome

Next, I would like to deal with the concepts of Anne Ancelin Schutzenberger, which are of importance in dealing with family resilience. She has written a book entitled *The Ancestor Syndrome* (Schutzenberger, 2000), which was written in response to the death of her 16-year-old son in a car accident. Schutzenberger proposed that people transmit a pattern of dysfunction, including family dysfunction, through the generations, and these can be traced back. She uses the family genosociogram to demonstrate this, which often traces, as Murray Bowen and Virginia Satir did, four and five generations of family patterning. This illustrates how people can conquer psychological and even physical difficulties, by discovering and understanding the parallels between their own life and the lives of their forebears.

There is an unconscious loyalty owed to previous generations that makes us unwittingly reenact their life events. Schutzenberger refers to narratives such as "The Crypt and the Ghost," "The Dead Mother," "Trauma of the Wind of the Cannonball," "The Anniversary Syndrome," and "Invisible Family Loyalties" (Schutzenberger, 2000). Yet another concept she refers to is the legacy of genealogical incest. She writes, "The genosociogram allows a visual sociometric representation of the family tree including surnames, given names, places, dates, landmark occurrences, bonds, and major life events such as births, marriages, deaths, important illnesses, accidents, moves, occupations, retirement. The genosociogram is an annotated representation of the family tree—a genogram—which highlights, through the use of sociometric arrows, the different types of relations the subject has with his or her environment and the bonds between the different people: co-presence, cohabitation, co-action, dyads, triangles, exclusions, etc. It pinpoints who lives under the same roof, who eats from the same dish, who raises whose children, who runs away and to where, who arrives—through birth or moving in—at the same time as another goes away—through death or departure, who replaces whom in the family, now things are shared—particularly through inheritance or donation after a death, who is favored and who is not, as well as repetitions and injustices in the family bookkeeping. . . . I work the genosociogram in great depth, in as complete a context as possible, and often reconstructing the past over two centuries, six to nine generations, and sometimes further. . . . We work with what is expressed through non-verbal communication, explore the 'gaps' in what has been said, what has been 'forgotten,' the splits, the break-ups, the 'broken hearts,' the synchronous events and the coincidences in dates of birth and dates of death, marriage, separation, accidents, onset of illness, failure in exams, reconciliation. We note the important anniversary dates in the client's personal world, in his family universe, in his social atom, in his social and economic environment, in his personal psychological reality, with the goal of helping that person better understand his or her life and give it meaning" (Schutzenberger, 2000, pp.10–11).

She demonstrated this very clearly in a workshop I attended wherein she first traced a lot of the psychological pain of a young depressed woman (Y) whose mother was dying. The woman's grandmother was imprisoned in Siberia. She also traced Y's near rape in Africa, to her grandmother being raped in Siberia. This woman's lack of resilience and fear of loss was understood as a multigenerational process. As it happened, in the genogram, Schutzenberger traced the woman's family being subjected to genocide in Russia. The genosociogram followed Y's life through five generations. Y was a living testament, bearing witness in the present to the past; her development following the therapy was an example of resilience being liberated (Schutzenberger, 2000).

Further examples of this invisible family loyalty include what Schutzenberger refers to as transgenerational terror. She refers to a case "The Wind of the Cannon Ball" (Schutzenberger, 2000, p. 25). This is an example, taken from the retreat of Russia in 1812, which left 20,000 survivors of an original 500,000 men sent to the Russian campaign. Napoleon's surgeons observed the traumatic shock experienced by soldiers who came within a hair's breath of death and felt "the wind of the cannon ball," which killed and massacred their buddies or brothers in arms. Some lost all memory of this experience, and others were frozen to their souls with terror. It seems as if the shock wave that hit them was transmitted to certain descendants who were sometimes frozen to the bone (Raynaud's disease) or feel sick, experiencing anxiety, throat constriction, or nightmares during certain anniversary periods by a kind of telescoping of generations and to a time collapse. Schutzenberger has said that she, as a clinician, has seen the countereffects of pathological and unfinished mourning in descendants and memories of loved ones who died without burial or went missing or when unfair deaths have occurred. Symptoms often appear in connection with commemoration of important events that occurred, such as the end of World War II. These vivid memories could be related to unfinished tasks. Sometimes parents carry these memories and invert the giving and receiving in their families.

In my own clinical work, I have observed that these patterns of dysfunctional coping shape family resilience in unconscious ways. While family members across the generations seek safety and security by following rigid rules for functioning, they unconsciously surrender cognitive, emotional, and behavioral flexibility and reliance on others. The resulting closed systems inhibit the natural resilience of the family.

In family therapy terms, resilience is a natural result when a family system operates in balanced, congruent ways. Each person in such a system is able to make effective choices in age-appropriate ways, with awareness of their own needs, the needs of others, and the context of the family system. The I HAVE component of resilience is present because the family system is able to reach outside itself for help, encouragement, and assistance because it is able to have a basic trust in others. The I AM component is present because the family system is internally supportive and cooperative, rather than competitive. Family members experience a strong identity and have a sense of autonomy such that relationships are felt to be among people who are equal in value. The I CAN component of resilience is present because the family system is able to initiate productive cognitions and actions based on a cooperative, networked ability to draw on the individual problem-solving skills of family members such that the system as a whole can accomplish more than the sum of its individual members' abilities.

References

Abramson, L. Y., & Alloy, L. B. (1981). Depression, non depression, and cognitive illusions: Reply to Schwartz. *Journal of Experimental Psychology: General, 110,* 436–447.

Alloy L. B., & Abramson, L. Y. (1979). Judgement of contingency in depressed and non depressed students: Sadder but wiser? *Journal of Experimental Psychology: General, 108,* 441–485.

Bowen, M. (1978). *Family therapy and clinical practice.* USA: Jason Erinson.

Bowlby, J. A. (1988). *Secure base: Clinical applications of attachment theory.* London: Routledge.

Constantine, L. L. (1986). *Family paradigm: The practice and theory in family therapy.* New York: Guilford Press.

Corrales, R. (1989). Drawing out the best. *Family Therapy Networker, 13,* 44–49.

Grotberg, E. H. (1995). *A guide to promoting resilience in children.* The Hague, The Netherlands: The Bernard Van Leer Foundation.

Grotberg, E. H. (1999). *Tapping your inner strength.* Oakland, CA: New Harbinger Publications.

Grotberg, E. H. (2000). International resilience research project. In A. L. Comunian and U. Gielen (Eds.), *International perspectives on human development* (pp. 379–399). Vienna, Austria: Pabst Science Publications.

Grotberg, E. H. (2001, Spring). Resilience and culture. *International Psychology Reporter, 12,* 13–14.

Grotberg, E. H. (2002). From terror to triumph: The path to resilience. In C. E. Stout (Ed.), *The psychology of terrorism* (pp. 167–189). Westport, CT: Praeger.

Hellinger, B. (1998). *Love's hidden symmetry.* Redding, CT: Zeig, Tucker & Co.

Hellinger, B. (1999). *Acknowledging what is.* Redding, CT: Zeig, Tucker & Co.

Kolevzon, M. S., & Green, R. G. (1985). *Family therapy models: Convergence and divergence.* Heidelberg, Germany: Springer Publishing.

Neil, S., & Silverberg, R. (1995). *The family chessboard.* (Vols. 1 and 2). Melbourne, Australia: Satir Centre of Australia.

Neil, S. E. S., & Neil, S. E. (2001). *A journey through three continents and four generations: A family reconstruction.* Melbourne, Australia: Satir Centre of Australia.

Satir, V. (1976). *Making contact.* Berkeley, CA: Celestial Arts.

Satir, V. (1983). *Conjoint family therapy.* Palo Alto, CA: Science and Behaviour Books.

Satir, V. (1988). *The new peoplemaking.* Palo Alto, CA: Science and Behaviour Books.

Satir, V., & Baldwin, M. (1983). *Step by step: A guide to creating change in families.* Palo Alto, CA: Science and Behaviour Books.

Satir, V., et al. (1991). *The Satir model.* Palo Alto, CA: Science and Behaviour Books.

Schutzenberger, A. (2000). *The ancestor syndrome.* New York: Routledge.

CHAPTER 4

Resilience in Families with Children Who Are Exceptional

Sharon Landesman Ramey, Stephanie DeLuca, and Karen Echols

The world over, the entry of a child into a family is a welcomed and celebrated event, especially when a family has good health, adequate resources (social, physical, and financial), and the prospect of future peace and productivity. Almost universally, a child represents joy and hope, as the family anticipates being able to give to and nurture the child and the child, in turn, being able to express love, bring forth happy times, and increasingly become capable and independent.

For families that have a child whose development is not typical, their own life course becomes altered dramatically: the prospect of joy, happiness, health, and independence for their children is far less certain (Borkowski, Ramey, & Bristol-Powers, 2002). Their child with special needs creates many unknowns and increases the demands on the family to provide additional and long-term care. For most families, their exceptional child is unlike any child they have known. Rarely do parents feel adequately prepared for or confident of their ability to parent this child (Ramey, Echols, Ramey, & Newell, 2000).

When faced with the serious challenges, frequent frustration and disappointment, and increased caretaking burdens for a child with special needs, what is so remarkable is that many families do this so well. These families that thrive are those in which the parents and siblings come to view their exceptional child as integral to their lives and as someone who brought new, positive opportunities into their family—opportunities that helped to transform and strengthen the family as a whole. Their children with special needs often thrive in wonderful and unexpected ways, and the families themselves establish mutually rewarding, lasting relationships with other families, professionals, and organizations. This process of transformation and strengthening is a remarkable one and affirms the fundamental value of the family as a vital unit in society (Flaherty & Glidden, 2000). This chapter is all about these families.

Here, we share our insights about those factors that distinguish families that are successful in their dual challenge—namely, *meeting the needs of their exceptional child while also sustaining the well-being of the family as a whole.* These insights come, in part, from an increasingly large body of research about how families adapt and adjust to their child with special needs over time, from first learning about their child's special needs through actively seeking special services and education through the transition into adulthood and aging (e.g., Farber, 1959; Floyd & Gallagher, 1997; Glidden, 1989; Keltner, & Ramey, 1993; Krauss & Seltzer, 1993). These studies have been conducted in many different countries and cultures, as well as at different times in history, with tremendous variation in the societal supports and attitudes toward children with special needs (Gallimore, Keough, & Bernheimer, 1999). Although the theme of resilience was rarely at the heart of these studies when they began, the information gathered often forced a reformulation of the way we think about families with children who have special needs. Although words such as *stress* and *coping* do apply to these families, terms such as *family strengths* and *benefits* also have meaning.

The research findings are ones we have seen firsthand in our experiences as clinicians who have worked with families and children directly, as professionals who have developed programs and services designed to improve the well-being of children and families, and as family members who have direct knowledge of what family life is like when there is a child with special needs. We have selected stories that bring to life the scientific findings, stories that we share in the hope that they will provide inspiration and practical guidance to families and professionals who seek to promote family resilience.

What Is Exceptionality in a Child?

There are many ways in which children can be exceptional. Undeniably, all children are unique individuals who have, from time to time, needs that are above average and necessitate active and sometimes creative and complex problem solving and adjustment on the part of their families. In this chapter, however, we use *exceptional child* and *child with special needs* to identify those children whose developmental needs are fundamentally outside the range of typically developing children and for whom the usual forms of education, health care, and recreation are not sufficient to ensure that they will realize their full potential.

These children have exceptionalities and special needs that motivate most parents to gather relevant information, seek expert and personalized advice, and learn effective and often new ways of nurturing, protecting, teaching, and guiding their children (Landesman, Jaccard, & Gunderson, 1991). These exceptionalities include children who have diagnosed physical, sensory, and intellectual disabilities, as well as children who are highly unusual in other ways, such as children who perform in the genius range in the realms of academic intelligence, music and the arts, science and invention, and athletics. As surprising as it may seem, parents whose children are extremely deviant from the typical course of development—regardless of the exact nature of these deviations—share a lot in common. These families rarely are well prepared in advance, and they must make special efforts and adaptations to accommodate their children's exceptionalities. Not only are the families challenged by their children's direct needs, but their extended family, their friends, and all too often their own communities are not well prepared either.

A child with special needs is one who necessitates a major alteration in the supports and activities in at least one (and often more) of the following areas: educational, social, physical, health care, and psychological/emotional. In addition, the special needs of a child change as the child develops, very often in ways that cannot be fully anticipated and that may fluctuate based on the adequacy of the child's supports and activities in earlier years. The additional efforts by families to plan for, take care of, and monitor their children's progress and well-being is thus likely to be a multiyear, ongoing endeavor, rather than something that can be permanently fixed or resolved. This fact of continuing (often lifelong) special needs, however, does not invariably lead the child and family into a state of constant distress, strain, or uncertainty. What, then, distinguishes those families that become the successful and resilient ones?

What Does Family Resilience Mean?

To be resilient as a family means that the family unit establishes active, healthy, and responsive ways of meeting the needs of an exceptional child, without compromising the overall integrity of the family and without neglecting the individual and developmental needs of the other family members (S. Ramey & C. Ramey, 1999). To create this type of balance and harmony in a family unit that includes a child with extraordinary needs requires vigorous, multiple, and often highly creative strategies. Family resilience is more than just parent commitment or mother resilience. Family resilience includes awareness and commitment from most (ideally all) family members, each contributing in his or her own way to the family's well-being and to the special accommodations that, in reality, make their family different from families with typically developing children.

Resilience in families represents the collective portrait of how people live their lives, despite unanticipated and serious challenges of having a child who is not typical and who is especially vulnerable if his or her needs are not well met. The families we have known that show lasting resilience are those that have tried lots of different ways of solving problems and helping their special needs child, while at the same time adjusting their view of life, re-evaluating their fundamental values and priorities, seeing the good side of things, and not giving up in the face of adversity or inadequacy in the supports for their child. These families do not deny that they initially experienced a range of negative emotions, deep concerns, and difficult times, or that these types of feelings do not recur over the years. Rather, it is the continued openness and optimism in many of these families that characterize their resilience and the great pleasure they derive in knowing that their child with special needs is living a valuable and valued life.

As we prepared this chapter and as we proposed our working definition of family resilience, rather than just parent resilience, we came to realize that we have known many children with special needs who have had a totally dedicated parent or relative who has vastly improved the child's well-being, but who did not have a resilient family. In these situations, the dedication of one parent sometimes has led to major family conflict, imbalance in meeting the needs of all family members, a breakdown in communication and honesty, or permanent disruption in or damage to the original family unit. In focusing on the total family, we do not deny the many heroic and important efforts often made by an individual family member, nor do we intend to imply that all families can become resilient simply by adopting the approaches that have worked for others. Rather, we hope the focus on family resiliency will allow others to see that the family itself is a dynamic system that seeks to establish an equilibrium and continually makes adjustments that, in turn, affect the lives of all family members, not just the child with special needs.

The First Recognition of a Child's Exceptionality

Much of the early research on families with children who had developmental disabilities, especially an intellectual disability or mental retardation, concentrated on how families first adjusted to the diagnosis (Ramey, Echols, Ramey, & Newell, 2000; Ramey, Krauss, & Simeonsson, 1989). Much of this research concentrated on a child born with a diagnosable condition, such as Down syndrome (one of the most prevalent forms of a chromosomally based exceptionality, which can be recognized at birth by the child's distinctive physical appearance and then confirmed by biological tests), or with early and severe delays in development leading to a diagnosis of mental retardation (or intellectual disability) within the first few years of life. These studies were guided by the view that the professional confirmation that the child was not just a little delayed or a little different, that their child would not grow out of this phase ("Let's just wait and see later how your child is doing"), would be devastating news to all families (S. Ramey, 1991). The reaction of grave despair was especially expected for families in which their child's major disability was intellectual and profound (e.g., Farber, 1959). This is because an intellectual disability is invisible, and from infancy through the early childhood years children are often quite typical in their appearance and other aspects of their behavior. For parents who have already suspected that their infant or toddler is not developing language and problem-solving skills at an age-appropriate rate, the diagnosis by a professional or team of professionals who has formally evaluated their son or daughter is often far from a surprise. The family's reactions thus can range tremendously. In reporting about their own experiences, parents frequently mention that they had many emotions upon learning about their child's condition, including a sense of relief ("We were right"), anger at others ("This should have been detected earlier, when we first mentioned things were not going well and that our child seemed different"), and self-directed anger ("I should have done something earlier when I first thought things were not right), and an eagerness for immediate information about what to do ("Who can help our child? What should we do to promote our child's readiness for school? Will my child be able to be independent as an adult?"). In addition, many parents and siblings remember overwhelming feelings of sadness or loss ("My child really will not be as bright as others"), fear ("My child may not be able to have a full and rewarding life"), and inadequacy ("I don't know how to raise a child with an intellectual disability"). Whether studies such as these can ever reveal the full and true range of feelings that parents and other family members have is not certain. What is clear, however, is that there are large differences in family reactions, and that the most serious types of negative emotions, such as self-blame ("I must be the one who caused this. What did I do wrong?"), blame of others ("Did the doctor do something wrong when I was pregnant or when my child was born?" or "This comes from my, or my spouse's, side of the family"), and rejection of the child ("This child with special needs is not really our child. This is not the child we wanted and we cannot continue to parent this child") are not universal. Far more importantly, the initial adjustment of the family to their child's special needs is something that requires time and depends, to a very large extent, on the degree to which family members feel they can take actions and provide supports that will improve their child's future.

In fact, there are a large number of different types of childhood disabilities and exceptionalities (e.g., Batshaw, 2001). Even the invisible intellectual and social-emotional disabilities have many different forms and ways in which they appear. One of the most surprising things to parents, as well as the general public, is that the overwhelming majority of children who have a major disability were perfectly normal at birth; that is, many childhood disabilities occur later as a consequence of childhood injury, illness, or extreme neglect (C. Ramey & S. Ramey, 1998). Thus, there are understandably many different ways in which families encounter the onset of their child's difficulties and differences (e.g., Glidden, Rogers-Dulan, & Hill, 1999). Furthermore, some childhood disorders are relatively static in terms of the impairment, whereas others involve a progressive or uncertain condition that may lead to a worsening in the child's overall health and behavior, a decline in activities, and a shortening of life itself. What almost all parents have told us is that the *uncertainty* that surrounds their child's condition is a huge factor—one that is frustrating at times, but also a source of hope and motivation.

Even for parents who have a young child who is exceptionally talented and academically gifted, an extremely atypical child can be a cause for concern. For example, when an 18-month-old or 2-year-old child is developing at double the typical rate, such that his or her language is like a 3-year-old or 4-year-old, respectively, along with other evidence of advanced reasoning and precocious onset of reading, spelling, or writing skills, such as young children who write poems and stories by the age of 3 years or less, parents are often confronted with a sense of inadequacy in nurturing this child's extremely high intelligence and simultaneously face criticism from many others who accuse them of pushing their child or of excessive bragging. This level of talent is rare, and such children often need extraordinary adaptations in their schooling, with a likelihood that they might enter college very early (some as young as 10–14 years old) or complete college-level courses when they are still in elementary school. Although there are obvious advantages to such academic capacity, there are complex social and emotional issues that exist for many such children as they seek to develop friendships and to find true peers. What parents of extremely precocious children have in common with parents of children who are delayed or disabled is their lack of preparation and their deep love and concern for their children whose differences make them vulnerable and whose needs require additional resources and time to meet well.

Professional Counseling and Guidance after Diagnosis

At different times in history, and undoubtedly in different regions and cultures, how professionals have told parents about their child's diagnosis and then offered counseling and guidance for the child and family has differed tremendously. For several decades, in our own teaching of medical students and students in many of the helping professions, including psychology, nursing, social work, physical and occupational therapy, speech and language therapy, and education, we have brought in panels of parents who tell their own stories and share their ideas about how things could have been done better. More often than not, these parents remember their doctors as being insensitive, inadequate, and/or uncomfortable in telling them the news that their child was not typical. Some of the stories parents tell are shocking regarding the rudeness and bluntness in the way their doctor told them their child had a serious problem. Furthermore, many parents have sensed that their child's doctor conveyed a sense of hopelessness, despair, and general negativity, as though their child was somehow less than a total child worthy of the same amounts of love, care, and investment as a child without a disability.

What we have observed is that this professional insensitivity and negativity, when they occur, reflect the deep and often unrecognized ambivalence and ignorance that the professionals themselves feel. Many cultures and societies have marginalized, ignored, and discriminated against individuals with disabilities or extreme differences (although this is not universal and many communities and countries have actively changed these negative views). The obstetricians, neonatalogists, pediatricians, and child psychiatrists—who typically are the first to tell parents the news that their child is different—often have had woefully inadequate preparation for this complex situation, even when they have been trained to make the diagnosis itself.

Indeed, some of the most revealing insights into these situations come from professionals in the field who later have a child with the very same type of serious exceptionality or developmental disorder that they have been diagnosing in other parents' children. One couple, where both parents are in the medical profession and work much of the time with young children with autism, told us that they were deeply ashamed of how they had spoken to and treated parents before they themselves became the patients. The father said that when his colleague spoke to him in the very same way that he himself had spoken to other parents in the past, he realized how indifferent, unfeeling, and almost annoyed the doctor seemed. Fundamentally, the doctor's behavior conveyed the following message: I don't really have anything that is going to help you, now that we know what the diagnosis is. There really is not anything that will much improve your child's life, given this diagnosis. Another mother, who for years was considered a highly compassionate and committed professional in her specialty field, remembers going home each night and thinking to herself, "I don't know if I could do what these parents have to." She felt huge relief that she did not have to live with the children she was helping during her work hours. Then she became a mother to a child with a major disability, a child whose needs were just like those she thought she could not handle. In fact, this mother and her family became one of the resilient families, after an initial period of great hopelessness and fear about the future.

Almost all childhood disorders are complex and poorly understood in terms of their biological origins, their optimal medical and behavioral management, and their long-term consequences, particularly in terms of the social and emotional impact on the child and the family. Professionals in their own training have rarely been prepared to understand what the day-to-day life of the child and families is like. Furthermore, the increasing evidence that there are positive stories—families that develop resilience and have their children do so much better than predicted—often is not featured in leading medical journals. The father of a child with autism, who shared with us his own personal transformation, has now begun to speak to other professionals, and he and his wife are planning to write a book with other professional couples who also have had the firsthand experience that has led to similar "awakenings" and a commitment to improving the communication between professionals and parents in the future.

Of course, not all professionals are inept in presenting the diagnosis to families. Furthermore, some professionals realize that there is no one best way to deal with all parents. Some parents are ready immediately for lots of information and are willing to meet other parents who have a child with the same or similar disability. But most parents initially want a period to absorb the information and take care of the most pressing issues, particularly if additional medical or physical treatment is needed. Gradually, parents then become ready for seeking out further information and considering making contact with other parents who have had similar experiences. It is also true that some parents still react in ways that once were considered to be the classic parental reaction, namely showing great denial and active resistance to accepting that their child truly has the given condition or diagnosis. For these parents who initially are resistant or deny the legitimacy of the diagnosis, the process of seeking out additional professional opinion and having time to reflect and think about their family and child are essential in the process of acceptance and eventual positive adaptation. We also acknowledge that parents sometimes are correct about errors in diagnosis or important things being overlooked in the early assessments of their child's condition.

Recently, we coauthored a chapter on the topic of early intervention in an excellent edited book written for parents (Ramey, Echols, Ramey, & Newell, 2000). Writing the first draft of this chapter was very rewarding, because we openly told parents about the many problems and limitations in both professional judgment and the services available and tried to do so in a way that would help parents understand why they often hear such different opinions (such as opinions about controversial new treatments, about what causes certain conditions, about some of the errors or mistakes of the past in how children were treated), and why it is so important that parents fulfill their role as a true partner in making judgments about their course of services, therapies, education, and other types of interventions. To our dismay, a great deal of what we wrote was never published. The editors thought the information would be too discouraging to parents, would confuse them, and cause them not to respect professional judgment. We argued with the editors (who are colleagues we hold in high esteem) and told them we already had several parents read what we had written, and they told us they wished they had been able to read something like that even earlier, to help them in understanding the world of professionals and why they received such differing opinions and attitudes (S. Ramey & C. Ramey, 1999). Alas, the truth is that professionals (like almost everyone else) do not like to be criticized or negated or to have their weaknesses revealed. In our judgment, the long-standing struggle and difficulties that can arise between and among professionals, families, and direct service providers reflect the fact that there are still so many uncertainties and unknowns when it comes to any particular situation. Furthermore, emotions are high on everyone's part, and the real answers and information that both parents and professionals would like to have simply cannot come quickly or easily without a great deal of investment of time, energy, and, often, money.

Just as impressive, however, is the fact that many families credit and thank the professionals who were there from the beginning with them. Parents can frequently tell how one therapist or one nurse or one teacher helped them to see their child and their child's potential for future positive growth and development, in a whole new light. These highly talented professionals are described as those who take the time to listen carefully to parents and to respect parents' observations of their own children, and then use this information as the basis for making thoughtful choices about the interventions and therapies that are promising to pursue. These professionals are in an ideal position to share practical information and real-life stories of other children and families with whom they have worked (while appropriately protecting the privacy of these families and their confidential relationships). Indeed, many of the early parent-to-parent and family-to-family contacts are facilitated by professionals who know of families willing to talk with others and who are aware of parent support groups and advocacy organizations and associations in their local communities. The transition for a family from their initial understanding that "our child is truly different," and that this fundamental difference is not just temporary, to a stage of active and open acknowledgment takes time. This need for time is constructive for many, because parents need to discover their own feelings about the situation, to learn as much as they can about sources of help, to share the news with other family members and close friends, and to become more confident in what they plan to do before they can move ahead.

For years, we have had major professional responsibilities for the conduct of specialized interdisciplinary clinics and services at a large, university child development center (Landesman & Ramey, 1989; C. Ramey & S. Ramey, 1998). We have experienced directly the benefits when families seek multiple opinions. We have even thought about the need to offer a "second and third opinion clinic," where parents can comfortably come and ask to have a different team of specialists evaluate their child and recommend a course of action. Also, it is true that children sometimes have better or worse days when they come to a clinic. Some practitioners are more or less experienced with a particular type of childhood disorder, especially when it comes to the rarer conditions. After parents have received a diagnosis, they often become more observant, and this, in turn, allows them to provide more detailed and useful information about their child's progress and special needs. Sometimes genuine mistakes are made or certain important pieces of information are not collected or are overlooked in reaching a clinical judgment. Other times, professionals themselves are not in agreement. There is nothing wrong with, and many things right about, parents seeking multiple opinions from different professionals and from different clinics. This process of obtaining advice and perspectives from many sources often leads parents to become skillful in their advocacy for their child and to recognize that the unique role they fulfill in their child's life is one that no one can assume.

In our opinion, the view that there is a typical course of reaction and eventual resolution related to a child's diagnosis is helpful only to the degree that this reminds parents and professionals that the very first reactions are not necessarily the most important or lasting ones. Rather, with increasing experience, knowledge, and reflection, many families will acquire new perspectives on their child and their own family life. Trying to predict whether this will take about two years, on average, such as the length of time an adjustment to the death of a loved one is supposed to take, seems to us to be too simplistic when thinking about individual families. We know some families that say that the process of adjustment is lifelong, while others say they were almost instantly comfortable with the news; far more important, in our experience, is the way in which parents interact with their child and discover ways to maintain or to create a balanced, dynamic family life.

We find it reassuring to remember how much better the world of care and acceptance is today for individuals with disabilities. We have witnessed the dramatic changes that have occurred in the arenas of civil rights, education for all children, increasing community and adult support services, physical accessibility, and the science-based treatments and interventions that have proven to make a significant difference in children's outcomes. This means there are multiple levels of support for a child's development and improved chance for a positive quality of life (Bronfenbrenner, 1979; Landesman, 1986). However, we may shudder in horror when we remember that it was not that long ago that parents were actively encouraged to give up their child—to an institution or to a foster family—so that their typically developing children or their future children would not be stigmatized or have any compromises in their own development because of the child with special needs. We also realize that this advice was given in an era in which there were few or no services to help families in meeting the additional needs of their children, and many parents trusted that the professionals truly knew that this was best for their children (rather than a well-intentioned guess based on little evidence).

The day that most dramatically changed me (Sharon Landesman Ramey) occurred just after completing a research study providing social and sensory stimulation to children whose parents were all told their children would die by the age of seven years old. None of these children had died, and they were teenagers or young adults when the study took place. On this day, I brought together the physicians who had made the predictions (prognosis) to meet the children who did not die—and had already lived more than twice as long as they had told parents would be possible. Each doctor was genuinely and deeply moved and concerned. They told me that no one ever had come back to tell them they were wrong or to let them see what happens to some of the children 10 or 20 years later. It was an experience I have never forgotten, because I realized that many doctors who are specialists also are limited in their own exposure to the life course of the children and families they treat. Once these children had been dismissed as "preparing to die" and sent home in the care of their families or placed in a long-term residential care facility, there was no more reason for the specialist to see the child. Even more compelling, I had conducted my treatment study (in the early 1970s) with these children because every child had been described in their written medical records, by at least two professionals, as being "hopeless," "not aware of surroundings," or "unable to benefit from any form of treatment or education." My research showed that these predictions also were woefully incorrect.

Making a Difference: Heroic Actions amidst the Everyday Reality

We also have conducted research on family strengths and resilience. The third author of this chapter (Karen Echols) identified a large group of parents throughout an entire state who had given birth to a child with Down syndrome. Each family was invited to share their experiences with the state's early intervention system, in which all of these children participated during the mid- to late 1990s. In addition, parents shared their own evaluations of how their family was doing, as well as their sources of strength. One of the major findings was that the families that were doing the best, in terms of their child's progress and their own satisfaction with the services and supports they were receiving, were also those in which the parents had been advocates and were more engaged in seeking out information and sources of help. These parents were more likely to join parent support groups and to become knowledgeable about their rights as parents of a child with special needs. This parental activism seems to be at the heart of many of the successful families. Why?

The role of parents is a paramount and sometimes daunting one. This is true of all parents with all types of children. It is even more apparent when a child has needs and exceptionalities that cannot be met with the usual amount of effort and the types of resources immediately available. The parents then have an added responsibility, in addition to providing the everyday love, care, and individual attention that every child needs. Rarely is it just one or two things that are needed, such as just purchasing the right wheelchair, learning sign language, scheduling corrective surgery, or finding the right combination of medications to control seizures. More often, a child with atypical development experiences special needs that extend far beyond the diagnosed condition itself. For example, a child with a severe neuromotor impairment often is not only limited in voluntary control of objects or locomotion, but may have difficulty in speech or vision, which in turn can impair the communication and social interactions with others; this may necessitate extra care to prevent secondary conditions in both the physical arena (such as a worsening of the child's health due to lack of proper positioning and adequate movement) and the social-emotional arena (such as developing behavioral problems as a way of coping with frustration and seeking additional attention or becoming withdrawn and depressed, due to the child's self-realization of the severity of the condition). The likelihood of these so-called secondary conditions is far from minor or small but indeed is what parents are acutely aware of in their child's everyday life.

Children who are different—despite the many positive changes toward acceptance and service that have occurred in many places in the world—still remain highly vulnerable to incorrect and sometimes negative judgments by others, reflecting a combination of other people's inexperience and their prejudices. To promote the social and emotional well-being of children with special needs usually requires vigorous, sensitive, and creative activities that parents will help structure during a child's younger (and sometimes older) years. Furthermore, parents almost always need to invest a huge amount of time to learn about and then make available as many types of assistance, treatments, and supports as possible for their children with special needs and for themselves and the child's siblings.

A positive outlook on life and a wholehearted acceptance of a child with special needs are invaluable tools within any family. Yet, often these qualities are not enough to maximize a child's and family's full potential. The terms *heroic* and *superparent* are not exaggerations or mere flattery about the many parents who become their child's successful advocate. When faced with extremely high needs on the part of their child, parents often are propelled into roles and actions they never imagined for themselves. Something we have noticed in the families we know, and something that is confirmed by many of the scientific studies, is that the presence of a child with special needs often takes at least one parent off her or his life trajectory in terms of the course of adult work or professional achievements. Most of the superhero mothers and fathers we have known have either stopped working outside the home or have reduced the amount of time they work in order to meet the needs of their exceptional child, at least during their child's first 6 to 10 years of life. Other families have relocated to live in areas where the services are markedly better for their child with special needs, even when this may limit the parents' options for employment or advancement within their careers or businesses.

Many fathers report taking less-demanding jobs so they can be supportive of their child and family. Others keep the same job, even with limited opportunities for advancement, in order to maintain continued health care benefits that would be lost if they shifted employment (often because of insurer rules that exclude preexisting medical conditions when a family enrolls in a new health care plan).

How to Promote Family Resilience, Based on True Stories

Thinking of the many remarkable and well-adjusted families we have known, we have struggled to discern what has helped them to be so successful. We have seen rich and poor, minimally educated and highly educated, first-time parents and experienced parents, parents who knew a lot about children and those who knew little, all become among the resilient, healthy families. There are many different types of families that become resilient. Among the many features we have seen, time and again, are that resilient families often have

1. a willingness to try new things and new ways;
2. the freedom from undue anger, guilt, resentment, or self-pity;
3. the participation of both parents, particularly if they live together or both are involved in the child's care;
4. a sense of hope that comes from personal belief and/or spiritual sources;
5. a sense of not being isolated from others or being limited excessively because of their child's disability;
6. a strong commitment to continuously seeking out ways to improve their child's well-being;
7. an appreciation that their child with exceptional needs has individual qualities that are positive and that have helped to strengthen and improve the family in many ways;
8. an openness and honesty about their situation, rather than concealing or hiding that their family is, in fact, special and not perfect in how they cope with every situation;
9. the persistence to establish multiple, positive, and often enduring relationships with professionals and teachers whom they see as partners or allies in helping their children and family; and
10. a sense of purpose or meaning in their lives that comes from their own experience of parenting a child with special needs, which often is expressed in altruistic ways by parents and siblings helping others and seeking to improve the supports and services for other children, as well as for their own child.

This seems like a long and daunting list of family characteristics. Yet the emergence of these qualities does not happen overnight, and many of these characteristics are not necessarily present from the start. Here are a few of the remarkable, but not rare, families who have shared with us about their lives and some of the unexpected good fortune they have experienced. (To protect the privacy of these families, we have changed some of the minor details and not revealed identifying information. The essence of what makes these families resilient, however, is reported as accurately as possible.)

The Family That Re-Evaluated Its Priorities

One family that has weathered ups and downs has a lovely teenage daughter, who until recently, was still in an elementary school, mixed-age class for fourth to sixth graders, a classroom where the teachers and the school's principal felt they could continue to help this young girl develop her academic and social skills. The family is from a prominent family in their city, and there were many other grandchildren in this large extended family who were quite accomplished academically, athletically, artistically, and socially, as well as being popular and attractive. Indeed, the parents themselves were highly accomplished and had never had first-hand experience with a child who had developmental delays or intellectual disabilities. Over the years, as the parents watched how the very fine public school system in their affluent community responded to their daughter and the social stigma that developed, largely based on the reaction of other parents and teachers, the parents began to question some of their own core values and priorities. The father began to take a keen interest in philanthropic activities, which included hands-on participation and improving the lives of those less fortunate, a direction he had not really considered previously. Indeed, he had a major career shift, and the family developed new interests that in many ways broadened their lives. The grandparents were highly accepting of their granddaughter, which was of immense support to the family. As the girl matured, the aunts and uncles became increasingly concerned about her immaturity and were alarmed and unprepared when she played in ways they considered inappropriate (but quite harmless) with their younger children. The family was remarkable in continuing to seek options for their daughter's summer activities, in finding strengths to build on (such as her love of tennis and helping others), and friendships. With painful awareness as adolescence progressed, they have placed their daughter in a residential school, but have their daughter come home often during weekends, vacations, and summer. They still face many uncertainties and sadness about their daughter's awkwardness in the teen years. Yet their pride and love for her, along with the balance in their own lives in taking care of their other children and continuing to be active in the community, are signs of their resilience. They helped to pave the way at the small, somewhat elite private school that was open to accepting their daughter, even when other schools were discouraging. Many of the classmates, although much younger, formed friendships with this young girl, included her in their birthday parties and sleepovers, and cherish their own expanded experiences. The years ahead still contain uncertainties, increasingly about adult independence and the degree to which their daughter might find personal satisfaction in work and long-term friendships. The family's strength of love, their strong faith in God, their active shifting of personal life values, and their perseverance in finding the right school setting and then actively monitoring their daughter's well-being are truly indicators of the family's overall resiliency. Although their daughter's disability might be classified as mild to moderate and has never contained serious threat to their daughter's life (although there is a seizure history and some medical complications), this family has learned to cope with an invisible disability that has for generations led to the social exclusion, devaluing, and marginalization of children and young adults who are filled with life, energy, and a genuine eagerness to learn and to participate.

The Family That Would Not Give Up Hope

Recently, we have come to know a family that was faced with a double crisis. The first was that their son was seriously injured and lost most of his voluntary control on one side of his body. Their son's condition was uncertain for a long time, but after extended hospitalization he demonstrated good recovery in terms of overall health and alertness. The family tried many types of recommended therapy, year after year. Despite the positive attitudes of professionals and their eagerness to help the family's child, their son did not progress in terms of neuromotor skills. In fact, the family was told that it would be best to amputate their son's arm and give him an artificial arm instead. These parents, who actively sought information and believed strongly that their son could regain some of his lost functional ability, found out about a new form of highly intensive therapy that we had developed. This therapy had just been adapted from a technique originally designed for adults who were

considered chronic stroke patients, and the first randomized controlled trial to test its efficacy had just been completed and reported
at professional meetings, but still was not published in peer review
journals (a process that can delay the sharing of new results by as
long as two years). The therapy, known as pediatric constraint-
induced therapy, involved six hours of highly structured therapy
each day for 21 consecutive days and required the child to wear a
complete arm cast on the functioning side during the course of treatment. The parents learned about this therapy from a professional
who had known another family who attended the clinic. The family
was willing to move to another city for the nearly month-long treatment, after investigating what the findings were to date. They
assessed the relative risk and felt they wanted to delay the decision
about amputation until they tried another approach. Remarkably,
their son, like other children treated thus far, showed very large and
immediate gains during his course of treatment.

These parents displayed their resilience in many ways. Both parents held high-prestige positions and remained active in their careers,
but were flexible about taking time off. Although the parents could
have been justifiably angry in the incorrect urging by the boy's physician for amputation, they did not waste energy on the past. Instead,
they interacted in very positive and very natural ways with their son
and did not appear to think that his life was compromised, despite the
serious impairment he had sustained. These parents showed both
gratitude and a practical approach to what they would need to do in
the post-treatment period, involving a large demand on their time
and their ability to request that their son exert extra effort to use his
newly acquired arm and hand skills. Although the therapy made a big
difference, their son was not and is unlikely to ever be normal again.
But it is the family's robust acceptance and positive outlook on life
that is salient, not a sense of regret or sadness or a feeling that their
son will live less than a very full, enjoyable life.

The Child Who Could Not Show Her Love Readily

In the above section, we described research conducted with children who were judged by professionals to be incapable of responding
to anyone and unable to benefit from any form of therapy. These clinical judgments were made in the 1960s and early 1970s, and our
intervention that involved providing physical contact from peers who
also were multiply disabled showed that the prediction was wrong.
One young woman had severe cerebral palsy and spent her days lying

on a mat in an institution. Her family was of American Indian heritage and had been told that their daughter would be able to be better cared for and to die more peacefully if they placed her in their special facility with other dying children. Her parents continued to visit and to stay in touch, even though they had a lasting despair about their daughter's uncontrolled seizures and her very limited responses to the world around her. They had always believed—and it turns out, they were correct—that their daughter did recognize them and was capable of emotions and perceptions that far exceeded her ability to show them. In fact, during the course of the research study, this young woman showed a very individualistic way of greeting people. She kicked her right leg when someone familiar and friendly approached her. Once this was recognized, we shared this with the caregiving staff, who confirmed that this was a form of "hello" and was used very selectively. In turn, the girl received increased amounts of attention, and her family increased their visiting. The family's own poverty and life circumstances did not allow them to take their daughter home, but she had lived her first 14 years with them (7 years past the time the doctors said she would die) and was part of their daily prayers, their thoughts, and all of their holiday celebrations (the whole family would come to visit). They came to appreciate that their daughter was, in a very real way, a teacher herself, for she taught others to look beyond the typical child behavior and pay attention to small cues and signs that reflected intelligence, love, and recognition. This was an extremely meaningful message and one that very likely extended to provide even better care for others for years beyond their daughter's eventual death, as a young adult. Before their daughter died, she formed several friendships with others at the state facility, which meant a great deal to her parents in their later life.

The Parents Who Taught Their Unteachable Child

This real-life story could be told many times over, but the family we have selected did this very independently and against professional advice. This family was a pioneer in the early 1950s when their daughter with Down syndrome was born and when schools routinely excluded children with mental retardation from public education. The parents had very modest means, but were highly intelligent and motivated. They found their daughter to be beautiful and delightful and included her, from infancy on, in everything they and their other children did. They made educating their little girl a family project, with the older siblings (who were highly intelligent) being engaged, as well, in teaching her everything from school subjects to how to be polite and how to do things such as dance the popular dances. The parents entertained a lot at home so their little girl could be included. The parents were so overjoyed in their child's progress, despite innumerable setbacks in her physical health, that their friends and extended family always enjoyed being with them. The parents defied the recommendations of the doctors to institutionalize her and never felt regrets. This was in an era in which children with Down syndrome were thought to be incapable of being toilet trained or being able to speak, much less learn to read, write, or eventually hold a job as an adult.

The Family That Chose to Adopt

As surprising as it seems to many people who have never cared for a child with special needs, there are thousands of parents who have chosen to adopt children knowing that they have very extensive special needs and will require a heavy caretaking burden. What would motivate these parents? Interestingly, for the researchers who have studied such families, it turns out that many chose to adopt another child who is exceptional. One family that chose to adopt already had four of their own biological children who were healthy and intelligent. The mother realized she loved caring for babies and offered initially to become a foster mother when she read about an urgent need in their community. She agreed to care for children who were medically fragile and were likely to die in the near future. After taking on the care of three such children, all at the same time (since she kept thinking one or two would not live long), she realized that these children were not just waiting to die, but were fully ready to live and to be loved. She was extraordinarily skillful at engaging their families, who often were detached and disheartened, yet she did not make the biological parents feel guilty that they could no longer care for their son or daughter. Furthermore, this was a family with a highly prominent father who traveled a lot and was in the public limelight, and one in which the older children were actively included in the decision making. At first, it seemed as though their mother was choosing a career, of sorts, at home, but the fundamental love and responsiveness of these children changed the hearts of everyone in the family. Soon, the older siblings were playing with the children and wanting them to be a permanent part of the family. The teens who at first were somewhat embarrassed by their home looking like a group home, with special beds and wheelchairs everywhere, no longer felt any shame and soon came to see their family as rather normal again. Remarkably, the strength of the mother was not the only feature of this resilient family. The family became a reservoir of knowledge for other families, both natural and adoptive families, and was a place that many professionals came to visit and bring their trainees to see the remarkable transformations that were possible. The transformations focused on were the children with special needs, yet those of us who came to know this family well realized that everyone's life had been immensely enriched as a result of extending care to a few children. This was a different type of blended family and one that practiced the art of childrearing with great exuberance, good humor, and openness.

These families are just a few of the many who have seen adapting to an unexpected major life event—the presence of a child with a life-long disability—in a positive light and would never turn the clock back. This does not mean that there were no moments of great fatigue, frustration, or sadness at the imperfect world and the imperfect supports for their children. Similarly, the families who have gone to great lengths to support exceptionally talented children often have experienced a major disruption, but often have sensed that there was personal gain and growth for other family members, as well as fulfilling their child's special needs. Adversity for most of these families simply is not something they dwell on. Their family life represents a can-do approach and an acceptance of the new challenges in their own lives, with a hope that often appears to illuminate the way and lighten the future load for other families and children.

A Word about Families That Struggle

Writing this chapter about resilient families warrants a serious reflection on families that have struggled and truly endured hardship as a result of having a child with exceptional needs. We do not see these families as weak or maladaptive, but rather wish that there were more vigorous efforts to help them learn new ways of coping and handling their interactions with others, including their own family dynamics. One pattern concerns the mother and father not agreeing on what is best for the child or the family. Another is that the parents are simply unwilling to get to know other parents who have faced caring for a child with similar needs. When families become isolated, when they deny the presence of a child who has special needs (often for fear of the social stigma for their typical children or the parents), or when they have a disproportionate amount of attention and energy go toward the special needs child and neglect the development of the other children, then they become more fragile as a family unit. The internalization of despair and guilt, without an opportunity for positive action, can take a lifelong toll on the family members. We can only hope that professionals and pioneers in understanding the idea of resilience will share lots of stories and gather the evidence about increasing resilience in families. The resilient families use help from others, as well as extend a helping hand. The resilient families are not naïve and do not deny their difficulties, but they keep a sense of optimism and, often, humor about their situation. They do find value in their transformed lives and have opportunities to think about the most profound aspects of why we are alive and what we value. There is no prescription for family resilience, but there are many encouraging paths and patterns that others can promote whenever possible. Some of our resilient families truly cannot imagine what they would be like without their child who has special needs!

As we were finalizing this chapter, a father called to discuss his endeavor to create a strong fatherhood network. This father of a child with Down syndrome, also a pastor, found that he and his wife were asked to step in to help with a parent-to-parent and family-to-family program (which had helped them) and then realized how urgent it was to have programs to reach out to and include fathers. This father now is launching a series of father networks and is hoping to study how fathers can be better supported and connected in ways that will improve family outcomes. Identifying the issues for fathers, such as health insurance or playgrounds, is vital to strengthening these families in the early years to promote engagement. What format will work best for sharing experiences and gaining knowledge is of high urgency, so that dads can make a difference. This is just another example of a family that has had its own life rearranged in positive ways and is now reaching out to help others.

References

Batshaw, M. L. (Ed.). (2001). *When your child has a disability: The complete sourcebook of daily and medical care.* (2nd ed.). Baltimore, MD: Paul H. Brookes.

Bell, R. Q. (1968). A reinterpretation of the direction of effects in studies of socialization. *Psychological Review, 75,* 81–95.

Borkowski, J. G., Ramey, S. L., & Bristol-Powers, M. (Eds.). (2002). *Parenting and the child's world: Influences on academic, intellectual, and social-emotional development*. Mahwah, NJ: Erlbaum Publishers.

Bronfenbrenner, U. (1979). *The ecology of human development: Experiments by nature and design*. Cambridge, MA: Harvard University Press.

Farber, B. (1959). Effects of a severely mentally retarded child on family integration. *Monographs of the Society for Research in Child Development, 24*, 71.

Flaherty, E. M., & Glidden, L. M. (2000). Positive adjustment in parents rearing children with Down syndrome. *Early Education and Development, 11*, 407–422.

Floyd, F. J., & Gallagher, E. M. (1997). Parental stress, care demands, and use of support services for school-age children with disabilities and behavior problems. *Family Relations, 46*, 359–371.

Gallimore, R., Keough, B. K., & Bernheimer, L. P. (1999). The nature and long-term implications of early developmental delays: A summary of evidence from two longitudinal studies. In L. M. Glidden (Ed.), *International review of research in mental retardation* (Vol. 22, pp. 105–135). San Diego, CA: Academic Press.

Glidden, L. M. (1989). Parents for children, children for parents: The adoption alternative. *AAMR Monograph 11*. Washington, DC: American Association on Mental Retardation.

Glidden, L. M., Rogers-Dulan, J., & Hill, A. E. (1999). "That child was meant?" or "Punishment for sin?" Religion, ethnicity, and families with children with disabilities. *International Review of Research in Mental Retardation, 22*, 267–288.

Keltner, B., & Ramey, S. L. (1993). Family issues. *Current Opinion in Psychiatry, 6*, 629–634.

Krauss, M. W., & Seltzer, M. M. (1993). Coping strategies among older mothers of adults with retardation: A life-span developmental perspective. In A. P. Turnbull, J. M. Patterson, S. K. Behr, D. L. Murphy, J. G. Marquis, and M. J. Blue-Banning (Eds.), *Cognitive coping, families, and disability* (pp. 173–182). Baltimore, MD: Paul H. Brookes.

Landesman, S. (1986). Quality of life and personal life satisfaction: Definition and measurement issues [Guest editorial]. *Mental Retardation, 24*, 293–300.

Landesman, S., Jaccard, J., & Gunderson, V. (1991). The family environment: The combined influence of family behavior, goals, strategies, resources, and individual experiences. In M. Lewis & S. Feinman (Eds.), *Social influences and socialization in infancy* (pp. 63–96). New York: Plenum Press.

Landesman, S., & Ramey, C. T. (1989). Developmental psychology and mental retardation: Integrating scientific principles with treatment practices. *American Psychologist, 44*, 409–415.

Ramey, C. T., & Ramey, S. L. (1998). Early intervention and early experience. *American Psychologist, 53*, 109–120.

Ramey, S. L. (1991). The family. *Current Opinion in Psychiatry, 4*, 678–682.

Ramey, S. L., Echols, K., Ramey, C. T., & Newell, W. (2000). Understanding early intervention. In M. L. Batshaw (Ed.), *When your child has a disability: The complete sourcebook of daily and medical care* (2nd ed., pp. 73–84). Baltimore, MD: Paul H. Brookes.

Ramey, S. L., Krauss, M. W., & Simeonsson, R. J. (1989). Research on families: Current assessment and future opportunities. *American Journal of Mental Retardation, 94*, ii–vi.

Ramey, S. L., & Ramey, C. T. (1999). *Going to school: How to help your child succeed*. New York: Goddard Press.

Ramey, S. L., & Ramey, C. T. (2000). Early childhood experiences and developmental competence. In J. Waldfogel and S. Danziger (Eds.), *Securing the future: Investing in children from birth to college* (pp. 122–150). New York: Russell Sage Foundation.

CHAPTER 5

Resilience, the Fourth *R*: The Role of Schools in This Promotion

Judy E. Papházy

Capitalizing on the Best Years for Resilience Promotion

Parents and teachers should be the providers of the stable environment (I HAVE) that allows children to develop their inner strengths (I AM) and their skills in problem solving and relating to others (I CAN). It is in the early school years that parents, teachers, and school personnel can work together to promote resilience in themselves and in the children entrusted to their care. The role of teachers is to help children develop a variety of problem-solving and social/interpersonal skills. Teachers do this by modeling and promoting resilience.

During the elementary years, children can really take hold of their environments, both in the physical and social sense. This is the time for learning. Children need to master the dual skills of academic work and social interaction with peers. It is a critical time in personality development. It is a time for children to develop competence, cooperation, and a sense of community. Children's sense of self-worth develops through their increased skills and competencies at school, at home, with peers, and with others. They are now involved in expanding their knowledge not only in a wide variety of school subjects, but also in their physical and social skills.

Schools that promote a sense of community, in which children and teachers have a strong sense of belonging, are places where bullying, delinquency, violence. and alienation are unlikely to exist. Those of us who have worked with children know that terror can exist in schools.

Children tell us that not knowing what might happen is terrifying. Not being accepted is terrifying. Not being able to make friends is terrifying. Being bullied is terrifying. Being at risk of physical violence and death is terrifying. As Edith Grotberg (2002, p. 167) indicated, "terror paralyzes . . . terror makes you lose your sense of safety and security." Resilience promotes the strengths needed to address these terrors. Resilience gives children skills that allow them to face, overcome, be strengthened and sometimes even transformed by adverse incidents, adverse events, and adverse environments. Resilience is essential for children during their school years.

Resilient children with active I HAVE, I AM, and I CAN resilience factors and behavior move into adolescence with greater trust, greater competence, and a purposeful sense of themselves as part of community. Such young people are very unlikely to behave in antisocial or terrifying ways.

The elementary school years allow parents and teachers to form a unique partnership in providing children with leadership, direction and discipline. Parents and teachers are the I HAVE people who help promote children's I AM and I CAN skills. The role of teachers and schools is to help children to not only separate from parents for many hours but also to become more independent and to broaden their range of skills in a number of areas.

Teachers become role models who teach and encourage children to improve and further develop their academic, physical, and social skills. It is from teachers that children receive respect and emotional support. It is teachers who help children learn to manage their behavior in the school setting. It is teachers who clarify the school's rules and expectations. It is teachers who provide an environment where feelings, problems, and issues can be respectfully listened to, discussed, and shared, and solutions found. It is teachers who offer help when children need it. It is teachers who help with mistakes and balance the consequences with empathy so that children can fail without loss of self-worth. It is teachers who encourage flexibility in problem solving. It is teachers who are optimistic about the future. So, it is teachers who provide the essential external supports children need to promote their resilience skills.

Teachers who model these I HAVE resilience behaviors provide a climate of trust in which children's internal strengths (I AM) plus problem solving and social and interpersonal skills (I CAN) grow and further develop. With such teachers, children realize that they are respected and likeable. They learn that they can not only make friends, but also share in and enjoy interactions with peers. They learn to show care and concern when friends and peers are in pain and discomfort. They feel and show empathy. They learn to be proud of themselves. They show self and others respect. They learn to show restraint and try not to do inappropriate things. They develop better self-control.

Encouraged by their teachers, children develop greater autonomy and independence and learn to accept more responsibility for their actions. They learn optimism, that things will turn out all right, and that they have an active role in making the future good.

Children's interpersonal and problem-solving skills will expand and increase in schools where the climate of resilience is evident. In such schools, children feel comfortable speaking about their thoughts and feelings. They can discuss and negotiate solutions to problems even if points of view differ. They are encouraged to be able to see other points of view and so are more able to accept the right to differ. They can ask for help when necessary. They can try out their thoughts, words, and solutions before acting on them. They can better manage their feelings and calm themselves when angry or distressed. They can think and not act too impulsively. They are better able to gauge their own and others' temperaments. They recognize caution, excitement, fear, and steadfastness as characteristics in themselves and others. They can look for trusting relationships with teachers, parents, peers, and others.

The research into resilience (Grotberg, 1995) indicates that children can promote their I HAVE resilience factors from about the age of nine years. Until then, they rely on adults for help, because adults show they are trustworthy, role models, encourage good relations with peers, and can put limits on behavior and help children learn to manage their own behavior.

How Do Teachers Learn to Promote Resilience?

Everybody has the capacity to develop resilience. Everybody can change behavior and language. Everybody can look at himself or herself and see which resilient factors are present and which need to be improved or developed.

Fifteen Elements of Resilience

To overcome adversities, children, youth, and adults draw from three sources of resilience: I HAVE, I AM, and I CAN.

I HAVE

1. people around me I trust and who love me, no matter what;

2. people who set limits for me so I know when to stop before there is danger or trouble;

3. people who show me how to do things right by the way they do things;

4. people who want me to learn to do things on my own; and

5. people who help me when I am sick, in danger, or need to learn.

I AM

6. a person people can like and love;

7. glad to do nice things for others and show my concern;

8. respectful of myself and others;

9. willing to be responsible for what I do; and

10. sure things will be all right.

I CAN

11. talk to others about things that frighten me or bother me;

12. find ways to solve problems that I face;.

13. control myself when I feel like doing something not right or dangerous;

14. figure out when it is a good time to talk to someone or take action; and

15. find someone to help me when I need it. (Grotberg, 1995)

Teachers are some of the major builders of our children's resilience. They have our children in their care for most of their waking hours; from kindergarten to the end of school, approximately 13 years. Their influence is profound. Their responsibility is awesome.

As a person, is the teacher someone people like, who is perceived as usually calm and good-natured? A person who plans for the future and is self- and other-respecting? A person who shows empathy and care for others and who behaves in a responsible way? And, above all, is the teacher a confident, optimistic, and forward-looking person? These are the internal I AM resilient factors that teachers need to promote and practice in their everyday interactions with children.

How are the teachers' I CAN resilience factors, their interpersonal and problem-solving skills? Can and do teachers generate new ideas, new ways of doing things? Do they recognize and encourage these skills in their students? Do teachers demonstrate persistence and encourage it in their students? Do teachers use humor in their teaching and interactions? Do they encourage their students to use humor as a tension breaker? Do teachers communicate their thoughts and feelings appropriately with their students? Do teachers control their personal behavior and help their students manage theirs? Do teachers show a range of problem-solving skills in various settings and encourage their students to explore a variety of ways of problem solving?

Do teachers reach out for help, for example, make use of colleagues when they need to and encourage their students to do the same?

Ideally, teachers would possess all these resilience factors and promote them in their classrooms, playgrounds, sporting fields, and throughout their schools. But, as with all human beings, teachers are not perfect at everything. Accepting their responsibility, teachers will look at themselves honestly and concentrate on improving those resilience factors that are not yet well developed. After all, teachers are in the business of promoting the values of lifelong learning.

The Early Years: Preparatory, Grade 1, and Grade 2

Because development is ongoing in children, the teachers' resilience-promoting language and behavior need to match each developmental stage. For example, by the time children begin school (around five years) they should have developed some trust, autonomy, and quite a bit of initiative (Erikson, 1985). But, as those of us who work with children know only too well, a number of children lack trust and autonomy and demonstrate little or no initiative. In these cases, teachers become critical and need to show very well-developed I HAVE resilience factors.

Trust is a basic need that enables children, and indeed adults, to cope with problems, to form relationships, and to develop a strong sense of self. Kindergarten teachers and first- and second-grade elementary school teachers have a unique opportunity to make their classrooms places of safety and trust. Using their I HAVE factors of being trustworthy and providing safe structures with clear rules, limits, and consequences, they provide an environment that encourages attempts at exploring, trying out new things, perhaps even some risk taking. Such an environment allows children to use their initiative to try moving out into a larger world. These teachers also model appropriate behavior. They show children how to do things—how to talk and listen respectfully, how to take turns and share, how to show care and concern for others, how to accept differences, and how to problem solve. These teachers help and encourage children to risk trying new things on their own and thus to become more independent. In such an environment children have the chance to take the risk to trust, thus furthering their development and resilience behavior. Children who already trust will increase their autonomy and initiative in leaps and bounds. Such an environment provides a win-win outcome for everybody.

Examples from Kindergarten, Grade 1, and Grade 2

In working with kindergarten and grades 1 and 2 teachers, I have often been asked to show how resilience can be used in problem situations. Here are a few examples the teachers gave me to work with:

1. Teasing (grade 1) about a lack of academic or social skills in the classroom.

   Teacher talks about how we are all different (e.g., color of hair/eyes, height, skills, etc.) and how we've inherited these from parents, grandparents, etc. Teacher uses self as an example: "I'm good at . . . , (and in light tones) not so good at. . . ."

   Resilience Factors: I HAVE - a teacher who wants me to learn, and
   - a teacher who shows me how to do things right.

   Teacher talks about different types of intelligence: "Some of us have inherited good math skills, so that it's easier for us to learn math. Some of us have inherited good writing/drawing/putting things together/music, etc. skills, which make it easier for us to learn to do. . . . Luckily, we've all inherited enough to learn and get along with each other. So for some of us some things will be easier and some things harder. That's why we all come to school so that we can all get to know more."

   Resilience Factors: I AM   - respectful of self and others,
   - responsible for what I do, and
   - optimistic about the future.

   Teacher talks about different types of people: "Some of us are noisier, some of us are quieter, some of us make friends quickly, some of us take longer to make friends. So again, we're all different, we have different ways of showing how we feel. At school, we learn to get to know all sorts of people and we learn to be fair to everyone."

   Resilience Factors: I CAN - problem solve,
   - control myself, and
   - work with our different temperaments.

Teacher: "My job as your teacher is to help you to learn to be fair in how you act with every other child in this class and school."

The teacher keeps a watchful eye on how all this is progressing. Consequences for not complying with "being fair" are invoked (e.g., time-out or missing out on a special activity).

Resilience Factors: I HAVE - trusting relationships,
                            - rules, limits, and consequences, and
                            - models for how to do things right.

2. Bullying on the kindergarten playground.

Teacher describes the behavior that needs changing: "Suzie you are hurting/being unkind to. . . ."

Teacher restates the rule: "At this kindergarten, we do not let boys or girls or teachers hit/push or call anyone unkind names."

(Teacher alternative): "Now Suzie, what else can you do if/when you want . . . ?"

Resilience Factors: I HAVE - a trustworthy teacher,
                            - limits to stop danger,
                            - a teacher who shows how to do things right, and
                            - a teacher who helps me learn.

Teacher invites/allows children to say what they feel: "Suzie, can you tell me what happens to you when you are not first/allowed to do want you want?"

Resilience Factors: I CAN   - talk about things that bother me.

Teacher insists on cooperation: "My job as a teacher means I have to make sure you stop hurting/being unkind to . . . , otherwise I'm not a good teacher."

Resilience Factors: I HAVE - a teacher who helps me,
                            - a teacher who keeps me safe, and
                            - a teacher who sets rules/limits.

Teacher accepts apologies and moves on: "Now because I know you want to be fair, tell him/her you're sorry."

Resilience Factors: I AM   - responsible for what I do.
                    I CAN   - control myself.

Teacher talks with children about how they are going to stop this behavior from happening again and offers help and support. Teacher keeps check on how/what progress occurs. Consequences are invoked if necessary.

Resilience Factors: I CAN   -   problem solve, and
                             -    control myself.

            I HAVE   -   encouragement to learn to do
                           things on my own.

            I AM   -   optimistic, sure things will turn
                           out all right.

3. A common problem in both kindergarten and elementary school is the child who doesn't listen.

Teacher moves to the child, touches his or her shoulder, or looks into his or her face, saying the child's name: "I need you to listen to me now. Remember the rule is when I (the teacher) speak you need to listen so you will know what to do." (If a hearing problem is suspected, check it out professionally.)

Resilience Factors: I HAVE   -   rules/limits, and
                              -    a teacher who helps me to learn.

Teacher insists on cooperation: "Okay, now let's get on with. . . ." If the child still ignores/does not listen, the teacher has the child tell the rule about when teachers talk. Focus the child's attention on listening to the teacher. As soon as the child has stated the rule, the teacher smiles and says, "Well done, (child's name)."

Resilience Factors: I CAN   -   control self.

            I HAVE   -   encouragement and help to learn.

Teacher invokes consequences if the above does not get cooperation: "(Child's name), when I've asked you to listen and you don't, the rule is you sit over there (time-out) until you can do as I ask *or* you sit right next to me so I can help you to listen."

Resilience Factors: I HAVE   -   limits and consequences, and help
                                   to learn.

Generally, to use resilience skills when coping with problem situations the steps, as appropriate for the situation, are to

* stop the behavior if it is dangerous;
* offer help if it is a problem for the child;
* be respectful of the child's feelings;
* describe the behavior needing to change;
* state the rule covering the situation;
* teach/discuss alternatives, for example, what/how else can you do/change. . . . Involve the child in problem solving if possible;
* insist on cooperation; and
* praise effort as well as success.

The Middle Years: Grades 3 and 4

Children between 8 and 10 years of age have generally developed more independence and a greater sense of themselves. They are well into Erikson's (1985) fourth stage, industry. Usually, they have mastered the ability to talk with others, to talk about their thoughts and feelings, to share in group tasks and play, to understand the school system and to ask for help, and even to help others. These skills are all not only the further healthy development of industry, but also of many resilience factors.

The sad fact is that some children have not developed adequate industry and so have begun to develop a sense of inferiority, a sense of not being successful enough, not good enough. There can be many reasons why children do not develop adequate mastery in these skills. The most common reasons are that parents, teachers, or other significant adults and other significant children have intentionally or unintentionally teased, made fun of, or in some way made these children feel not good enough. The further sad fact is that these not good enough–feeling children carry these feelings over into their schoolwork and their relationships with peers. Now they focus on their limitations, instead of their strengths. These children really need teachers who know how to promote resilience. Inferior feeling–prone children need to be turned around before adolescence hits.

Teachers need to engage them in rediscovering or beginning to establish strengths and a will to learn. Otherwise, these children will withdraw from learning and relating with peers. Alternatively, they will become behavior problems. They will become at-risk adolescents, adolescents who might turn to some form of deviance to escape from their not good enough feelings.

Today, teachers are expected to fulfill many roles. They are parents, counselors, social workers, marriage guidance counselors, coaches, mentors, and meeting attendees. Their role is constantly changing. More and more demands are being made of them. They are overloaded and often overwhelmed by legal requirements and paperwork. Many classrooms are overcrowded, many schools underequipped. More than ever, teachers need to be resilient to cope with the multitude of demands without losing control of their environments. Some teachers really suffer from the fear of losing control. This is a fear that can also be overcome by reaching out for help from a trusted and competent source—perhaps a fellow teacher, partner, principal, or friend, someone who is a competent I HAVE and I CAN person.

Third- and fourth-grade children learn a great deal by watching what behavior and language their teachers model. Teachers who practice resilience promotion will encourage the further independence in children's learning. They model and encourage good social skills: listening to and speaking with each child respectfully, looking at how problems can be solved, encouraging children to try out solutions and having them persist until the task is finished.

Teachers need to encourage children to cooperate not only with classroom tasks and rules, but also with fellow students. Group activities, group assignments, and group productions are easier for the more extraverted children and harder for the quieter, more reserved children. The more introverted, reserved, or shy children are less likely to enjoy or want to participate. Hence, special teacher attention and care (I HAVE) are necessary with these children. Teachers may initially need to set specific tasks or instructions for these quieter children to help them into the group or activity. In time, and with repeated practice, these children will find it easier to risk being more actively involved in groups. Cooperation needs to be established in children who have trouble controlling and limiting their behavior.

Teachers help children to learn how rules, limits, and consequences apply and that mistakes can be corrected, forgiven, made up, and that we can all move on with optimism because past mistakes will not be held against them. Cooperation also means the social skills of getting along with others, resolving arguments and difficulties, and being able to control one's behavior.

Children's I CAN skills—communicate, problem solve, and persist; manage own feelings; and ask for help when needed—can really take off in these early elementary years.

As in the previous section, teachers asked for help and guidance with behavior in which they wanted the resilience promotion skills demonstrated. Here are the examples they gave me.

Examples from Grades 3 and 4

1. Swearing

   Teacher states the rule about language usage. The rule exists for two reasons—first to be respectful to others (*fair* is a word that younger children better understand) and second because the role of school is to teach and improve proper language skills.

   Resilience Factors: I HAVE - rules, and
   - a role model to show how to do things right.

Teacher asks child using inappropriate language privately whether he or she would use those words with parents. Child will probably answer no because he or she would get into trouble. (If a child answers yes, say, "Well at this school such words cannot be used.")

Resilience Factors: I CAN   -   control myself.

Teacher: "So you know it is wrong to use those words." The child may say, "Don't know." "What do you think I have to do, as it is my job to see every child is treated respectfully/fairly? You need to tell me that you won't use those words again. If you need me to help you stop, I'm happy to help you." (The child may need help in recognizing signs that lead to swearing and have a process to stop it: for example, at the first sign of frustration/anger use the STOP/THINK and only then DO method).

Resilience Factors: I HAVE -   rules, and
                                                -    a role model to show how to do
                                                      things right.

             I AM   -   respectful and responsible.

             I CAN   -   control myself.

2. Exclusion from games

    This can be a twofold issue: (1) children who feel they are not good at games, or (2) children who are not readily included in activities.

    Teacher talks about how we are all different and that's why we have different skills (inheritance) in sport, art, math, music, computers, etc.: Have class discussions on how we can be fair to people who might not be good at . . . (whatever).

    Resilience Factors: I HAVE -   help to learn to do things right.

                 I AM   -   respectful.

    Teacher and class: Can an activity/role be found for all children? Can they be taught skills that might improve them? Who would be prepared to teach them? Would excluded children like to learn skills? Can excluded children think of ways to help themselves?

    Teacher: Set a time frame for change.

    Resilience Factors: I HAVE -   trusting relationships, and
                                                    -    help to learn.

                 I AM   -   empathic, and
                                -    respectful.

                 I CAN   -   problem solve, and
                                 -    take action.

As always, use the resilience factors that are appropriate for the problem or issue needing solution. Remember,

- stop the behavior if it is dangerous;
- offer help if it's a problem for the child;
- respect the child's feelings;
- describe behavior needing to change;
- state the rule relevant to the situation;
- teach/discuss alternatives, for example, what/how else can you do/change? Involve the child in problem solving if possible;
- insist on cooperation;
- accept apologies/restitution; and
- praise effort as well as success.

The Final Elementary Years: Grades 5 and 6

In their 11th and 12th years, many children have begun adolescence. They are more critical in their thinking and more uneven in their moods. Now they need teachers who are flexible, not about rules and limits, but about application and interpretation. Teachers continue to be role models who encourage their students to be independent and to continue improving their academic and social skills. Fifth- and sixth-grade children can more readily be responsible and accountable for their own behavior. These increasing skills build integrity and allow for further I CAN development. Children learn to stay with tasks until finished. They problem solve in both academic and social situations. They ask for help when they need it.

Concomitant with their greater I CAN skills, they demonstrate I HAVE resilience behaviors. They are trustworthy, accepting of the need for fairness, safety, and order (rules/limits). They model appropriate behaviors, especially to the younger children on the playground, in school buildings, and on buses. They, as the senior students, encourage younger children to try out at games, activities, and groups. They offer help to younger children as necessary.

The three Cs, competence, caring, and community, must be given prominence by teachers every day. These Cs underpin every program, whether academic, social, or sporting. Children need to really feel a connection with their school. They need to fit in and belong in their school community. They need to see and feel purpose in their role as active participants in their school. They need to feel able to contribute in some way to the daily life of their school. Such budding adolescents would be well anchored in the sense of themselves (I AM).

Much useful work can be done in class discussions, examining ways in which fifth- and sixth-grade children can improve the life of the school community. The challenge for teachers in these years is to capitalize on the altruism young people show at this age, to direct them into looking outside themselves, to see what can be done to change or improve aspects of classroom or school life, so that it is fairer, better, more inclusive for everybody.

Examples from Grades 5 and 6

In dealing with the examples teachers put forward, I explained that issues now become somewhat more sophisticated in behavior, approach to problems, and outcome. Additionally, the children need to be actively involved in finding solutions to the issues or problems. Here are the teachers' examples.

1. Lack of respect for peer/teachers.

    Teacher states the rule of *fair:* "Because we are all members of the class/school we behave fairly with each other. I (teacher) believe everyone in this class/school can be fair and I expect you all to be fair." (Make sure as the teacher you model *fair* in your behavior.)

    Resilience Factors: I HAVE   -   trust, and
                         -   a role model.

2. Child who is lacking in respect.

    Teacher: "I hear/see (name) you're being rude/mean/unfair to . . . and that upsets me. What's causing you to do this?"

    Child: May answer, may shrug and say "don't know," or "he's/she's a nerd."

    Teacher: "Do you really think this is an O.K. way to behave?"

    Child: May say "yes" or say nothing.

    Teacher: "You know my job as a teacher is to see that you're all fair to each other. How can you and I do that?"

    Child: "Don't know." Shrugs.

    Teacher: "Well for starters, let's talk fairly to and about (name). You can do that (name)!"

    Resilience Factors: I HAVE   -   trust, and
                         -   rules.
               I CAN   -   control myself.

Note: How this moves on depends on how the child responds to these statements and how well or willing he/she is to continue. Teachers need to know the steps for a number of possibilities.

3. Aggressive response to minor accidental incidents

Teacher: "(Child's name) that's enough now. Please stop."

Child: May say "Why should I?"—"Its not fair"—"He/she is a. . . ."

Teacher: "Be that as it may, you can calm down and stop."

Child: "I won't, you're on his/her side. . . ."

Teacher: "(Child's name) I need you to stop right now and listen to me. So and so was wrong/unfair (whatever) in what he/she did. That part you have right. But I cannot allow you to misbehave because (whatever) happened. Now let's deal with (whatever)." (Use resilience skills as appropriate.)

Resilience factors: I AM   -   empathic and caring, and
                            -   respectful of others.

              I HAVE   -   trust, and
                       -   limits and rules.

              I CAN   -   control myself.

4. Gang versus gang: verbal slanging match.

Teacher: "It has come to my notice that there's much verbal abuse (in class session) going on between . . . and. . . . You all know that the rules state that people speak fairly, using proper words, at this school. I know it's easy to get worked up, especially when you're in a group and are name calling the other group. But this is not appropriate and we're going to work out a way to solve this problem. Now, who can offer a sensible start?" (Class process.)

Resilience Factors: I AM   -   empathic and caring, and
                           -   respectful of others.

             I HAVE -   trust, and
                     -   limits and rules.

             I CAN   -   problem solve.

5. Reluctance to complete tasks assigned by teacher.

Teacher: "(Child's name), I see you're having a bit of difficulty doing. . . . Do you know what to do or do you need me to help you?"

Child: "I can't do it"—"I don't want to do it"—"I hate. . . ."

Teacher: "What part can't you do?—It's hard to make ourselves do things sometimes, but we need to do it. So can I help you get going?—Well I can understand you don't like . . . but it's part of what you have to learn/do this year. Let me give you a bit of help. Now, let's start."

Resilience Factors: I AM   -   respectful of others, and
                           -   empathic.

                I HAVE -   trust, and
                        -   learned to do things.
                I CAN   -   seek help when in need, and
                        -   problem solve.

6. Children destroying displays of work from other children.

   Teacher: (If child who did damage is known, name him/her.) "(Child's name) you must not take down/ruin displayed work. That is not fair to the people who have done it."

   Child: "Didn't do it."—"I think it sucks."

   Teacher: "Nevertheless, you are not allowed to ruin or remove displayed work. Well, how can we resolve this problem?" (Go through steps of rule/consequence, child involved in solution, apology/repair/restitution, etc., as appropriate.)

   Resilience Factors: I HAVE -   trust.
                       I AM   -   responsible, respectful of myself, and
                               -   confident and optimistic.
                       I CAN   -   problem solve.

Guidelines for Dealing with Problems

The following use of resilience behavior when coping with problem situations are as follows:

- Dangerous behavior must be stopped.
- Get the child's attention.
- If there is a problem for child, offer help.
- Be respectful of child's feelings.
- State rule covering the situation.
- Describe the behavior that needs changing.
- Teach alternatives.
- Allow child to express his/her feelings.
- Insist on cooperation.
- Involve child in problem-solving process.
- Accept apologies.
- Praise effort as well as success.
- Talk about (teacher) feelings regarding the child's unacceptable behavior.
- State a time frame for change.

Examples of How Teachers Can Start Using Each Problem:

Dangerous behavior:

"I need you to stop that right now!"

Child's attention:

"(Child's name), listen to me please."

If there is a problem for child, offer help:

"I see you're finding it a bit hard. Can I help?"

Be respectful of child's feelings:

"Can you tell me how it feels for you if/when . . . ?"

State the rule:

"At (school's name) we do not allow. . . ."

"As a teacher, I cannot let you/this . . . to go on/happen."

"My job is to see that everyone's safe/fair. . . ."

Involve the child in problem solving:

"What is/are something(s) we could do to help/change, etc., this situation?"

Accept apologies:

"Okay now, we'll need to let (child's name) know you're sorry for (whatever). How do you want to do that?" (If child is unable, help with possible words/behavior.)

Praise effort as well as success:

"Good try."

"Glad to see you try."

"Gosh, that looks hard. Well done!"

"Great work."

Sometimes just smile and nod!

Teacher's feelings about unacceptable behavior:

"I worry when I see. . . ."

"It makes me feel sad when. . . ."

"I'm really upset by. . . ."

State time frame for change:

"Now this will need to be done by. . . ."

"The change has to happen by. . . ."

"What time frame do you think is fair with . . . ?"

The Self-Discovery Years: From 12 Years On

Adolescence is a challenging time for young people. During these years, they experience great physical, mental, and emotional changes.

These are the years that are full of excitement, discovery, turbulence, and achievement.

The adolescent years can be likened to young people sailing through uncharted waters in search of themselves and their identity. It can be a very exciting journey for everyone involved. The role of teachers and other wise adults is to help these young people make this journey safely and to help them reach the shores of adulthood successfully.

What is the role of the school in furthering these young people's experiences in their secondary school years? School provides many of the environmental aspects in which adolescents live out their daily lives. School provides for many of the needs of adolescents. School gives direction for the growth, safety, skill building, and self-discovery that adolescents go through on their way to becoming well-adjusted individuals. Adolescents can learn to become resilient in the school setting. Then they are able to face, overcome, be strengthened by, and even transformed by the experiences of adversity.

School can be likened to a laboratory in which adolescents are encouraged to try out and experiment with their thoughts, attitudes, skills, and behaviors that lead them to maximize their developmental potential. As a result of their experiments in the school setting, adolescents have the opportunity to form a strong connectedness with their school community. Research in the United States (Resnick et al., 1997) and in Australia (Fuller, McGraw & Goodyear, 1998) indicate that family and school connectedness are the best protective factors against distressing thoughts, for example, suicide and violence, and against substance abuse.

Identity in Adolescence

Because the major task of adolescence is the quest of identity, (Erikson's fifth stage, 1985), they need their teachers and schools, even more than peers, to help them answer many of their questions about identity. Some of the important questions adolescents have to face in their quest of identity are as follows:

1. Who am I? The am I as good as, as accepted as, as attractive as, etc., questions.
2. How do I measure up against peers?
3. What are my newly forming adolescent relationships with my teachers and other important adults?
4. What have I accomplished and achieved?
5. Where do I go from here? What is my future?

Adolescents are preoccupied with who they are and if they are appreciated by their peers, their teachers, and their schools. They feel a strong need to be recognized as individuals, each valued for himself or herself. They need to feel that they are accepted by their peers and teachers.

Adolescents are able to seek their identity in a number of ways, beginning with academic and social skills. They are able to compare their behaviors to accepted standards. They are able to be supportive of others. They are able to dream of a good future. If they can recognize the role of idealism in their thinking and planning, they are well on their way to resolving their quest for identity.

The problems and adversities of life to which resilience applies can be real or perceived to adolescents. Threats to actual survival, whether emotional or physical, affect their sense of security, their self-image, their sense of control, their social status, and their relationships with others. Developing and using the I HAVE, I AM, and I CAN resilience factors will contribute significantly to answering the five "who and what am I" questions. For example, an adolescent who can handle an adversity, such as failing a subject, by seeking help from a teacher or a friend or by spending more time studying, becomes responsible and, if successful, more confident. Confidence and responsibility are both I AM resilience factors.

Research indicates that four main causes of adversity adolescents face are

1. feelings of not belonging to or being connected to family, school, and the community;
2. engaging in overly stimulating activities and substances;
3. having few social and problem-solving skills; and
4. having no future plans or goals.

These adversities are characteristic of their age, and facing them, dealing with them, gaining mastery over them, requires both the promotion and practice of resilience. The school (and the home) contribute to this promotion and can capitalize on opportunities for practicing resilience. Adolescents are also quite able to contribute to the promotion of their own resilience, just as they are increasingly able to assume responsibility for their own lives. Let's look at ways to address the four adversities with suggestions as to how school can help overcome them.

Not Connected

Adolescents who do not have a sense of belonging to or fitting into school are likely to exhibit antisocial behaviors, failure with schoolwork, lack of social skills, and a desire or need to escape into destructive behaviors.

Though research shows that adolescents feel a strong need to keep connections with family, school, and their community, these needs are often in direct opposition to their need to be independent. However, if the connections are kept intact, adolescents have a greater chance to mature a future healthy identity. It is unlikely, then, that they will need to engage in destructive behaviors whether sex, violence, graffiti, or substance abuse.

How do teachers and schools develop and maintain connections with adolescents? Teachers can do this by

1. using open-ended questions that promote thinking and stimulate the adolescents' problem-solving skills. It is in this role that teachers can contribute significantly by providing class environments in which adolescents feel safe to try out their new thinking and reasoning abilities (I HAVE and I CAN);

2. communicating their belief and confidence that their students can make sensible choices (I HAVE, I AM, and I CAN);

3. negotiating and discussing with students what limits need to be set and why they need to be set (I HAVE, I AM, and I CAN);

4. encouraging students to problem solve and to search for solutions (or at least ways to manage) tough issues (I CAN);

5. being aware of their own biases and fears so that these do not adversely interfere with their students' freedom to explore their range of thinking (I AM and I CAN);

6. discussing high-risk behaviors in a factual, honest manner rather than in a moralizing way (I AM and I CAN); and

7. modeling resilience promoting speech and behaviors and being available for help, guidance, and discussion (I HAVE, I AM, and I CAN).

Risk-Taking Control

Teachers know that adolescence is a risk-taking period. Teachers know that some adolescents crave more excitement and stimulation than others. Teachers know that some adolescents are more heedless of, or indifferent to, the consequences of dangerous behaviors. Teachers know all of this because adolescents' temperaments, like those of all people, vary from very active to very passive. Teachers need to ensure that adolescents taking excessive risks are diverted from destructive to constructive interests and activities.

Diverting adolescents from one path to another is a challenge for any teacher. One of the ways to achieve this is to actually challenge the adolescents' advanced thinking and reasoning skills. Discussion about morals, values, and ethics need to be a part of daily school life. Engaging and broadening adolescents' understanding and knowledge of how morals, values, and ethics form the fundamentals of society; how laws are arrived at, why life is held sacred, why each of us has the right to move about freely, why we respect the rights and property of others, why we have elected representatives, why we are a democracy; what does that mean/entail, etc., are topics of discussion.

The teacher's role is not only to extend and challenge, but also to help adolescents to learn to plan and think ahead, to have values that further their I AM and I CAN resilience factors. Then, adolescents will grow in integrity and character, and their identity will be more firmly established.

Social and Problem-Solving Skills

The adolescents' social skills and social life take on new dimensions. Questions such as how do I get on with peers, how far do I go along with peers, how far do I go in sexual relationships, how often do I skip a class, and how do I say "no" occupy them.

When adolescents know their own emotions, they can recognize the need to use strategies that keep them within reasonably safe boundaries. Their social skills need to include the ability to make friends with people like teachers and peers who challenge them physically, intellectually, and emotionally in constructive ways. They need to learn how to listen, how to express anger without belligerence, how to express disappointment or disagreement, and how to express empathy. All these skills should be modeled by teachers as part of their resilience.

Forming constructive friendships and expressing emotions appropriately help adolescents avoid excessive risk taking while learning social skills that will help them not only through their student years, but also through later life.

Their problem-solving skills now include hypothetical, analytical, and critical abilities. Class discussions need to involve reflective thinking and teachers should ensure that there are many opportunities for inferring what might have happened in a given situation, from a number of perspectives and from a number of alternatives. In this way, adolescents' higher mental-processing skills develop appropriately. Their I CAN skills continue to mature. It is worth noting that should adolescents not develop this higher mental-processing capacity, they are likely to fall victim to confusion, loss of initiative and industry, and, saddest of all, loss of self-trust.

Planning for the Future

Adolescents need to be able to set goals for themselves, to plan not only for the day or week, but for their long-term future. Teachers should give opportunities for exploring future options so that adolescents can practice planning. Examples of the types of questions adolescents feel worth exploring are: What is exciting to think about doing? What are challenges worth taking? Who can help with goal setting and planning?

The Role of Schools and Teachers

The fact that schools and teachers play a dominant role in the lives of adolescents is well researched. Generally, the expectations of schools from adolescents are that they are

- accepting responsibility for own behavior (I AM),
- learning and developing mastery in academic and social settings (I AM, I CAN),
- working with and being part of a team (I AM, I CAN),
- accepting authority and school rules (I HAVE, I CAN), and
- being involved in school community (I CAN).

And adolescents need from their schools

- respect and even being liked (I HAVE),
- acceptance of what they are (I HAVE, I AM),
- sense of belonging (I HAVE),
- being and feeling understood (I HAVE),
- support and encouragement (I HAVE),
- responsibility and independence (I AM, I CAN),
- problem-solving skills (I CAN), and
- rules/limits/norms/values (I CAN, I AM).

It is obvious that this set of expectations and set of needs intersect and can be brought even closer. It is also obvious that whenever a teacher offers help and guidance to adolescents experiencing difficulties, that teacher is building confidence and mastery, both essential skills in dealing with adversities. That teacher is promoting resilience skills in adolescents. However, if adolescents misbehave and their punishment offers no insight, alternatives, or improved problem-solving skills, real opportunities for resilience promotion have been lost.

As can be seen from this section on adolescents, the role of teachers and school becomes less directive and more expansive and inclusive. By modeling I HAVE, I AM, and I CAN behaviors, teachers show how resilience is promoted and used. They encourage adolescents to demonstrate greater independence and breadth in problem solving, in responsibility, in managing their behavior, in expressing their thoughts, feelings, and wishes, in helping others, and in involvement in as many aspects of the school community's life as possible.

Effectiveness of Resilience Programs

To show how effective resilience can be in school communities, let us share some of the outcomes in a rural region with 32 elementary and secondary schools. The manager of schools in this region indicated that he received between four and eight serious bullying notifications each week. Subsequent to our work on resilience promotion, which the schools decided would underpin their student welfare policy, no bullying notifications were received in the following eight months.

Examples in Resilience Promotion

Teachers asked me for specific resilience responses to these examples. We found it more useful, however, to include them in finding resilience responses. When working with teachers it is wise to let them see and experience their responses, many of which already include resilience. However, it is in the naming of these resilience factors that teachers become conscious of the I HAVE, I AM, and I CAN factors. And it is the conscious use of resilience that is important in its promotion. A second benefit of this process is that teachers also become aware of the resilience factors that are not so well-developed and what they can do to improve them.

A 15-year-old girl, Marjie, is often absent from school. Her parents and teachers report that she often spends all night out of the house. What should the school do?

A little further probing indicated that there was quite a bit of marital discord. So, maybe Marjie's absence from home was her way of getting away from the parental fights, and then she was too tired to come to school.

The school needed to bring the parents in for discussion about the problem (I HAVE). Then if the parents were willing, suggest marital or family therapy (I CAN). Finally, Marjie needed help to explore alternate ways to cope with her parents. For example, perhaps another temporary home could be found while the parents were out of control. Perhaps Marjie could go to part of the house where the sounds of the fighting were muted.

The teachers came up with quite a useful set of suggestions to help Marjie. They became real I HAVE and I CAN people and even offered to have Marjie telephone one of them if things got too bad (I HAVE).

> The second example was Jason, a 13-year-old who was so shy and anxious that he could not answer in class. He would go very red in the face, mumble something, and sit down overwhelmed by embarrassment. One of the teacher's suggested a gentle way to begin would be to talk to Jason alone, to ask questions when no one else was present. In this way, Jason could experience the satisfaction of being able to answer without embarrassment. The I HAVE setting could provide the safety Jason needed to feel free enough to answer. This success, praised by the teacher, needs repetition at various times and by various teachers. Building up Jason's confidence, I AM and I CAN factors, could be used to transfer his success solo into a class setting as he showed sufficient willingness to try.

A comment that is often made by teachers involved in resilience workshops is their lack of time, that they cannot invest so much time and effort into one child or adolescent. Our answer is always the same—giving the necessary time to a needy student models a number of resilience factors. It tells the recipient that he or she is worthwhile. It demonstrates to other students that teachers care irrespective of the behavior or problem. It will save the student from possible harm or loss, and it will certainly benefit society. Young people who are not kept constructive and focused on options toward a good future are likely to move into some form of deviance or escape, and that cost to society will be infinitively greater than the time and cost to the teacher or teachers.

Putting It All Together

Adolescence tests both the young people moving through these potentially turbulent years and the adults who have the task of guiding them. Teachers and schools help them to become more responsible, independent, broad thinking and socially skilled. In brief, to become more competent, caring and community minded individuals.

Resilience plays an important role in helping adolescents cope with the inevitable adversities that will occur during these years. Resilience will give them the skills and strengths to face and over-come difficulties and adversities. Resilience will help them face their future with greater confidence and optimism. What a wonderful gift to the adolescent is the resilience promoting teacher.

Resilience Programs in Schools

To introduce any program into schools involves a number of steps and stages. First, approval from the local education authority or school principal is necessary. This is best achieved by face-to-face meetings. The person responsible for giving such approval needs to hear and see not only the value of resilience promotion but also your passion and commitment. At this meeting, the resilience promotion information needs to be covered.

Resilience Promotion Information

What Is Resilience?

Resilience is the human capacity to face, overcome, be strengthened by, and even transformed by the effects of adversity.

How Does It Work in Schools?

- With resilience children can triumph over adversities (small and large problems as well as crises and traumas).
- How teachers respond to situations and how they help children to respond separates those teachers who promote resilience in their students from those who destroy resilience.
- The three sources which promote resilience are I HAVE—I AM—I CAN (Grotberg, 1995). Each is briefly described.

I HAVE (external supports)
  - teachers I trust, who like and respect me,
  - teachers who set limits for me, explain rules and apply appro-priate consequences,
  - teachers who show me how to do things right by the way they do them,
  - teachers who encourage me to do things on my own, and
  - teachers who help me when I am sick, in danger or need to learn.

I AM (internal strengths)

- a person who can like and love, generally be good natured,
- a person who shows pleasure and concern for others, has empathy,
- a person who is self- and other respecting,
- a person who accepts personal responsibility, and
- a person who has faith and optimism in the future.

I CAN (problem solving and social/interpersonal skills)

- share my thoughts and feelings and problems with others,
- work out problems for myself and persist with tasks,
- control myself when I feel like doing something dangerous or wrong,
- know when to talk or when to act, and
- find help when I need it.

Why Is It Important?

Children need resilience to face many common problems (e.g., teasing, bullying, self-doubt, no friends, etc.) academic problems, (e.g., reading/writing/comprehension problems—memory or processing problems—other learning difficulties) and common crises (e.g., death, divorce, drugs, illness, accident, etc.). Children often feel lonely, fearful and vulnerable. These feelings are less overwhelming for children who have the resources of resilience.

What Are the Outcomes?

Teachers who promote resilience encourage children to become more autonomous, independent, responsible, problem solving and caring. Thus children can become more active in promoting their own resilience. Building resilience safeguards children against depression and runaway behaviors. It gives children optimism and the ability to move forward confidently.

In the school environment the whole school culture improves. Resilience impinges on all facets of school—better behaviors, better cooperation, better work and curriculum outcomes. Resilience promoting schools develop a culture that promotes belongingness that in turn promotes a sense of community.

How Can It Be Promoted—By Whom?

Resilience is a basic human capacity nascent in all children. Initially parents but later and often more importantly, teachers can awaken and form this human capacity in children into an active, coping resource.

Teachers promote resilience in children through their words, actions and the environments they provide. They learn to use the resilience set of tools. Able to use the language of resilience, teachers help children to identify resilient behaviors in themselves and others. The more teachers understand resilience, the greater their opportunities for acting and speaking in ways that guide their own and children's behaviors. This helps children meet and often resolve their problems and crisis with strength and hope.

What Does the Program Contain?

1. Resilience promotion for each stage:
   - (a) Prep to grade 2
   - (b) Grades 3 and 4
   - (c) Grades 5 and 6
   - (d) Grades 7 and 8
   - (e) Grades 9 and 10

2. Each stage will have the following five steps plus reference material:
   - a. *Tasks of the age*—description of where the child is in developmental terms—what tasks are being mastered and how these relate to resilience.
   - b. *What teachers can do*—actions and language teachers need to take and use to enhance resilience at children's different stages.
   - c. *Examples of resilience responses*—how positive/negative responses foster/fail to foster resilience in children at each developmental stage.
   - d. *Results*—what happens when resilience has been promoted? What skills have children learnt? How do they feel about themselves?
   - e. *Checklist*—for perceptions of resilience in children.

This overview process is twice repeated. First to the senior staff and senior administrators, then to the whole school staff. The next step is to break the teaching staff up into the appropriate developmental years. In our Australian experience that is the preparatory year and grades 1 and 2 children, from 5 to 7 or 8 years. Then grades 3 and 4 children from 8 to 10 years, and finally, grades 5 and 6, the 11-plus years. The secondary school divisions are grades 7 and 8, from 12 to 14 years, and grades 9 and 10, from 14 to 16 years.

Each group focuses initially on what resilience factors are needed for children at these ages. How can teachers best promote these?

What are the resilience factors teachers already promote? Which ones need more development?

Having achieved a broad outline of what the children need and how teachers meet these needs, the group focuses on itself. Usually teachers will give either personal or classroom examples of adversities they have experienced. These are treated with care and respect. In guiding teacher groups, it is essential the leader models resilience in both language and behavior. For example, a young grade 1 teacher gave this situation:

> Dillon, a six-year-old boy, had climbed onto a shelter shed roof. His classmates were screaming "Jump, Jump" when the teacher came on the scene. She was annoyed with Dillon and told him to get down at once. She saw Dillon was upset and then offered to get a ladder to help him down.

In examining this example further, it was obvious that there were many opportunities for resilience promotion. Discussion centered around safety, rules, other children's participation and so on. Further teasing out of these issues resulted in how to make Dillon feel safe. I HAVE—people who keep me safe. The leader then offered this alternative:

> The other children needed to be moved away. A quick way to move the other children out of earshot could be the teacher clapping her hands, pointing to the edge of the court, saying "I need you all to line up along the white line by the time I count to ten." Having moved the children out of immediate hearing, she turns to Dillon, "Can I help you down or would you like me to fetch a ladder?" If Dillon refuses, she says, "Well, you'll need to come down safely. I certainly don't want to see you hurt [I HAVE—trust/help/safety]. If you need a quiet place for a while, you could just sit in the shelter shed and I'll come and get you in a few minutes."

The emphasis is on letting Dillon know he is important and worth caring for, then giving him time and space to calm down. Only after these safety issues are met does the next step happen. What made Dillon climb onto the roof, what needed to be done by both Dillon and the teacher to resolve this. Finally, rules and consequences regarding this issue need to be sorted and applied.

In these early school years, I HAVE teachers can really help strengthen children's I AM factors, which, of course, are attitudes, beliefs, and inner strengths that exist in each child. They can help children see themselves as likeable, caring, achieving, respectful, becoming more autonomous, and optimistic. To further the children's problem-solving I CAN factors, teachers need to be people the children trust, so that they can not only talk about things, but also try and work out solutions. Children need to feel safe enough to reach out for help, knowing and trusting that the teachers will do something to help. Throughout these early years, children see their teachers as role models and form images of and memories about how they see them behaving. Though not yet able to promote their own resilience, they are learning and storing what is modeled for them.

In examining situations and examples, teachers review the following steps:

- The event—what happened?
- The action—what did you do?
- The emotion—how did you feel?
- Others' actions—what did the other person do?
- The other's emotion—how do you think that person felt?
- The result—how did the event end/resolve?

By grades 3 and 4 teachers are teaching children who have some capacity to promote their own resilience. Now children are expected to demonstrate more ability to accept responsibility, to use their thinking for not only school work, but for negotiation and problem solving with peers. They are expected to listen to teachers, to obey rules and to be self- and other respecting. How is this achieved? As always, by teachers modeling resilience in their speech and behavior. Letting children see and hear what is respectful, what is self-control, and what is problem solving.

Again, teachers can use more personal experiences of classroom examples with which to work. Two grade 3 teachers working together with 45 boys and girls indicated that they had difficulties with some children working in groups. Here is their example:

Four children, two boys and two girls all aged nine years, could not cooperate and work together. Initially these children were put into four separate groups but always disrupted others. In desperation the teachers put them together. Their task was to describe and build a model of a pioneer's hut. The girls wanted to make a model out of paper cut-outs. The boys laughed at that and said it had to be made from wood. They would make the hut, and the girls could describe it. The girls were not having a bit of this, they wanted to do the building. The teachers decided to let them each build their version and describe it as well.

Neither group wanted to write descriptions so for the sake of peace the teachers agreed to just the building. How could resilience skills be used here was the question.

It was obvious that each pair was able to cooperate in a physical task—building the hut. The problem was the written task. It seemed that none of the four children felt able, safe, or comfortable to write. So step one was how to provide a safe environment that might allow them to try. One of the grade 4 teachers suggested each pair describe on tape how they built their hut. Another teacher said the children could dictate the steps and one of the teachers could write them down. The second step was to interest the four to stay with the writing task, to finish it. Then, it was hoped, this success could be transferred into other settings, so that these children could start to become involved in learning, in taking the risk to write, or at least steps toward writing. Discussion by the teachers indicated they felt the lack of cooperation was a fear response and that once that was addressed, things would improve. What the teachers decided was the interaction between the I HAVE—safe/helpful; the I AM—confident/hopeful; and the I CAN—problem solve/seek help set of resilience skills.

In our work in primary schools, especially with 9- and 10-year-olds, we have found many resilience factors useful in modifying and changing children's behaviors. We have involved children, teachers, and parents in resilience promotion and used the skills to solve problems and change behaviors. The following is an example that details how resilience promotion can make a real difference to a school and community.

A particularly unpleasant but often encountered problem in schools is bullying. Let us share with you the process we used to help some groups of 9- and 10-year-olds deal with this serious problem in a country school. We started by asking these children, Why do games have rules? Their answers, condensed after brainstorming were

- so people can't cheat,
- so it's fair to everyone,
- so it can be played,
- so people get turns, and
- so no one gets hurt.

Our next question was, Why are there rules about driving cars? Their answers were

- so there are no crashes,
- to keep us safe,
- so we can get where we're going,
- so we know what to do, and
- so there's order.

Finally, we asked, Why did they think schools had rules? Their answers were

- to stop people getting hurt,
- for safety,
- because things would be out of control,
- to help us learn,
- to keep us quiet, and
- to keep the school tidy.

Much discussion of these reasons for rules followed, after which it was rather easy to ask the children which of these reasons they thought were really important and why they thought them important. Their three-reason final selections were chosen

- so it's fair to everyone,
- so everyone is safe, and
- so no one gets hurt.

I HAVE—I AM—I CAN
These three reasons led into our three questions:

- Is bullying fair?
- Is it safe (especially for the victim)?
- Does anyone get hurt?

The children agreed that bullying wasn't fair, that it was not safe for the victims, and that people got hurt when bullied.

Our next task was to remind them of our earlier discussions about the I HAVE elements and ask them to list some of the I HAVE people in their lives. Many children listed parents, grandparents, teachers, sports coaches, club leaders, relatives, and peers. This led to asking them if they were, or could be, an I HAVE person to anyone (e.g., a friend, a younger brother or sister, to a little child at the school, etc.).

Having established that they could be I HAVE people in a variety of ways, we asked if they could be I HAVE people to bullies and victims. Needless to say, this caused heated discussion. After some time, when the need to be punitive was exhausted, many practical ways of being an I HAVE person emerged. They could

- be trustworthy,
- stop people being hurt,
- show people how to behave sensibly, and
- help victim kids to feel safe.

Now we came to crunch time. Our question was, Is it possible to be fair to both bullies and their victims? Again, a rather natural tendency to deny fairness to the bully had to be worked through. However, this was much easier because the children were seriously trying to use I HAVE factors. Agreement was reached that if we really meant *being fair to everyone* it had to include bullies.

The task the children set themselves was to come up with "ways of being fair so no one gets hurt" ideas. They brainstormed and filled sheets of paper with suggestions. We worked through these with them. Their final result was as follows:

- Everyone is responsible to keep things fair and safe.
- Everyone needs to stop bullies.
- Everyone needs to help the kids being bullied.

Actually, their three points used many I HAVE—I AM—I CAN factors. The I HAVE factors were

- I have people I can trust who help me;
- I have people who set limits to stop dangerous things/behaviors; and
- I have people who show me how to do things right.

The I AM factors were

- be respectful of myself and others,
- be willing to be responsible for what I do, and
- be sure things will turn out okay.

The I CAN factors were

- to talk to others about things that bother me,
- to find ways to solve problems, and
- to find someone to help me when I need it.

Our view of these children was that they were serious in dealing with bullying and wanted practical ways to achieve a good outcome. Once more brainstorming about ways to get everyone involved, everyone responsible, and everyone helping occurred.

As is often the case, if young people are given the direction and opportunity to problem solve, the results are amazing. These wonderfully inventive and well-intentioned children came up with the following:

- Anyone who saw bullying was to use a group (because bullies can be tough and a bit frightening) of peers, always more than the bully or bullies, and go up to the bully and say, "Stop, that's not fair."
- This was to happen every time bullying was seen.
- The victim was to be invited to come away with the group. (And after a time one of the children suggested that maybe the bully should be invited to join the group also.)

I HAVE—I AM—I CAN

Our sessions with these 9- and 10-year-olds were regular over six weeks. A check up some three months later found that bullying among the 9- and 10-year-olds was almost nonexistent. That bullies were now more regular class members who, if they did a bit of teasing, were quickly reminded to be fair and that was the end of it. Other classes noticed the changes and asked what was going on, so these children were showing other children what could be done. Teachers reported better cooperation and classroom behavior.

The children said they were learning better, and those who had been frightened now felt safer. The final reporting came from parents. They said their children seemed happier at home and at school and that aggression between siblings was much less.

The outcome for the groups at this school was an overall improvement in the lives of all concerned. Resilience, we found, improved not only their skills, attitudes, and behaviors, but also built a sense of community. In consciously promoting resilience, these children and adults worked together and learned to overcome a challenging problem.

Preparing for Secondary School

In the final two years of elementary school teachers need to prepare children for secondary school. Not only do the children's academic skills need to be well established, but also their ability to organize themselves, to persist, especially with tasks that may not always be exciting, to be responsible and respectful, and able to accept authority. Their social skills and ability to communicate effectively with peers and teachers also need to be well established. Secondary school can be a dislocating experience, especially so for children who lack the necessary independence or social skills. How then are teachers to maximize their student's resilience? What will they need to do to not only promote resilience, but to help children strengthen and promote their own resilience?

Much emphasis must be placed on developing problem solving skills in academic, creative, social, sporting, and community settings. Children need practice in, and success with, a variety of tasks. They need to expand their communication skills, to listen and speak appropriately, to be able to stand up for themselves—being assertive but not aggressive. They need to be able to show friendly interest and know when to ask for help.

Teachers Using Intuition

Children at 11 or 12 will often not say or try to show what bothers them. It is often seen as uncool by peers to ask for help. Teachers need some detective skills and intuition to discover what is really going on. Here are two typical examples that illustrate this point.

In a grade 5 English class, the teacher is discussing a story called "Marty's Unusual Toys."

Child: "This story is dumb."

Teacher: "No it isn't. it's an interesting story."

Child: "I hate reading. It's boring."

Teacher: "Nonsense, you read easily. I've heard you read well."

Child: "It's too long."

Teacher: "Now that tells me you're lazy and not trying."

Interpretation: This child's I AM and I CAN factors are not very evident. The teacher, full of good intent, is missing the point. The child is discouraged and needs the teacher to be more of an I HAVE person. Let's replay this event:

Child: "This story is dumb." (Child is really saying "I need help.")

Teacher: (Recognizing child's negative feelings.) "What don't you like about the story?"

Child: "It's boring reading about toys."

Teacher: "Sounds like 'Marty's Toys' isn't interesting to you." (I
    AM–respectful of self and others.)

Child: "No, I like animal and adventure stories."

Teacher: "Well, we'll have to make sure that our next book is about
    animals, adventures, or both!" (I HAVE—people who want me to
    learn.)

In the replay, the teacher recognized the child's negative feelings and
began to build trust (I HAVE). Encouraged, the child was able to say
what bothered him or her (I CAN). Helping the child through the
problem, but allowing the child to face the problem (I HAVE/I CAN),
the teacher showed forward planning and gave the child optimism (I
AM/I CAN).

The second example was a physical education class with a sixth-
grade girl.

Teacher: "Hurry up and get changed."

Child: (Sitting on the bench, not moving.) "I am."

Teacher: "You're not, you're not moving, get a move on."

Child: "I don't feel well."

Teacher: "That's what you say almost every P.E. lesson. How do you
    expect to keep fit and healthy if you don't exercise."

Child: "It's too hot today."

Teacher: "The others don't find it too hot. See, they are ready."

Child: "I feel sick."

The girl is deaf to reason at the moment. She is resistant to P.E. The
teacher is trying to get her to face reality, but it's not working. Let's
replay this:

Teacher: "Hurry up and get changed."

Child: "I don't feel well."

Teacher: "I bet you wish it wasn't P.E. now."

Child: "I can't do those gym exercises."

Teacher: "That must make it hard for you to start. It takes a lot of
    practice to develop the muscles needed for these gym exercises."

Child: "It would take me forever."

Teacher: "What say you help me with holding the ropes for the others
    and see if later there's something you'd like to try."

Now the teacher hears the girl's fears and uses the I HAVE/I AM
and I CAN skills to help the girl face her problem with trust in the
teacher. The teacher facilitates the girl, engaging her I AM and I

CAN, making it possible for her to participate and be more optimistic about her chances of trying out an activity.

When teachers in these or other years ask us if it is their job to have to deal with their students' feelings, our answer is "Yes." When teachers spend time dealing with a student's feelings—whether appropriate or not—in an I HAVE way, it often stops those feelings getting out of control. And no, it is not wasting class time: it is meeting a need. And yes, teachers need to make clear distinctions between feelings and behaviors. For example, students (and teachers, too) have the right to feel anger, frustration, and disappointment. They have the right to express their feelings. But they do not have the right to do anything that attacks or hurts the other, whether physically or verbally.

Putting It All Together

We can see that teachers promote resilience when they

- encourage autonomy and independence,
- allow for differences respectfully,
- have clear rules, limits, and consequences,
- teach skillfully,
- offer support and encouragement,
- are predictable and reliable,
- proactive in planning,
- are good role models who lead by example,
- work for a positive school community culture,
- have realistic expectations, and
- provide varied opportunities for children to succeed.

It is self-evident that resilience development is a lifelong task and that we can all strengthen our resilience skills and promote them in everyone we meet. It is also self-evident that none of us will escape adversity. It is hoped that our years of working with children have not only deepened and expanded our understanding of these I HAVE, I AM, and I CAN factors, but also enabled us to promote them in children in clear, confident, and caring ways.

References

Erikson, E. (1985). *Childhood and society.* New York: Norton.

Fuller, A., McGraw, K., & Goodyear, M. (1998). *The mind of youth. Resilience— A Connect project.* Turning the Tide, Victorian Government Strategies against drug use. Victoria, Australia.

Grotberg, E. H. (1995). *A guide to promoting resilience in children*. The Hague, The Netherlands: The Bernard van Leer Foundation.

Grotberg, E. H. (1999). *Tapping your inner strength: How to find the resilience to deal with anything*. Oakland, CA: New Harbinger Publications.

Grotberg, E. H. (2002). From terror to triumph: The path to resilience. In C. E. Stout (Ed.), *The psychology of terrorism* (pp. 167–189). Westport, CT: Praeger.

Papházy, J. E. (1994). *Coping with children: Parenting from 3–12*. Victoria, Australia: Flactem.

Papházy. J. E. (1993). *The troublesome years: Parenting adolescents*. Victoria, Australia: Flactem.

Resnick, M. D., Bearman, P. S., Blum, R. W., Bauman, K. E., Harris, K. M., Jones, et al. (1997). Protecting adolescents from harm: Findings from the National Longitudinal Study on adolescent health. *Journal of the American Medical Association, 278*, 823–832.

CHAPTER 6

RESILIENCE FOR THOSE NEEDING HEALTH CARE

Bette Keltner with Leslie Walker

Introduction

The capacity to face, deal with, overcome, learn from, and be strengthened by adversity suggests a robust constitution. However, good health is not necessarily required for a person to be resilient. Indeed, a health problem is sometimes the agent that provokes resilience. Similarly, persons with certain fragile health characteristics may prove themselves strong in enduring, even using, illness or disability to propel special accomplishments. The public is enchanted and inspired by stories of Beethoven composing music while deaf or young adults racing their wheelchairs. The honor and recognition that comes from these achievements despite adversity powerfully reinforces an individual person's resilience and illuminates for the collective mind the depth and breadth of human capacity. In this chapter, we will provide an overview of the tremendously varied types of health challenges children and adults face, examine how the need for health care can mediate resilience, describe protective factors that operate particularly for children with special health care needs, pay special attention to the critical transition period of adolescence and young adulthood, and address the health system intended to support optimal health and resilience. This broad look at resilience for those needing health care gives insight to special circumstances of adversity and ability.

Health Care Needs

Encounters with death and disability can inspire acts of heroism, motivate a desire for scientific discovery, and seed great literature. Some people become famous for their resilience. Craig Ventner, who mapped the human genome, became determined to know more about health while serving as a medic in Vietnam. With a wheelchair and ventilator, Christopher Reeve galvanizes support for persons with spinal cord injury and encourages people with disabilities to live a full life. St. Therese of Liseaux faced fatal illness as an adolescent by writing about the spiritual meaning of pain, suffering, and death. In different ways, resilient people may do more than just make their own lives better. Occasionally this inspiration is a case of genius at work, that is, people with special natural abilities or lifelong training who are destined to overcome any adversity in their path. One of the most intriguing aspects of resilience is that it is apparently not reserved for those select few. There is evidence that resilience is a human capacity that everyone has. Resilience may be demonstrated in the context of a range of adversities that include economic hardship, violence, family disruption, discrimination, and by a serious health disorder.

The types of health needs associated with resilience are amazingly varied. It appears that almost anything that can create major obstacles to normal functioning may create a crucible for resilience. For the purpose of this review, we will consider chronic long-term conditions in the development and expression of resilience. Situations such as a near-fatal injury with rapid recovery clearly constitute adversity. Many times these experiences are very dramatic and act as a call to change behavior in some way. Surviving a car crash in which other people die sensitizes many individuals to health threats.

However, the adversity we examine in this chapter is the experience that issues constant challenge and requires daily adaptation. Chronic conditions force some lifestyle change. Not every person who adjusts to lifestyle change becomes resilient. In fact, for children and youth, daily hassles and worry combined with the worry and supervision from caregivers and health care providers set up a situation where a child or adolescent can easily become fearful and fragile.

Chronic conditions, sometimes referred to as special health care needs, share certain defining characteristics. One characteristic is that health services are needed, either for treatment, monitoring, or to prevent worsening of the condition or additional problems. Childhood cancer, cerebral palsy, and asthma are conditions that call

for high use and a wide range of health care services. Note that these examples include conditions that may be cured (e.g., cancer) or diminish over time (e.g., as asthma sometimes does); they may be lifelong (e.g., cerebral palsy) or may even be fatal (as cancer and asthma sometimes may be).

The second defining characteristic is that there are everyday considerations related to lifestyle that must be considered whether or not the condition limits functioning every day. Epilepsy and Tourette's syndrome, for example, do not necessarily cause daily problems, but do involve vigilant caregiving in childhood and translate to special self-care requirements as children grow up. Resilience related to health needs is most likely to be apparent among youth.

We are reasonably comfortable with health problems that follow a natural life course. For the vast majority of people, health care is an intermittent and often predictable need. Getting older is part of that prediction. Aging, season, and history (epidemics or war) affect the amount and nature of health needs. Common acute conditions and serious disease associated with aging occur in generally rhythmic patterns. These can have an extremely high impact for patients and families, as in cases of Alzheimer disease, requiring adaptations for patients themselves and also for their entire families. Resilience in childhood is special because it falls outside the parameters of predictability. It interferes with expectations and, for a society, causes concern for many reasons, including lost productivity and perpetuating cultural and social communities.

Health care services are used predominately by persons with chronic conditions. Many health problems occur as a result of aging, but other conditions originate in childhood; some are the result of early disease or trauma. These are the cases where resilience is most likely to be found. Adaptation to health problems may itself be a primary stressor, separating different coping and lifestyle responses. Facing childhood cancer, multiple sclerosis, or paraplegia can be an all-absorbing adjustment or the first step in finding a meaningful life path that accommodates or uses the disability. Adapting to debilitating and exacerbating conditions such as asthma and sickle cell disease pose particular challenges. Knowing how to prevent or contain a crisis health event is all important. Conditions such as these also can be generally debilitating, affecting normal growth and development. Serious disease and disability among children, adolescents, and young adults are chronic conditions that require both personal adjustment and, if available and accessible, high use of health care

services. Two factors are important indicators of public sentiment about health problems. One is the age of the person affected, and the other is whether or not the illness or injury is easily identifiable by the general public. The phenomenon of unexpected adversity is clear for serious childhood disorders. We expect children to be healthy and grow in their capacity to be productive. The other defining aspect of the disease is its visibility. Western culture, especially the United States, tends to celebrate achievement over adversity that is visible. The dominant Western culture is much less sympathetic to limitations that are invisible, especially if they can be interpreted as being lazy or slow. This means that the age at which disability occurs and the type of disability will evoke different sympathies and support from the community at large. There are interesting cultural variations on this theme. We will examine culture as a protective and risk factor related to the nature of disability that children and youth experience.

Children with special health care needs (CSHCN) have recently become a focus of attention, both in terms of research related to chronic disease care, family issues, need for special education or social services, and health care use. Insurance programs often carve out children with special health care needs because they have high volume and sometimes high expense requirements that are atypical of others in their age cohort. Rates of disability and chronic illness commonly start to climb at about 45 years of age. Yet, the National Health Interview Survey shows that 4.4 million children in the United States or 6.5 percent of the noninstitutionalized populations under the age of 18, have chronic conditions that limit their activities to some degree (Newacheck & Neal, 1998).

The most common chronic conditions were respiratory disease and mental impairments, with proportionately more cases concentrated among older children, boys, and children from low-income and single-parent families. Whether as an agent to provoke resilience or another barrier to overcome in the expression of resilience, health problems can be paramount in the study of resilience. Chronic conditions now represent a significant shift in causes of death, disease, and health care resource use. It is expected that health care services that cannot fix or cure a problem will enhance functionality or quality of life. In many ways, this expectation suggests that health care services—a truly vast array of different professionals doing different things—can help people with chronic conditions to face, deal with, overcome, and learn from their disease.

Inherent in the changing health care system is the idea that health services can support or build individual resilience. This idea is implicit rather than specifically articulated. There is not yet a systematic practice for promoting resilience nor evidence-based intervention strategies to accomplish this for children and youth with special health care needs.

Conceptual Models of Resilience

Stress and coping has been the primary theoretical paradigm that has examined resilience among children with special health care needs (Keltner & Ramey, 1992, 1993). A critical aspect of coping in this model is adjustment to the limitations that arise from chronic disease or disability.

Stress and coping models allow insights that describe the varied ways in which coping is acquired and supported. Coping with a chronic health problem begins with the premise that the disease or disability cannot be cured or that it will be very long in duration. Consequently, the term *adaptation* or *adjustment* is prominent in this literature. It is recognized that the child and the family must make lifestyle changes. These adjustments follow a certain psychological path of facing and mentally dealing with a diagnosis. This type of adjustment for many people is monumental and ongoing. Coping with a health problem means that there is a physical or significant psychiatric disorder.

Use of health care services is presumed, and upon the child and family comes the task of learning to manage the disorder. This sometimes requires enormous sophistication and skill. Children who are ventilator dependent in order to live, now often live at home and sometimes even attend school. Tasks that once were the exclusive domain of licensed health care providers are transferred to the patient and his or her family. Routine intravenous transfusion of factor VIII for persons with hemophilia may be provided by a family member. Medication that must be self-injected (e.g., for diabetes or some neurological conditions) is part of adjustment to a health need for the child and adolescent. Therefore, coping has elements of the practical as well as psychological and social factors.

The idea that there is something toxic about a strong violation of expectations (Stone, 2000) is supported by concepts such as normalization. Normalization actually became a slogan and approach to services adopted by advocates for persons with disabilities. This has prompted changes in public arenas such as schools where children with special needs are no longer segregated. It was a key stimulus in the widespread structural changes such as wheelchair ramps and legislation such as Americans with Disabilities Act.

Research continues to explore the normalization concept as one that supports optimal functioning and quality of life—in short, important aspects of resilience. Among a small cohort of ventilator-dependent children, child and family coping were strengthened by "adopting a normalcy lens." A normalcy lens in this case was established by a context that defines what is normal for this child and by engaging in parenting behaviors and family routines that are considered normative in the household and communities they live in. Fitting in was an important model for shaping daily life and understanding the situation (Morse, Wilson, & Penrod, 2000).

Risk and Protective Factors

Risk for disease and injury is a common approach to knowing how likely it is for people to experience a health problem. Certain children are more likely to develop asthma or injury based on both genetic and experiential factors. Risk is also a concept for deleterious and nonoptimal outcomes associated with chronic conditions. That is, for people who have asthma or who have become paraplegic, some will become more handicapped than others, even when the disease or injury is relatively the same in terms of the biologic limits it places. This is especially true for children and youth who face long duration or lifelong conditions. Exposure to stress or psychic challenge is fundamental to the definition of resilience. Using this notion, there are some researchers who believe that regular experience with stress bolsters or builds resilience for humans or for particular people who have a resilient nature. Others find little evidence for this school of thought but recognize that the expression of resilience occurs only in the face of adversity. Certainly, children and youth who have chronic health needs will most likely have daily demands and different challenges that give regular experience with stress. Some health problems have episodic flare-ups. Asthma, for example, may contribute to general low levels of energy and poor nutrition, but asthma attacks can be acute, life-threatening occasions. Typically, experience occurs over time for the child and his family. They may learn to predict or, sometimes, prevent the frequency and severity of these episodes. Paralysis consequent to spina bifida, however, occurs at birth, and though it may predispose a child to bladder infection or skin breakdown, the disorder itself is constant rather than episodic. The number of health professionals who will work with children who have either of these conditions may be quite extensive: physicians (primary care and specialists), hospital and home health nurses, rehabilitation specialists, social workers, nutritionists, physical therapists, respiratory therapists, and others. Special education or recreation accommodations are likely to be called for. Special equipment and special training for parents are needed. In both examples, children are exposed regularly to different types of stress associated with their health needs and a range of different services and service providers.

Protective Factors: The Development of Resilience

The question has been posed as to whether risk and protective factors are merely mirror images of each other, essentially the same phenomenon at different points of the continuum. There is an increasing body of work that describes, predicts, and explains resilience (Grotberg, 2002). Analyses of data from Werner's landmark study of children in Kauai (Werner, 1989) classified three types of protective factors that characterize resilient children: (1) dispositional attributes of the individual, such as activity level and sociability, at least average intelligence, competence in communication skills (language and reading), and an internal locus of control; (2) affection ties within the family that provide emotional support in times of stress; and (3) external support systems, whether in school, work, or church, that reward the individual's competencies and determination and provide a belief system by which to live. The dynamics and development of resilience has been described differently, but with certain common elements involving confronting challenge or challenges, problem solving, and some type of ego growth or strong intraspychic quality. A qualitative study of 28 males and females with catastrophic illness examined how these young people managed their personal and social world (Dewar & Lee, 2000). Three phases were identified in bearing their situation: finding out, facing reality, and managing reality. There appears to be great fluidity in experiencing these phases, with individuals moving in and out, and re-experiencing the primary emotions and challenges associated with each.

Positive coping strategies were defined as protecting, modifying, and boosting. *Protecting* is the term used for insulating oneself from further emotional pain, especially in interaction with others. *Modifying* encompassed learning to manage the physical, emotional, and social aspects of a condition. *Boosting* involved building courage by various self-generated strategies of encouragement and elevating self-esteem. One of the ways this occurred was by comparing self to others in a similar situation. Even profoundly disabled persons (and their families) paint the experience of others as having more difficult circumstances to bear. There are certain health-related conditions that appear to be generally incompatible with resilience. Depression has been associated with death, disability, and generally worse outcomes when associated as a comorbid condition with other health problems (Stone, 2000; Meijer, Sinnema, Bijstra, Mellenbergh, & Wolters, 2002). Yet even this is not a certainty. Some great artists, for example, have been known to have clinical depression, though often of the manic-depressive type.

Gender is associated with resilience and its varied expressions. Though there is well-supported concern about women's health, males experience higher frequencies at an earlier age of most serious health disorders. This is true across the life span. For example, young widowers (25–64) are the most vulnerable to early death from a wide range of conditions: suicide, heart disease, accidents, and alcohol-related illness. Indeed, though measures of women-specific or child-specific indicators are standard barometers for societal well-being (maternal mortality rates and infant mortality rates that directly reflect education, economics, sanitation, health care), one researcher refers to young men (who are typically the lowest users of health care services) as the social-sensitive canaries, since they, as a group, are expected to be resilient. For at-risk groups and children with special health care needs, girls more often than boys pursue higher education and get involved in service organizations. Some interesting coping behaviors contribute to resilience for some young people. High social anxiety and low social self-esteem have predicted poor psychological adjustment for adolescents with chronic illness (Meijer et al., 2002). However, adolescent survivors of childhood cancer have been found to be less anxious than peers who had not faced a life-threatening illness. Age, gender, and specific illness variables (such as age at diagnosis and time since treatment) were strong predictors of psychological outcomes. Unlike research that finds resilience associated with boldly confronting the health threat and associated difficulties (Meijer et al., 2002), these adolescent cancer survivors were more likely to use avoidance strategies to manage their problems (Bauld, Anderson, & Arnold, 1998). In several ways, however, this corresponds to the concept of protecting or insulating oneself from additional emotional pain.

Culture and a cultural community contribute to resilience. A strong ethnic affiliation, intergenerational support, and connectedness to a faith community correlate with resilience for children and adolescence (Frison, Wallander, & Browne, 1998; Engle, Castle, & Menon, 1996). Ideology and nationalistic fervor have been associated with childhood and adolescent resilience, particularly in the face of violence, but has less sustaining effect than resilience that arises from religious orientation and belief in a sense of higher purpose in life.

Protective Factors: The Expression of Resilience

The literature that describes the development of resilience for children with special health care needs has been approached conceptually through models of stress and coping. As researchers and clinicians adopt a more integrated perspective, there have been new ways of viewing how resilience can be demonstrated. A useful view in examining the expression of resilience is Grotberg's categorization of resources in three dimensions: inner, social, and external. These dimensions have also been labeled as I AM, I CAN, and I HAVE. Children with special health care needs can claim deficits in all three of these dimensions. Yet, some of these children demonstrate resilience by overcoming the obstacles their health problem poses. Resilient children will face adversity and their health problems using a dynamic and balanced interaction of these three factors. I AM qualities are those of inner strength. For children who are not resilient, simply facing the health problem and addressing the overt needs becomes dominant. Tough avoidance and denial strategies sometimes may be used, chronic conditions force at least some level of acknowledgement in order to manage required lifestyle changes. A young child with diabetes and her family must give daily injections and attend specifically to diet and blood sugar monitoring in order to live. Overcoming and being strengthened by the health need is more extraordinary than facing and dealing with special health care needs. Facing a disability and adjusting to it can be normative not only for the person with a disability but also to the family members. In interviews among a Great Plains Indian tribe, a family member indicated that there were no members of his family who had a disability. The interviewer asked about his blind mother. "Well, yes," was the response, "but she was always blind so she wasn't really disabled." Many accommodations for this disability became routines for the family.

The I AM qualities are personal attributes that foster resilience. Children who have an appealing temperament, an achievement orientation, and feel themselves to be lovable have the kind of inner strength that helps them overcome adversity. An internal locus of control, feeling that they can influence their destiny, is a key feature of resilient children. Resilient children have been depicted in art and literature. In a new view of disability and the humanities Mark Jeffreys (Snyder, Brueggemann, & Garland-Thomson, 2002, pp. 36–37) describes his brother, who was born without legs. Their parents wanted him to wear artificial legs to look the same as everyone else at school. Some classmates only saw Jim sitting and didn't know he had a disability until he went out for the wrestling team. Not long after that, Jim recounted, is when he started making friends. Two points are remarkable about this story. One is that family protection eventually became inhibitive. The other remarkable point is that it is difficult to say what abilities should be cultivated. It would be natural to suggest that Jim work on art or music. He followed his own interests and then received positive social reinforcement, and possibly affirmation and assistance from the coach. Inner strengths follow patterns, but they are not necessarily prescriptive. This offers great creativity and opportunity for individual expression. I CAN refers to social and interpersonal skills. Rooted in personal attributes, these qualities have been reinforced and honed through social interaction. Persistence, humor, communications skills, impulse control, and creativity can be acquired and enhanced by most children. Social experience originates with families or primary caregivers. It is remarkable that some children who have dysfunctional families or limited caregiving can use social reinforcement from alternate sources very effectively. Extended family, neighbors, nurses, and teachers have all been named as social mentors by resilient children. The frequency and nature of social reinforcement is pivotal to creating an I CAN ability for children with special health care needs. Joanne is a school-aged child with a severe limp consequent to a domestic violence injury she experienced when she was a baby. Joanne has been in a series of foster homes, some good and some not so good, and has returned to her mother's care from time to time. She cannot run or climb and has serious difficulty with stairs. Joanne has maintained a strong, affectionate relationship with her blind grandmother who prays for her every day and knits clothing for her. When she started school, Joanne's first-grade teacher made a point of spending extra time helping her learn to read. Joanne loves words.

She loves to read and loves to talk and listen. The reading skills help her achieve in school, and her pleasure in conversation facilitates social relationships in many spheres. The I CAN qualities are fostered despite difficult life circumstances.

The I HAVE aspect of resilience is a result of trusting relationships and formal and informal supports. Families, schools, faith communities, and health services contribute to children and youth who overcome adversity. The family relationship is a common source of resilience for children and youth with special health care needs. One emerging field of study and practice in health and human services and public policy relates specifically to family theory and family support for children with special health care needs. Mothers are often primary caregivers for children with special health care needs. Some become public policy advocates or even pursue special study in order to make life better for their children. It is interesting to note that the family itself experiences certain vulnerability and adversity when they have a member with serious chronic health problems. One domain in the field of family support for CSHCN is the study of and services for siblings. When so much of the family focus goes to a child who needs special care, other children in the family may need to be enlisted in delivering care or may be neglected in some ways because of high demand. In either situation, these circumstances profile that adversity is experienced not only by the child with health problems but also by the other family members. Sources of both informal and formal supports are the community systems that surround a child with special health care needs. Culture has a powerful impact on resilience for children with special health care needs. It is worth noting that resilience is often demonstrated by people who experience adversity because they are part of a marginalized community.

Culture often has its own definition for the origin or purpose of serious health needs. Cultural values are expressed in ways that foster or inhibit the development of resilience based on particular beliefs. Culture also affects risk for adverse effects among siblings. The sibling relationship is more prominent in non-European cultures, and there is less family and community emphasis on treating children equally and less reluctance to give siblings major caregiving responsibilities for children with special health care needs. In the dominant U.S. culture, overcoming obvious disability is imbued with a sense of worthiness as well as achievement. The visibility of a condition is one marker that evokes community support. Community and cultural meaning and support are universal in their ability to promote resilience. In other cultures, the visibility of the condition may not be the most salient factor.

Sam is a Navajo child with epilepsy. He needs to take medication everyday, but he has had at least one seizure at his Head Start class and one at a tribal meeting when he was a toddler. Because in the traditional way of thinking epilepsy was a sign of incest, community support and even support within his extended family is absent or lukewarm.

Etta is a classmate of Sam's, also a Navajo child with a disability. She was born with a dislocated hip that wasn't treated early because her mother died when she was an infant. This was a relatively common disorder that for years was thought to facilitate horseback riding. The fact that so many people had trouble walking and that the community ascribed a positive character to it made the disorder one that evoked cultural and community support, building the I HAVE dimension of resilience. Religious beliefs have powerful community influence for I HAVE characteristics. Religion has some of the most important ways to give meaning to pain and suffering, including chronic disease in children. Not every person uses faith to bolster resilience, but for those who do, it is often the predominant or paramount force in overcoming adversity. Ideas about sacred pain exist in all faiths, serving as a foundation for spiritual meaning (Glucklich, 2001). Though religion and other group expressions of faith and spirituality have a strong influence in developing positive I HAVE characteristics, children and youth with special health care needs may or may not be exposed to them by their caregivers. This exposure may also be episodic as the youth moves through stages of spiritual development and enlightenment within the life of the family. In contrast the ever-present need to work with health and human services can have an additional profound impact for many youth with special health care needs. This impact can be protective and lead to further development of resilience, or it can be an added risk factor, adding tension to the development of self-determination.

Potential of Health Care Services to Promote Resilience for Children and Youth with Special Health Care Needs

The hallmark characteristic of children and youth with health care needs is that they will or should have fairly frequent contact with health care providers. Generally, they will also see a wide range of health care providers.

The potential to do more than treat a problem is enhanced by the fact that, increasingly, patients, families and professionals are concerned with promoting optimal functioning and quality of life. Health care services, however, are part of complex systems that are not always conducive to capitalizing on this common goal.

Ron S. is a 16-year-old young man who came to a doctor's office front desk to check in for his scheduled physical. The front desk asked where his parents were, and he stated he came alone that day. Unfortunately, it was his first visit in the clinic, and there was no documentation from his parents that he could be seen alone. The front desk staff said he would have to reschedule. Ron S. asked if there was any way he could be seen because he really felt he needed a checkup, he needed asthma medication refills, and had come a long way for the appointment. He stated he always went alone to his previous doctor visits because his mom was busy with other younger sisters and brothers at home and usually couldn't get away. The front desk called the physician and asked if anything could be done. The doctor said if his parents could be reached by phone to give a verbal consent for him to be seen it was okay to check him in. His mother was at home and gave the verbal okay; the physician then saw Ron S. This could be described in terms of I HAVE, I AM, and I CAN. It is possible to help people develop different perceptions of their environment that will shape the I HAVE. For Ron, he perceived he had a health care system that was supposed to work for him, to aid in his care, and he had a family that was supportive of him developing independence. Ron also realized I AM in terms of believing he was worth the time the front desk was going to take to see if there was any way for him to be seen. An I CAN quality was exhibited in his understanding that he could state what he needed, and he would expect his request to be taken with respect. In this case the health care system acknowledged the person's resilience, and he was successful. The extent to which the experiences with the health care system fosters, inhibits, or is neutral in contributing toward resiliency can be varied.

Successfully negotiating health care systems in the United States is a difficult task for many. It takes resilience to be a successful consumer of the health care system. In this chapter, the health care system is defined as the places people go to get health care and the process involved in securing that health care. Also included is the process of accepting and being able to follow recommendations given by health care providers.

There are three main checkpoints that people must pass in trying to get health care: the initial financial access to health care, the inter-personal interaction with a health care provider, and the process of carrying out health care recommendations and treatments.

In the story, the young man and his family had successfully accom-plished the first checkpoint, they had insurance and picked a provider, but the second checkpoint, actually interacting with the provider, was not guaranteed. It was only because of the teenager's determination and his resilience and solid self-esteem that he was able to see the doctor that day. Had he been less assertive he would have left the health care office and not had his health needs met.

While all of these checkpoints are difficult for an adult, there are additional barriers that can make the process hostile when a teenager tries to access health care.

Teaching youth at a young age to be assertive when accessing health care is essential. This will lead to a lifetime of making sure health needs are explored and met. While traditional medicine con-centrates on risk factors, there are now concepts that directly look at resilience in the health care system. These have mainly focused on interpersonal interactions and adherence to recommendations and treatments. One example of this shift is seen in discussing health care promotion with people living with chronic illness. Instead of empha-sizing the person's illness and looking at the person as a chronically ill man or woman, it is more helpful to reshape the perception by see-ing a whole person who happens to also have a chronic illness. One example could be of youth and young adult celebrity spokespeople living with HIV or AIDS. People such as Magic Johnson have put their lives on display and have continued to live meaningfully and productively beyond the chronic illness. This might best be explained with the stress and coping model. Many of the strengths may have arisen as a direct result of the stress the special health care need has caused. Exploring the person's strengths, both those they bring to the special health care need and those developed because of the stress of the health care need, seems to produce much more positive health and lifestyle outcomes in some studies.

In a study done by W. E. Mourdian, health care providers are encouraged to look at personal narratives as a way to promote a dis-covery of sources to increase resilience for those with incurable con-ditions. That means that a medical professional would take the time to explore the person's perception of their life and how they have coped with the special health care need or debilitating illness. Through this exploration, strengths that would fulfill the I AM attributes are revealed to the doctor and can be used to help support the person's challenges through his or her illness.

Financial access to health care is a barrier, and confidence and coping are extremely important in helping to get care that is needed.

Samuel P. is a 20-year-old young man who was previously healthy before he was hospitalized and almost lost his life. He had a grave infection that even doctors didn't know that he could survive. After being treated in the hospital for three weeks, he was finally ready to go home. The doctors still felt it was essential for his life that he continue antibiotics at home to fight infection for a month and to return to the heart doctor to check on the damage done to his heart. The doctor caring for the young man wrote a prescription for the medication and told him to come to his office for follow-up care in one week. Seven months later, the young man appeared in a new doctor's office with many serious complaints, and he wanted to fill the medications written half a year earlier. He stated he didn't have health insurance when he was in the hospital and couldn't afford the medications that were prescribed.

To access health care a person must have some financial resources to pay for the care; private or government insurance plans are used, but for many traditional health care is delayed or passed up because of lack of financial resources. This young man was unable to tell the doctor he didn't have health insurance to get the medications, and the doctor did not make sure Samuel had the ability to get medication once he was home. As a result, this young man lived in fear of dying every single day for seven months. He clearly understood and wanted to follow the directions the doctor had given him, but did not have access to medical care once he was discharged from the hospital.

When considering protective factors that promote access to health care, internal I AM and I CAN attributes such as hardiness and self-determination may prove useful. Becoming one's own advocate and pushing the medical system to provide services that do not seem readily available takes self-empowerment. This is not easily taught to those that are lacking in this area.

It may be possible, however, to look at environmental factors in the health care system that could promote increased resilience in those that need access to the system. One possibility would be for health care facilities to increase social support in accessing health insurance plans. This could be done for those who have been unsuccessful in the

past by providing guidance and support for accessing private or government insurance plans.

Sherrie R. is an 18-year-old young woman who had recently come
to her doctor to ask for a referral to have an adult-focused specialist
to manage her diabetes.

She had had diabetes since early adolescence and felt she was ready
for an adult doctor since she was living on her own and working as
an adult. She had a history of being very nonadherent to any diabetic
regimen that was recommended, but now she appeared to have more
concern about improving her health. She was given a name and telephone number of a specialist with whom her regular doctor was
familiar, and an appointment was made for the new doctor at this
visit. Two months later Sherrie appeared again at her regular doctor's office requesting more insulin and diabetic supplies. It was then
revealed she had gone to her new doctor and felt he just didn't take
enough time to know who she was and didn't seem as attentive as her
previous doctor.

She was not interested in trying any other new doctors and wanted
her care to continue from the pediatric service. Transitions from
childhood to adolescence to young adulthood in those with special
health care needs can be described in terms of resilience. There are
recent recommendations that stress the value of focusing on resilient
traits of individuals with chronic health care needs. A focus on factors
that foster this resiliency is also important (White, 2002).

As mentioned earlier, historically the focus on those with special
health care needs has been directed toward the deficits the person
has, not the resilience that they have or can attain. This has been the
case even though there are studies that show evidence that patients
who focus on positive attributes, even in the face of chronic illness,
now lead more productive lives (White, 2002). In the transition from
youth care to more adult care, many young adults find it difficult for
many reasons. One reason is that a youth who has grown up with a
special health care need has learned how to best care for that special
health care need. When they reach young adulthood, they have usually educated friends, family, and even health professionals on the best
way to assist them in their care. Between the pediatric primary care
provider and the youth exists, many times, a partnership in which
both learn and grow from the experience. When this partnership has
to be broken and a new relationship forged with adult providers, the
expectation of partnership is not always present. Primary care
providers, such as internists, are not always trained to partner with

their patients in the same way as the pediatric providers, and the youth with a special health care need is not always prepared for a provider that may not be interested in past triumphs the youth has achieved. The resilience of the youth will be tested at this juncture of their development as they encounter a new health care system that is more focused on self-reliance and less family involvement. For some this transition is very traumatic and leads them back to the original pediatric providers many times before they are able to identify a professional with whom they can partner. During this time, they have to accept a readjustment of expectations for the health care system and develop new positive factors that will aid in their success in the health care system they must enter because of age. Also during this time, the family must develop more resilience as the I HAVE attributes may change. Namely, the insurance coverage for an emerging young adult with special health care needs may disappear or offer fewer needed services that were relied upon to assist in daily life needs. This stress placed upon the family will increase resilience in some as they learn to navigate new systems of care. For others it may increase family stresses and delay full emancipation of youth with special health care needs who can and want to attain autonomy as an adult. The protective factors for those with special health care needs that were associated with having resilience included having a self-perception as not handicapped, involvement in household chores, having a network of friends both disabled and not disabled, and support from caring adults without overprotectiveness (Ungerer et al.,1988).

Though these protective factors are not directly related to the health care system, they can be promoted by the health care giver. Lack of resilience factors is more likely to be the cause of difficulty coping with a disability rather than the chronic condition itself.

Janet is a 15-year-old sexually active teenager who comes to the doctor with her mother after telling her mother she is having sex and wants to get birth control. They have discussed methods of prevention of pregnancy and sexually transmitted infections as well as the risks of having sex as a teenager. Above her mother's objections Janet has told her mother she is not willing to stop having sex. Indeed, her mother is aware that once a teen begins a sexual life, they rarely completely abstain from the behavior. Her mother decides to make sure she does not get pregnant while she continues to work with her daughter to refrain from having sex. After both have counseling with the doctor and have picked a birth control method, they are seen three months later for a follow-up. Janet is still using a birth control method but has recently broken up with her boyfriend and is considering abstaining for a while.

Siera is a 15-year-old teenager who also is sexually active. Her mother finds out by accident and demands she stop having sex. She brings in her daughter for a physical exam. On evaluation it is found Siera is seven months pregnant and has a sexually transmitted infection.

Though we have been speaking of those with chronic illness and those with special health care needs, it is important to remember the majority of people—youth and adults—who enter the health care system with a particular problem or concern.

Most are usually healthy, but have a temporary concern that is in need of health care. These people are sometimes those for whom it is hardest to develop resiliency. Their concern is invisible or perceived as being the result of preventable behaviors.

Another example would be smokers who are unsuccessful or not yet ready to quit smoking behaviors. Because some of these temporary concerns develop into life-changing problems and even chronic illness, it should not be forgotten that resilience could also be promoted in these people as well. The support and encouragement to adopt positive attributes for those with episodic concerns is not as enthusiastic as the support for someone just diagnosed with cancer.

Resilience of adolescents with high-risk behaviors is beginning to be defined in an effort to reduce the risk of bad health outcomes. Teenage pregnancy prevention has long been an area of concern, and most recently there has been some evidence that positive factors such as school connectedness and parental connectedness promote delayed sexual initiation of adolescents. There are programs now underway trying to develop or increase these characteristics in youth at high risk for teenage pregnancy. There is another area that needs attention: those that have high-risk behaviors with medical needs as a result, but who do not always access health care. Addressing these unmet health needs of those youth that are otherwise healthy is difficult. Most teenagers who become sexually active do not receive any health-related care until at least one or more months after their first sexual encounter (AGI, 1994). This means that some will first come to medical care pregnant or with a sexually transmitted disease that could have been prevented had they had medical attention before or soon after the first sexual encounter. Enhancing resilience factors may be helpful here as well.

References

AGI, *Sex and American's Teenagers*, New York: AGI, 1994, pp. 19–20.

Barnett, W. S. (1993). Toward a more general model for research on the well-being of siblings of persons with disabilities. In Z. Toneman & P. W. Berman (Eds.), *The effects of mental retardation, disability, and illness on sibling relationships: Research issues and challenges* (pp. 333–354). Baltimore, MD: Paul H. Brookes Publishing Co.

Bauld, C., Anderson, J., & Arnold, J. (1998). Psychosocial aspects of adolescent cancer survival. *Journal of Paediatrics and Child Health 34*, 120–126.

Bernard, B. (1995 August). *Fostering resilience in children. ERIC Digest.* Retrieved 10/10/02 from http://ericps.crc.uiuc.edu/resnet/library/benard95.html (ERIC Document Reproduction Services No. EDO-PS-95–9).

Bernard, B. Resiliency Associates. (n.d.). *Turning it around for all youth: From risk to resilience. ERIC Digest.* Retrieved from http://ericps.crc.uiuc.edu/resnet/library/dig126.html

Dewar, A., & Lee, E. (2000). Bearing illness and injury. *Western Journal of Nursing Research 22*, 912–926.

Engle, P., Castle, S., & Menon, P. (1996). Child development: Vulnerability and resilience. *Social Science & Medicine 43*, 621–635.

Finley, M. (n.d.). *Cultivating resilience: An overview for rural educators and parents. ERIC Digest.* Retrieved 10/10/02 from http://ericps.crc.uiuc.edu/resnet/library/edorc945.html (ERIC Document Reproduction Services No. ED372904).

Frison, S., Wallander, J., & Browne, D. (1998). Cultural factors enhancing resilience and protecting against maladjustment in African American adolescents with mild mental retardation. *American Journal on Mental Retardation 102*, 613–626.

Gallo, A., & Knafl, K. (1993). Siblings of children with chronic illnesses: A categorical and noncategorical look at selected literature. In Z. Toneman & P. W. Berman (Eds.), *The effects of mental retardation, disability, and illness on sibling relationships: Research issues and challenges* (pp. 215–234). Baltimore, MD: Paul H. Brookes Publishing Co.

Garmezy, N. (1993). Children in poverty: Resilience despite risk. *Psychiatry 56*, 127–136.

Glucklich, A. (2001). *Sacred pain.* New York: Oxford Press.

Grotberg, E. H. (1999). Countering depression with the five building blocks of resilience. *Reaching Today's Youth 4*, 66–72.

Grotberg, E. H. (2000). International resilience research project. In A. L. Comunian & U. Gielen (Eds.), *International perspectives in human development* (pp. 379-399). Vienna, Austria: Pabst Science Publishers.

Grotberg, E. H. (n.d.). Resilience and culture/ethnicity examples from Sudan, Nambia, and Armenia. *ERIC Digest.* Retrieved on 10/10/02 from http://ericps.crc.uiuc.edu/resnet/library/grotb98b.html.

Keltner, B., & Ramey, S. L. (1992). The family. *Current Opinion in Psychiatry* 5, 638–644.

Keltner, B., & Ramey, S. L. (1993). Family issues. *Current Opinion in Psychiatry* 6, 239–634.

Meijer, S., Sinnema, G., Bijstra, J., Mellenbergh, G., & Wolters, W. (2002). Coping styles and locus of control as predictors for psychological adjustment of adolescents with chronic illness. *Social Science & Medicine 54,* 1453–1461.

Morse, J., Wilson, S., & Penrod, J. (2000). Mothers and their disabled children: Refining the concept of normalization. *Health Care for Women International, 5,* 659–676.

Newacheck, P. W., & Neal, H. (1998 April). Prevalence and impact of disabling chronic conditions in childhood. *American Journal of Public Health 88,* 610–617.

Paddock, D. (n.d.). Bent not broken: Building resilient adoptive families. *Families with a Difference.* Retrieved 10/10/02 from http://www.adopting. org/DeePaddock/html/bent.html.

Snyder, S., Brueggemann, B., & Garland-Thomson, R. (Eds). (2002). *Disability studies: Enabling the humanities.* New York: The Modern Language Association of America.

Stone, R. (2000). Stress: The invisible hand in eastern Europe's death rates. *Science, 288,* 1732–1733.

Ungerer, J. A., Horgan, B., Chaitow, J., & Champion, G. D. Psychosocial functioning in children and young adults with juvenile arthritis. *Pediatrics* 1988 Feb; 81 (2): 195–202.

Werner, E. E. (1989). High-risk children in young adulthood: A longitudinal study from birth to 32 years. *American Journal of Orthopsychiatry, 59,* 72-81.

White, P. H. Transition: a future promise for chldren and adolescents with special health care needs and disabilities. *Rheumatology Disease Clinics of North America* 2002 August; 28 (3): 687–703, viii.

CHAPTER 7

Resilience and Biculturalism: The Latino Experience in the United States

Francisca Infante with Alexandra Lamond

In 1997 Carlos arrived in Washington, D.C., from Los Angeles to live with a friend of his father. Carlos was escaping from his old gang because they refused to allow him to quit. He had emigrated to Los Angeles five years earlier from Colombia. Once in Washington, D.C., he realized his father's friend had enough problems himself and that he was not really welcome at that house. As a way to survive, he found a community-based organization that worked with Latino youth and a transitional living house for homeless youth. In March 1997 he was living in the residential home and taking General Equivalent Degree (GED) classes to receive his high school equivalent certificate. Carlos is a very friendly and outgoing youth. He is polite, always offering help at the Center. After a month participating in the community-based organization, everyone knew him and was trying to help him with his studies, helping him to find a job, and trying to get him a scholarship to go to college. Because of his ability to reach out for support and resources, Carlos was able to discover opportunities available to him within and outside the center. His being a lovable, friendly person made people want to help him. Carlos is an excellent example of a resilient youth and a model for youth workers and service providers who can learn to identify the resources, skills, and inner strengths that can be provided and promoted to help Latino immigrants settle down and succeed in the United States.

Life stories like Carlos' give new insights to think about how individuals react and behave when experiencing adversity. In the area of human development, Carlos' story is an example of the importance of promoting human potential for social adjustment. Carlos' resilience, demonstrated by his optimism, creativity, and trust, his planning skills, his capacity for establishing meaningful relationships with other people, and the availability of social services for Latino youth, together provided him transitional housing, college resources, and the opportunity to leave the gang and become an active participant of U.S. society.

This approach to social adjustment, focusing on human potential, presents a stark contrast to the one prevalent in support of strategies that would have focused on Carlos' troubled background in Colombia and Los Angeles as explanations for his involvement in risky gang behaviors. Current thinking emphasizes the importance of providing social support to immigrants, drawing from values and practices from their countries of origin, and developing biculturalism as a source for successful adaptation. Together, the focus on human potential and on the values and resources from other cultures will bring a better understanding of the relationships among the different races and cultures that make up the United States.

The purpose of this chapter is to provide insight into how the social services can be more effective in promoting resilience in the Latino population by drawing from the personal, cultural, and social strengths of this community. To do so, we will analyze the stories of Latinos in the United States, the difficulties they experience, and the strengths they develop in the process of becoming part of their new country. By describing the Latino experience of immigration and their transformation into bicultural individuals, we want to contribute to the understanding of the specific factors that allow resilience to develop. The conceptual framework considers resilience as a social phenomenon, and through the analysis of cases like Carlos' we will show that extended family support, oral traditions, optimism, and cultural attachment, among other factors, can be used by social services to promote resilience in the Latino population.

A Brief Review of the Concept of Resilience

In this chapter, we follow Grotberg, who defines resilience as "a human capacity to face, deal with, overcome, learn from, be strengthened by or even transformed by experiences of adversity" (Grotberg,

2001). Researchers have organized different factors that enhance resilience in three categories: the inner strengths developed, the external support provided, and the social and problem-solving skills acquired. Resilience and its three categories of factors are enhanced by the individual interaction with social resources that allow a positive adaptation despite conditions of extreme adversity.

The history of resilience shows that there have been two generations that differ on the questions they use to guide their research (Masten, 1999; Luthar, Cicchetti, & Becker, 2000; Luthar & Cuching, 1999; Luthar, 1999; Kaplan, 1999). The first generation was led by the question, "Among high-risk children, what distinguishes those who do well from those who do poorly?" (Luthar as cited in Kaplan, 1999, p. 69). They conducted research to identify risk and resilience factors present in those individuals who did well despite adversity and organized them in the three categories of factors mentioned above. The second generation, which began publishing in the second half of the 1990s, wanted to learn by trying to understand how risk and resilience factors interacted, allowing resilient behavior to occur in order to address risk. The second generation focused on understanding the underlying processes and mechanisms of positive adaptation and at the same time continued with the interest of the older generation by asking which factors are present in those at-risk individuals who are able to deal with the adversities of life.

A review of the evolution of the concept clearly shows that Edith Grotberg (1999, 1995, 2001) has been a bridge between the two generations. Through her International Resilience Research Project she was a pioneer in the field in three different ways:

1. She was one of the first researchers to question the cultural specificity of resilient adaptation. She started asking whether resilience varied among countries and cultures and conducted research and field testing of the concept in 22 countries around the world.

2. As part of the first generation of researchers, she identified the sources of resilience and translated them into an easy-to-understand vocabulary. She translated inner strengths into I AM, the external supports and resources into I HAVE, and the interpersonal and social skills as I CAN. Furthermore, she added that resilience could be promoted and developed a guide for service providers and parents to promote resilience in clusters (Grotberg, 1995).

3. Following Michael Rutter's theory (1987) of resilient mechanisms, Grotberg suggested that resilience is a dynamic adaptation that occurs by the interaction among three sources of resilience, I AM,

I HAVE, and I CAN, suggesting what the second generation calls "resilience as a process" (Infante, 2001).

The second generation of researchers, represented in particular by Luthar and Cuching (1999), Masten (1999), and Kaplan (1999), focuses on the process or dynamic by which individual and environmental factors interact (Bernard, 1999), allowing a person to adapt despite adversity. In this chapter we will take the main contributions from the second generation, identifying resilience factors in the Latino community and trying to understand how these factors interact. To better understand the process of developing resilience we will examine the Latino experience: the sources of adversity, such as the country of origin, the motivation for coming to the United States, experiences of discrimination and adaptation, and social and economic status. Furthermore, we will examine the resilience factors that help Latinos adapt to the new culture and develop biculturalism. In our view, identifying the sources of resilience will help to better understand the process of developing biculturalism and its contribution to the United States.

Understanding the Latino Immigrants: Their Struggle between Acculturation and Biculturalism

Latinos are considered to be "U.S. persons whose origins can be traced to the Spanish-speaking regions of Latin America, including the Caribbean, Mexico, Central America, and South America" (Flores et al., 2002). By defining *Latino* as immigrants from Spanish-speaking countries in the Americas, we are not considering the territorial definition of Latin America that includes Brazil and does not include the Caribbean. Neither are we considering the U.S. Census term *Hispanic*, which emphasizes only the European influence of Spanish colonialism without taking into consideration the diversity of ethnic and cultural groups living in Latin America and the Caribbean (Flores et al., 2002; Suárez-Orozco & Páez, 2002). For the purpose of our analysis, the term *Latino* will include immigrants from Spanish-speaking countries (including Caribbean countries such as Cuba and the Dominican Republic) and also indigenous people whose ancestors do not come from Spain.

As mentioned in the definition, the experience of being Latino exists only in North America. Outside of the United States, Latinos are Mexicans, Salvadorans, Dominicans, Peruvians, and Argentineans, among others. Only on North American territory does the immigrant become Latino—a label that brings together different countries of origin, ethnic background, class, race, and language in one minority group category. Although there is constant reference to Mexicans in Los Angeles or Dominicans in New York, I would say that only in the past five years, have studies and publications (Suárez-Orozco & Paéz, 2002; Rumbaut & Portes, 2001) begun to specify that the Latino populations cannot be generalized. Latinos are white, black, and indigenous, and they come from Latin America and from the Caribbean. Latinos include highly educated groups that tend to have higher education degrees than native-born Americans and also include poorly schooled, semiskilled workers who come to this country with a ninth grade education or less. However, the growing number and youthfulness of the Latino populations and its impact on the North American culture have brought increased attention from politicians, sociologists, economists, pediatricians, and health care professionals.

According to the 2000 U.S. Census, Latinos are the fastest growing minority group in the United States. They comprise 13 percent of the population today and are projected to be 25 percent of the U.S. population by 2050. About 5.5 percent of the Hispanic population is between 10 and 24 years old, compared with only 3.5 percent of non-Hispanic whites (U.S. Census Bureau, 2000). According to the projections, two generations from now the United States, after Mexico, will claim the second largest population of Latinos. Even though not all Latinos speak Spanish as a first language, research has found that Latinos are the immigrant group most committed to retaining their language (Suárez-Orozco & Paéz, 2002). The fact that Latinos speak primarily Spanish in the United States today certainly holds this group together and presents strong differentiation from the rest of the population.

Latinos have gained political importance in recent years. There is now clear awareness about the need to incorporate Latino issues into political discourses in order to capture the Latino vote. For example, in May 2001, President George Bush delivered his weekly radio address to the nation in Spanish, marking a new milestone in the history of U.S. presidents (Suárez-Orozco & Páez, 2002). Latinos currently constitute 7 percent of the American electorate, but with a sustained effort Latino voters can be multiplied by targeting those who are new voters through promoting voter registration (National Council of La Raza, 2002a). However, research finds that giving political discourse in Spanish or advertising in the Spanish media is not

enough. According to Raul Yzaguirre, president of the National
Council of La Raza, "there is a need to do research and respond to
issues that affect Hispanic families" (National Council of La Raza,
2002a).

There is also a developing awareness and effort to train Latino youth
in leadership and advocacy, both at the community level and at the highest levels of the political decision-making process. In both cases programs are seeking to empower Latino families and neighborhoods to
achieve economic success through education, leadership, and fostering
altruistic values (National Council of La Raza, 2002b; National
Foundation for Teaching Entrepreneurship, 2002; Hispanic Association
of Colleges and Universities, 2002). All these efforts strengthen Latino
communities, promoting their resilience by strengthening external support, providing social opportunities, promoting social skills, and building inner strength.

Economically, Latino immigration, which comprises the largest
wave of newcomers in U.S. history, has two interesting features. One
is a new framework for understanding economic trade among countries, or what economists call the *transnational framework*. This framework recognizes the economic impact of money family members in
the United States send to their countries of origin. In some countries,
such as the Dominican Republic, El Salvador, and Mexico, Latino
remittances have been an important contribution to foreign exchange
and country income (Hinojosa Ojeda, 2001). A second area of interest for economists is in relation to employment and wages, or the
impact of Latino labor in U.S. businesses ("The Longest Journey,"
2002).

From the sociological perspective, research and programmatic
interest have focused on the interpersonal dynamics created by the
new wave of immigrants, who come from Latin America, the
Caribbean, and Asia (Suárez-Orozco & Suárez-Orozco, 2001).
Different from the old wave of immigrants, who came at the beginning of the century from Canada and Europe, the new wave of immigrants are ethnically, culturally, and linguistically diverse,
contributing a whole different range of concepts to the acculturation
process.

Until the past two decades, the process of Latino immigration was
compared with the European immigration, where people, mostly
white, were able to assimilate relatively easily after the second or
third generation in the United States. They came to the United
States, got a job, and settled down. Even though at the beginning

they would also be discriminated against because of religion or culture, the second or third generations of European immigrants would
learn the language and become part of the North American culture
(Suárez-Orozco & Suárez-Orozco, 2001). Now that new immigrants
are mainly people of color, they have brought new races and racial
awareness to the country, changing the historical racial dichotomy
between blacks and whites (Sánchez, 2002). However, according to
Sánchez, it does not matter how well the new immigrants learn the
language, or whether or not they have a job, because they cannot disappear into the white mainstream of the country, which makes the
different generations more exposed to discrimination and harder to
assimilate or Americanize.

"Acculturation is . . . [the process of] changes in cultural attitudes,
values, and behaviors that result from immigration experiences"
(Ainslie, 2002, p. 291). Researchers used to understand acculturation
as a linear process, assuming immigrants arrived with well-defined
identities and would increasingly assimilate to the new culture.
Moreover, researchers thought immigrants who did not resolve
whether to maintain an identity with one culture or the other would
be exposed to a larger amount of stress and alienation (Ainslie, 2002,
p. 291). This model of acculturation assumes that immigrants leave
their old identities behind, acculturate, assimilate, Americanize, melt,
or camouflage themselves within the new mainstream identity, which,
in the case of the United States has to do with the white American
culture. However, recent studies find that the longer immigrant generations have been in the United States, the greater the possibility
they will engage in risk behaviors (Flores et al., 2002), especially
when Latinos or other immigrants live in poor neighborhoods and do
not have access to opportunities to better understand the North
American mainstream culture. Along with these new studies there
are emerging trends in understanding successful acculturation,
which refers to Latino identity as a combination of the old and the
new culture, or biculturalism. Understanding biculturalism is the
transformation process of the cultural attitudes, values, and behaviors
as a result of immigration experiences, with the objective of dealing
with both the new and the old cultures (Ainslie, 2002; Suárez-Orozco,
2001).

According to Carola and Marcelo Suárez-Orozco (2001), the
process of developing biculturalism and creating a new identity
requires combining two frames of reference: the culture from the
country of origin, usually represented by the parents, and the new

society expectations of the American culture. Though first-generation parents can deal with this dual frame of reference by learning skills to live better while maintaining a strong sense of identity with the country of origin, for children, and especially for adolescents, there is an enormous need to belong to the dominant culture, to be accepted. This need to be accepted is strengthened by the family's need to settle down and at the same time clashes with the forces of discrimination, especially with the new immigrants that are stigmatized by color or ethnicity.

For example, José, a light-skinned 11-year-old born in the Dominican Republic but raised in the United States from age two, experiences the dichotomy of having a strong Dominican family and identity while feeling the pull of assimilating into the predominant culture of his Brooklyn neighborhood. As the oldest of three boys in a single-parent home (José's parents divorced and his father moved out of the home and to the Bronx when José was four), José is encouraged by his extended Dominican family to take on the role of man of the house; being responsible for supporting his mother emotionally while looking out for his younger brothers. His paternal grandparents play a significant role in José's life as part-time caretakers while José's mother works two jobs. They also strengthen his Dominican identity through instilling in him the stories and rituals of his native country. José was mainstreamed from a bilingual to a general education classroom in the fifth grade at age 10. José struggles academically, making it hard for him to achieve the social and familial expectations of being a good student. José's hope was that the mainstreaming would stop the bullying he was experiencing because of being in an English as a Second Language class and maybe would allow him to become friends of the tough guys in the class. José was beginning to exhibit concerns of preadolescents, marked by a need to be part of a peer group in his school and neighborhood. The tough guys achieve high social status because they challenge authority and bully girls and more passive boys. According to the adaptation process, José is a Latino boy at a pivotal point in his development of identity. He feels the pull of belonging to the "in crowd," which would mean denying his biculturalism, camouflaging with the peer group, and probably engaging in risky behaviors, such as violence and drug abuse. At the same time, he feels a strong attachment to his family and Dominican heritage. In wanting to belong to this peer group, José is also jeopardizing the expectations of his family for academic achievement and family support.

José's case represents the struggle Latinos, especially youth, have as they are torn between denying their cultural background or accepting their family and cultural traditions in order to develop biculturalism. On the one hand, they have the challenge and desire to belong to American groups, and on the other hand they have their race, family, and networks that connect them with their culture of origin. Providing opportunities to understand and value biculturalism allows recognition of the positive values and traditions present in the American culture and the Latino culture. Allowing people like José to be comfortable with their race and culture becomes an asset for him and for the country that can better learn positive values and traditions present in other cultures.

For sociology and psychology, understanding biculturalism and the Latino experiences means examining the place of immigrants of color in the United States and how new immigrants are challenged by racism, poverty, and discrimination, as well as by the effort of becoming competent and adapting to a new set of cultural values. However, from a resilience perspective we would argue that it is possible to recognize that for some Latino groups, biculturalism is a resilient outcome because it implies a set of values, behaviors, and social service availability that allows positive adaptation despite the constraints given by poverty and discrimination.

The Living Conditions of the Latino Community

Even though different countries, education levels, and socioeconomic status comprise the Latino communities, almost a quarter of Latinos live under the poverty line, in poor housing, attending lower-budget schools. Furthermore, they are more exposed to health risks as a result of their nutrition and the environmental conditions of their neighborhoods. In the following section we will analyze the health and welfare conditions that affect the majority of Latino families. We will describe the case of the Ramirez family, which has, as many other Latinos, walked the difficult and often adverse path toward successful adaptation.

Poverty

Part of the American Dream for Latino immigrants is to leave behind social and economic inequalities. However, after arriving in the United States, they are still left behind in terms of family income. In 1998, 22.7 percent of Latino families lived below the poverty line, compared with 6.1 percent of non-Hispanic whites;

Latino unemployment was 6.7 percent, compared with 3.6 percent unemployment for non-Hispanic whites; the median income for Latino males was $18,430, compared with $31,486 for non-Hispanic whites. Household income in 1998 was $28,430 for Latinos and $42,439 for non-Hispanic whites (Suárez-Orozco & Páez, 2002, p. 25). The tension between the American Dream Latinos had before coming to the United States and the actual living conditions they have once in the United States can be represented by the Ramirez family.

Eva Ramirez is an 11-year-old Mexican American girl who came from Guerrero, Mexico when she was six years old. She came with her mother and siblings to join her father, who worked as a custodian in a Manhattan office building. The family settled in Fort Greene, Brooklyn. When Eva arrived in Brooklyn, she knew no English and was enrolled in a public school in a bilingual preschool grade class, where she received instruction in Spanish. Her father worked three jobs, her mother, two. After school, she helped care for her three-year-old brother, who had a neurological disorder related to his exposure to high lead levels. Besides better educational and economic opportunities for their children, Eva's parents cite the need for medical attention of their youngest child as hastening their decision to come to the United States. Like Eva and her family, many Latinos immigrate to the United States looking for better-paying jobs. Immigrants estimate that a job in the United States can generate the same or more money than several months of work in their country of origin.

The Ramirez' decision to come to the United States was fueled by a desire to achieve higher economic, educational, and health status for their children, which could explain their motivation, optimism, and commitment to doing well in the new land. However, though they make considerably more at their jobs here than they did while employed in Mexico, the Ramirez still live way below the U.S. poverty level. They live in low-income housing in a rapidly gentrifying neighborhood and struggle to pay rent each month. Like the Ramirez, who are unskilled laborers, many recent immigrants arrive in the United States to confront a rapidly technologically advancing society where their skills are not valued monetarily. Unskilled laborers are no longer easily absorbed into the U.S. job market and are the most vulnerable when an economic downturn occurs. The Ramirez family's low household income and their difficulty in rising above the poverty line is exacerbated by their undocumented status, low educational level, and lack of language skills. In today's social and economic context, education and skills seem to be the factors differentiating between those immigrants that adapt and move into good jobs and those immigrants experiencing poverty.

Health

According to the Latino Consortium of the American Academy of Pediatrics Center for Child Health Research, the most important health priorities and challenges regarding Latino children are to gather culturally specific research, promote access to quality health care, and develop policies to decrease the amount of risk factors associated with living in poor neighborhoods (Flores et al., 2002).

Latino children and youth spend more days in bed for illness than do their white counterparts; they make fewer visits to the doctor and have lower chances of receiving vision screening, prescription drugs, and being adequately medicated for pain (Flores et al., 2002). Related to mental health issues, 20 percent of Latino youth report having considered suicide compared with 18 percent of white youth and 15 percent of black youth (Flores et al., 2002). In particular, Latina adolescents make a concrete plan or attempt suicide 1.5 times more often than African Americans and non-Hispanic whites (National Coalition of Hispanic Health and Human Services Organizations, 1999). When describing the living conditions of most Latinos, risks such as exposure to outdoor and indoor pollutants, hazardous waste sites, pesticides, and mercury explain morbidity and even premature development of asthma, lead poisoning, and cancer. The disparity becomes obvious when realizing that three of the five largest hazardous landfills in the United States are in Latino and black neighborhoods and that the percentage of Latinos and blacks living in areas with toxic waste is double that for areas without toxic waste (Flores et al., 2002).

Given these health conditions of the Latino populations, it is important for social service and medical agencies to reach out to Latino communities in poverty-stricken areas. Luckily, this was the case with the Ramirez family. A brother, diagnosed with a neurological disorder, benefited from a school-based program that served as a bridge to an early intervention diagnostic treatment center in the community that accepted uninsured, undocumented children. The early diagnosis and consistent high-quality follow-up services facilitated his placement in a general education, rather than a special education, preschool classroom.

Education

Latino youth have the highest dropout rate—29 percent compared with 13 percent for blacks and 7 percent for whites; and the disparities persist after adjusting for socioeconomic status (Flores et al., 2002). The high dropout rate for Latinos is affected by important variations within the group because Hispanic immigrants tend to drop out more frequently, 44 percent, than U.S.-born Latinos, 21 percent. According to Suárez-Orozco and Suárez-Orozco (2001), a large amount of the dropout rate for Hispanic immigrants has to do with the lack of documentation, which prevents them from going to college.

The White House Initiative on Educational Excellence for Hispanic Americans report mentions that school achievement in this group is influenced by less participation in preschool programs, lack of English proficiency, and/or poverty. For example, Latinos under age five are less likely to be enrolled in early childhood education programs than are other groups. Once they enroll in school, teachers indicate that they do not have the skills or training needed to meet the needs of students with limited English proficiency. Four percent of public school teachers are Latinos, compared with 15 percent of the student body. Latino youth borrow less financial aid money to pay for their education. Fifty percent of first-year Latino college students received grants, compared with 60 percent of African Americans and 46 percent of whites. Only 30 percent of Latinos received college loans, compared with 42 percent of African Americans, and 31 percent of whites.

The lack of preschool attendance as a factor in lower academic achievement for Latinos can be found in the example of Eva's eight-year-old cousin, Sergio, a sensitive, soft-spoken boy, who came to the U.S. at age three. Unlike Eva's parents, who enrolled her in a bilingual preschool in the United States, Sergio's parents made the decision to keep him at home until he was old enough to enter kindergarten. Sergio's first experience with socialization outside his extended family, and outside Mexico, was in a kindergarten classroom in a low-performing, urban U.S. school. It was very hard for Sergio to develop autonomy and to build relationships outside of his family, especially because he lacked the knowledge of social and cultural norms that his classmates had mastered, such as assertiveness, being able to defend himself in a nonconfrontational way, and verbalizing his needs and opinions.

On the other hand, within three years of entering a bilingual classroom, Eva had mastered English well enough to be placed in a general education fourth-grade class. She was able to form meaningful relationships with classmates and adults in the school. In particular, her relationships with her English as a Second Language teacher and the social worker who had worked closely with her family around her brother's medical needs facilitated her involvement in leadership activities at the school. In her fifth-grade classroom, Eva ran for class president and won. Her blossoming leadership skills and interest in science were tapped when she became a member of a student-led Environmental Committee at the school, which started and ran a school garden. Her extracurricular activities, strong English language skills, and good academic performance led to Eva being accepted into a competitive program at a Brooklyn middle school for children interested in careers in science and mathematics. Eva's personality, supportive family, and access to a supportive school helped her to successfully biculturate; moreover, Eva became a leader to other Latino children who saw her develop and succeed.

Strong and supportive schools seem to have a greater influence on Latino youths' academic performance than they do on other minority groups (Institute for Mental Health Initiatives [IMHI], 2002a). Research has shown that Latino youth are especially open to participating and cooperating with other students in school activities when they are given the opportunity (IMHI, 2002a). The school, then, is an important place for Latino children and youth to develop strengths and acquire skills in dealing with problems they face and in providing hope for the future.

As illustrated by these three children in the extended Ramirez family (Eva, Sergio, and Eva's brother), the importance of access to quality health care, supportive schools, and policies to provide opportunities for low-income Latino families, while working with supportive families, help Latino youth come closer to achieving successful biculturation. However, although health and welfare are key factors in successful biculturation, they are not the only factors. For example, differences in the motivation for coming to the United States, whether the individual or family is documented or not, and whether the individual has a strong support network impacts how the person or family experiences the process of adaptation and possible development of biculturalism. Moreover, once in the United States, variations can be found according to the country of origin, the number of generations the individual or family has been in the United States, and how Latinos experience discrimination.

The Latino Experience in the United States: Sources of Adversity and Social Adjustment

When we look at constraints and the role of resilience in the process of adapting to the new culture, it seems that the most important factors that determine how Latinos succeed in the United States are the motivations that bring families to emigrate, their legal status, and the tension between the optimism to forge ahead and the difficulties inherent in discrimination. The motivation to emigrate/immigrate is what Carola and Marcelo Suárez-Orozco (2001) call the "pathway" to becoming Latino. They distinguish two main pathways for coming to this country: the immigrants and the refugees.

Immigration as a Pathway to Becoming Latinos

The Latino immigrants are usually motivated by socioeconomic reasons, such as the notion of opportunities, the American Dream, and a better tomorrow, by giving special emphasis to roads of success and achievement, either economically, educationally, or both. Immigrants are also often motivated by transnational connections of relatives and friends who have already departed to the new land. Both the socioeconomic motivations and the connections among family and friends explain the large groups of Dominicans in New York, El Salvadorans in Washington, and Mexicans in Los Angeles. Unfortunately, in many cases, this American Dream of coming to a new country and becoming rich and successful encounters several constraints upon arrival. For example, a lawyer from Honduras ends up in a cleaning company or an Argentinean psychologist ends up as a Yoga instructor, both making more money in real terms than in their country of origin, but with a significantly lower status. It is common for Latino parents to postpone their personal dream to do well in the United States once they realize the limitations they have (such as age, language, and professional accreditation). Usually, parents adapt their dream, hoping that their children have a better future.

Nora, a Mexican woman who came to the United States several years ago, has as her home voice-mail message the perfect English-speaking voice of her six-year-old daughter. Nora was determined to learn English and have a good job in the United States. As soon as she arrived here, she realized learning the language was very hard and that the kind of jobs she could have without speaking English were not as good as she expected. After a few years in the United

States she got the green card and became pregnant. Both life events together made her decide that her daughter would have all the opportunities she could not have. Today Nora works in two different jobs in order to save money for her 11-year-old daughter to go to college. Even though Nora speaks excellent English today, she does not want to change the voice mail because she feels proud of her daughter's accent, which represents a very important achievement for them as a Latino family and allows them to present themselves as a bilingual family. Nora counts on the school to teach the skills and competencies necessary for her daughter to go to college, while she, as a mother, assumes the responsibility of teaching family values and culture. Nora's example emphasizes English, education, and schooling of Latino children as a priority and as tools for success for the whole Latino immigrant family.

When Latino groups emigrate from their country of origin, motivated by a search for freedom or escape from fears, they take the pathway of "asylum seekers, or refugees" (Suárez-Orozco & Suárez-Orozco, 2001). The asylum seeker is motivated by fear of persecution based on political, ethnic, or religious affiliations, which does not necessarily guarantee he or she will succeed in gaining formal protection and rights in the United States. Those who are not accepted by the United States are usually sent back to their country, sent to a third "safe" country, kept in Immigration and Naturalization Service (INS) detention camps and jails because their country of origin does not want them back, or simply immerse themselves in the world of the undocumented Latinos or illegal aliens, which adds a whole new reality to their arrival.

The involuntary process of the asylum-seeker's path creates intense stress in Latino families. This stress could be due first to feelings of failure and guilt for leaving others suffering at home; second, to a resentment toward the country of origin, leaving a bitter and justifiable feeling of retaliation; and third, the constant hope of returning home. It is not rare that refugee Latinos are victims of political violence in their own country, which might provoke enormous consequences to their physical and mental health while in the United States. A clear example of the effects of posttraumatic stress was the panic wave after September 11, 2001, when many Latino immigrants who had suffered torture, political violence, or had experienced war in their countries of origin sought psychological help in Latino clinics around the country. That is the case of "Señora María."

Señora María came to a Washington, D.C., community center to participate in a group discussion two weeks after the September 11 attacks. The discussion centered around how to help children to process the violence they were seeing on television and in the streets. After the discussion, Señora María stayed behind and asked one of the facilitators to help her "get rid of the tape." In her words,

> When I left my country I thought I had left the tape in the closet. I closed the door of the closet, then made sure I was locking the main entrance door of the house and came to the U.S., knowing that here it would be different. After September 11, I keep seeing the same images of violence I thought I had left in the tape in Nicaragua. I am driving my car and see Managua, and cannot stop crying. I do not want my girls to notice I am crying because I would have to tell them about the tape and the images that it has. I thought I had left the tape in the closet in my house in Managua, now I realized I have carried the tape with me and I want to get rid of it. (F. Infante, personal communication)

Señora María had come to Washington, D.C., at the end of the Sandinista Revolution in the mid-1980s, trying to find a place of peace and freedom. Once here she could not receive political asylum as was the case with many other Nicaraguans, and became an illegal alien, working in a cleaning company. Even though she left her house and family members in her country, she has always felt it was worthwhile coming to Washington. Every time she remembered her town or her house she would try to think about something else. She wanted to forget her life in Nicaragua and start a new life as a Latina in the United States. She was being successful in leaving behind the sources of fear and stress, but then the events of September 11 revived her memory. Señora María began therapy in order to validate the pain and abuse she experienced in Nicaragua and when crossing the border. Talking about the horrors she lived through in Managua within the confidentiality and security of therapy sessions, she could also revisit her life history in her country and slowly start talking about it with her children. After a few months, she could start sharing her childhood and pleasant images she had left next to the tape in her house's closet.

The example of Señora María illustrates the struggles and mechanisms of adaptation the refugee Latinos have to go through in order to do well in this country. For Señora María, to become a Latino and assume a new identity helped her find a job, have a family, and have a new house. However, in order to accomplish this, she had to deny parts of her past and history. It was only when she could validate the pain and trauma that she had experienced, that she could have long conversations with her daughters regarding their country of origin, their extended family, and their history as Nicaraguans. Using the three categories of resilience factors outlined by Edith Grotberg, Señora María began repairing her I AM. By accessing her memories as a Nicaraguan woman who had experienced trauma and was still optimistic, hopeful, and confident, she was able to connect more with her family and build a stronger cultural identity.

Nora and Señora María are both examples of the path of becoming Latino, one as an immigrant, the other as a refugee. Both share the interest in giving hope and opportunities to their children, while learning from the new culture themselves. Both became responsible for sharing their family history and culture with their daughters. Therefore, both mothers are on a path to achieving biculturalism using the three categories of resilience factors. By recognizing the values and rituals of their countries of origin and recognizing the opportunities their children will have living in the United States, both women provide resources for developing resilience and biculturalism.

However, dealing with history in the country of origin and motivations to forge ahead in the new land are only some of the issues of becoming Latino. Other important issues are the political and social situations immigrants encounter in the pathway to becoming Latino. Señora María and Nora, as well as other immigrants and refugees, are conflicted by their illegal status once they arrive. According to the research, their legal status influences the experiences and life opportunities of adapting to the new land more than does their national origin or socioeconomic background. Undocumented Latinos cope not only with the danger of crossing the border, but also with the daily threat of deportation and exploitation by employers who take advantage of the situation. These daily threats often translate into a constant guardedness and distrust of service providers, such as teachers, social workers, or doctors, who represent the United States mainstream and can be potential informants. In the case of Latino youth, being undocumented in the United States strongly influences their hope for the future, making it almost impossible to enroll in college, obtain financial support, or have access to well-paid jobs. In cases like Señora María's, dealing with her posttraumatic stress has to be postponed because of another obstacle, which is the lack of trust in social institutions.

Overcoming Discrimination and Building a New Identity

Once Latinos are living in the United States, they have to deal with two often-contradictory forces as they develop their new identity. One is the optimism, effort, and energy to move ahead and succeed, which was described as the motivations for initiating the pathway to becoming Latinos. The other force is social discrimination, which places a number of obstacles to settling down. The dynamic among the motivation for settling down and the different forms of discrimination, combined with issues noted earlier, such as life stories in the country of origin, the experiences lived in the pathway to becoming Latino, and the expectations and resources they find in the new land, together determine how Latinos form their identity and acculturate.

Many Latino youth consider that discrimination is their main source of adversity or difficulty while adapting to this country. This discrimination is expressed in bullying in school, difficulty finding work, limited participation in the social life of their school, and low expectations on the part of adult authority figures, especially teachers and the police (Infante, 1997; IMHI, 2002a). Even though most Latino immigrants have experienced this or other forms of discrimination, not all of them react to them in a destructive manner. When negative social expectations coexist with troubled backgrounds, such as lack of positive role models, living in poor neighborhoods, lack of family support, and lack of access to social resources, youth have fewer resources to cope with discrimination.

Reaction toward discrimination in a destructive way could be interpreted as a reaction to mainstream expectations where youth cannot or do not want to belong to the mainstream culture and seek marginal subgroups such as gangs. Like José, there are many other Latino adolescents who would like to belong to or join with other minorities in the inner city, adopting an adversarial reaction against white middle class society (Suárez-Orozco & Suárez-Orozco, 2001). For youth who develop reactive identities, "embracing aspects of the dominant culture is equated with giving up one's own ethnic identity" (Suárez-Orozco & Suárez-Orozco, 2001, p. 107), but at the same time it is very hard to embrace their own culture because they are no longer the Guatemalan, Mexican, or Dominican. Unfortunately, a common denominator for these youth who tend to develop these contradictory identities is to have troubled backgrounds or lack of positive role models who can help them thrive and come to terms with the stress and challenges of adolescence and discrimination.

Though social discrimination can become hazardous to the health and education of Latinos, there is also the possibility to become competent in both the new and the old culture, without necessarily developing the identity of the majority group, in this case white Americans (Ainslie, 2002; Suárez-Orozco, 2001). Furthermore, maintaining a strong connection with their Latino culture, meaning developing a bicultural or multicultural identity, demonstrates resilience and the possibility of doing well in the United States (Ainslie, 2002; Suárez-Orozco, 2001; National Research Council, 1995). For example, Latino youth who are able to learn and practice social skills from both Latino and Anglo cultures are less likely to abuse drugs, drop out of school, be depressed, or have bad nutrition (National Research Council, 1995) and can be motivated to be agents of change in their own communities.

Bicultural youth start developing a sense of identity that allows them to thrive in the expectations and demands to the new culture while behaving and keeping the attachment to the family and community where they live. In some cases, bicultural youth learn the rules of the game and realize that because of race or ethnicity they are discriminated against. In these cases youth tend to develop a stronger sense of identity and associate with others facing discrimination in order to fight against it (Suárez-Orozco & Suárez-Orozco, 2001; Falicov, 2002). In our experience, bicultural youth with an understanding of discrimination are the community or school leaders who are advocating for Latino rights and equity.

In summary, Latinos' experiences of immigrating and adapting to the United States are marked by the history lived in the country of origin, the motivation in coming to the new land, the experience in crossing the border, whether they are documented or undocumented, and the kind of identity they develop. The Latino identity usually develops around the experience of discrimination. When identity is based on negative images or anger against discrimination it could be expressed as antisocial practices such as gang involvement, violence, or other risk behaviors. When their identity is based on recognizing discrimination, the constraints of being an immigrant, the strengths of the culture of origin, and at the same time recognizing the good aspects of American culture, then there are possibilities of developing biculturalism and resilience.

Resilience in Latino Communities

Studies on resilience suggest that the strengths of the Latino populations reside mainly in their shared set of values that prevail regardless of the country of origin or income level (Children's Safety Network, 1999). Even though each family or individual shares a different history determined by ethnicity, class, nationality, education, religion, occupation, and motivation for coming to the United States, it is possible to identify shared characteristics for each Latino group. In this last section we attempt to bring together the main elements of resilient adaptation showed in previous stories, by organizing them into the basic categories of resilience: (1) inner strengths, (2) social skills, and (3) support networks. Furthermore, we will provide evidence to demonstrate the important role that the social services can play in bridging the gap between the two cultures by recognizing biculturalism and fostering resilience in the Latino communities.

Individual Strengths That Seem to Distinguish Latinos

Personal characteristics that help Latinos cope with adversity and to adapt to the new culture are based on psychological variables. We will not address whether these characteristics are only individual based or are shaped and developed in the relationship with other people, the environment, or the culture. But instead we will try to identify the personal characteristics that Latinos themselves report as resilience factors that help them in the process of developing biculturalism and adapting to the new culture.

A recent study conducted by the IMHI (2002b) found that Latinos coming from El Salvador, Mexico, Cuba, and the Dominican Republic all have a strong *sense of responsibility, optimism, autonomy, and the confidence that they can create a positive change.* The sense of optimism, responsibility, and confidence that they can generate a positive change in their lives can be understood because of the motivation to achieve a higher economic and educational level than in their country of origin. As was stated in the stories of Nora and Señora María, both came here aiming for better opportunities, although when they realized it would be hard for them to have well-paid jobs, both turn their motivations to their children and became responsible for giving hope and opportunities to their children. Together, the motivation to settle down in the new country and the fact that the United States has a history of waves of immigrants who adapt and succeed, both become thriving forces that could explain the inner strength found in Latino immigrants. Optimism, responsibility, and belief in the possibility of change could be understood as the fuel or basic resource that, when combined with external support, can help the individual acquire the skills necessary to adapt to the demands of the new country. As was mentioned before, some of the elements that promote biculturalism are the skills acquired to move from one culture to another and the capacity to understand the benefits of participating in mainstream U.S. culture while recognizing discrimination and culture of origin. Schools and other social services are key players in recognizing the importance of the culture of origin while providing education and better opportunities for immigrants to channel their inner strengths, develop skills, and facilitate access to mainstream U.S. society.

Social Skills

From the study of different subgroups carried out by IMHI (2002b) the main factors related to problem-solving skills and successful adaptation despite having experienced adversity were found to be *communication skills*, which include *expressing feelings* and *communicating expectations* and the *capacity to reach out and find resources available* to them. Another important social skill observed especially in Latino youth is their *capacity to charm and establish strong relationships* with service providers (Infante, 2000).

The best example of social skills is Carlos, the youth described in the introduction, whose ability to reach out for help, personal charm, his capacity to communicate his needs, along with the existence of social support, enabled him to gather the resources necessary to learn English, study for the GED, and adapt to this new culture. Another important example was provided by the Ramirez family, who were able to reach out for help and communicate their needs, allowing Eva to join preschool education and her brother to receive medical health care for his neurological problem. In Señora María's case, her fear because of the emerging images of violence experienced after September 11, motivates her to seek for help and support, going beyond her fear of being reported to the INS, and starting therapy to work on her posttraumatic stress disorder. Moreover, Señora María's therapy allowed her to develop the skills necessary to recall her pleasant experiences in Nicaragua, to talk with her daughters, and to promote the sense of biculturalism.

In the three cases discussed, Carlos, the Ramirez family, and Señora María, they used their social skills as a bridge between their internal strength and the existing resources and support available for them. Social services, at the same time, played an important role connecting the family, personal characteristics, and capacity to adapt to the new culture with social opportunities and structure to participate in U.S. society.

Support Networks

Members of the Latino community place high value in maintaining a link with their culture of origin and its traditions, at the same time they are in the process of learning and adapting to the new culture. Irrespective of the characteristics of their emigration or the history they carry, the Latinos keep a sense of family, a regard for their roots. Thus, strong family relationships and deep cultural attachment to the culture of origin are key elements upon which resilience can be constructed.

Strong Family Relationships

Strong relationships within the family seem to have an important effect on the Latinos' process of adaptation (Children Safety Network, 1999; Falicov, 2002). This connectedness works by ensuring basic needs for attachment and security necessary for human development. Connectedness is also a source for developing the sense of identity and biculturalism that is often challenged in the process of acculturation. According to Smith and Krohn, with youth, for example, family support seems to keep Latinos off the path of delinquency more than it does non-Hispanic youth (cited in IMHI, 2002a); it also keeps them away from illegal drugs more than it does African American youth, according to a study by Brook (cited in IMHI, 2002b). A perfect example of family connectedness and its importance on identity development is José, whose grandparents were the main voice for the Dominican culture. Even though José had his grandparents, he struggled with his Latino-Dominican identity and wanted to belong to another American group, which happened to be a group of peers involved in violence and other risk behaviors.

The notion of family connectedness and sense of identity in Latino families does not necessarily correspond to the traditional image of a nuclear family, but rather a net of national and international relationships with relatives.

When the family is in the same country, maintaining a notion of cultural identity and keeping family values and rituals associated with the culture of origin, it might well develop biculturalism. This biculturalism tends to promote resilience when both cultures relate in a coherent and flexible dynamic within the family. While acting according to the white American culture, it is possible to develop a sense of continuity and knowledge about cultural identity. Something similar is presented by the research results conducted at IMHI (2002), where youth and service providers mentioned the importance of taking the positive aspects of each culture and learning how to use them together. For example, developing the value of truth and assertiveness present in the American culture and the importance of family relationships and love present in some groups of the Latino culture creates a strong relationship based on unconditional love and open communication.

Another factor that seems to play an important role in family connectedness in the Latino communities is the sense of family history and oral tradition. According to the IMHI (2002b) study, youth, parents, and service providers highlighted the importance of oral communication among Latinos. This factor could be translated in the sense of family tradition as a story to keep the family identity. For example, the story of the grandfather who sacrificed his life for work and is able to make it in the new land usually serves as a model for effort, motivation, hard work, and optimism for future generations. Other family stories could be related with the country of origin, how rituals have passed from generation to generation, independently of the country where the family is living. Family connectedness, family history, and rituals are all different ways to develop biculturalism by keeping traditions from the culture of origin while learning from the new country. For example, Nora and Señora María leave to the schools the responsibility for developing competencies in their children enabling them to go to college and to socialize in the North American culture, while they take the responsibility as mothers of socializing family values and culture of their country of origin. Both cases show how culture, along with the importance of family connectedness, seems to be a key element for developing resilience and biculturalism.

Cultural Attachment

Researchers and people who are working in the field have raised questions about the components of biculturalism and successful adaptation. They are concerned with developing cultural specific measurements of successful outcomes in the midst of adversity. Garcia Colls, Akerman, and Cicchetti (2000) suggest that the understanding of the role of culture in human development has used developmental milestones based on Eurocentric theories. In the case of the Latino populations, a good example is what was considered the acculturation process and now is called *Americanization*, where a positive outcome for immigrants was to behave according to white American values and expectations, denying or leaving behind the history and culture from the country of origin. It is in this context that biculturalism has emerged as a new paradigm of successful acculturation, which promotes respect for the culture of origin and recognizes it as a key element of success in the new culture. This new paradigm of biculturalism focuses on the elements immersed in cultural attachment and how cultural influences contribute to the development of resilience.

According to Falicov (2002), the Latino experience of acculturation is charged by feelings of loss and grief for what is left behind in the country of origin. Thus, connection with Latino culture allows Latinos to better cope with the adaptation process and allows the individual or the family who immigrates to connect with a social community and ethnic neighborhood that reproduce the sounds and smells of the old land. Falicov (2002) calls these "pockets of remembrance," alluding to neighborhoods and networks that replicate the country of origin's culture. According to Beauvais and Oetting (1999), for children these cultural attachments also mean a place to learn competencies, develop strengths, and incorporate norms that will be useful when growing up. In moments of crisis for the family or the child, there is support and assistance by other members of the community or the family. For example, a family with cultural attachment usually means that its members are meeting cultural demands that are meaningful for them; they usually belong to a larger community that helps as a support network and provides a stable environment for children to grow. These factors, connected to the communication skills mentioned previously, bring clarity regarding the expectations as a Latino immersed in two different cultures. The pockets of remembrance help as a source of socialization in the culture of origin as well as a source to learn about the new culture's expectations and skills to achieve these expectations.

Along the same lines, Emde and Spicer (2000) explain possible resilience factors underlying the relationships between caregiver and child when they are from similar cultural backgrounds. When the child is exposed to the cultural ways of the Latino family, the values and behaviors are acquired. Thus, the child receives rewarding feedback and establishes a better relationship with the caregiver, which is one of the elements for developing a secure attachment. Later, as the child is exposed to the acculturation or biculturation process, the child has a strong foundation and can accept some different ways of thinking and behaving.

In the specific case of Latino youth, cultural attachment and a strong sense of community play important roles in their development. Marin and Marin (1991) found that the Latino culture emphasizes the values and characteristics of the group over the individual, stressing interdependence, cooperation, conformity, empathy, and trust for others in the group. Infante (2000) found that Latino adolescents and youth had a specific characteristic of being able to reach out for help, setting them apart from other groups. As was stated before, cultural attachment and identification with the Latino community allows developing a sense of leadership and active participation against discrimination in some Latino youth. Eva and Carlos recognized the struggles Latinos go through and became active advocators for biculturalism and the need to be proud of the Latino culture. In José's case, biculturalism and his family background are sources of constraint; however, he might develop the same capacity as Carlos to overcome the need to belong to "tough groups" and, instead, become a leader in the Dominican community. This pride to be Latino, along with the importance of language and cultural attachment, might be some of the elements that are challenging politicians and economists to start targeting the different Latino cultures to either vote for them or buy their products.

In conclusion, we have provided evidence of the potential in Latino communities that, when properly recognized and valued, can be used as part of the comprehensive process of promoting resilience and biculturalism. As the fastest-growing immigrant community, the potential of this social group must be recognized and promoted as a major contribution to American society and culture. Social services, such as school and health care, can act as bridges between the capacities of Latino communities to adapt to the new land and North American social structure that allows and encourages Latinos to be successful participants in the U.S. culture and economy. In enhancing the elements that promote resilience lies the possibility of developing biculturalism and a constructive adjustment that will enable a maximum opportunity for contribution to the United States.

References

Ainslie, R. (2002). The plasticity of culture and psychodynamic and psychosocial processes in Latino immigrant families. In M. Suárez-Orozco & M. Páez (Eds.), *Latinos remaking America*. Berkley, CA: University of California Press.

Beauvais, F., & Oetting, E. (1999). Drug use, resilience, and the myth of the golden child. In M. Glantz & J. Johnson (Eds.), *Resilience and development: Positive life adaptations.* New York: Plenum Publishers.

Bernard, B. (1999). Applications of resilience: Possibilities and promise. In M. Glantz & J. Johnson (Eds.), *Resilience and development: Positive life adaptations* (pp. 269–277). New York: Plenum Publishers.

Children's Safety Network. (1999). *Youth violence prevention in Latino communities: A resource guide for MCH professionals.* Newton, MA: Educational Development Center, Inc.

Emde, R., & Spicer, P. (2000). Experience in the midst of variation: New horizons for development and psychopathology. *Development and Psychopathology, 12,* 323–331.

Falicov, C. (2002). Ambiguous loss: Risk and resilience in Latino immigrant families. In M. Suárez-Orozco & M. Páez (Eds.), *Latinos remaking America.* Berkley, CA: University of California Press.

Flores, G. et al. (2002). The health of Latino children. *JAMA, 288,* 82–90.

Garcia Colls, C., Akerman, A., & Cicchetti, D. (2000). Cultural influences on developmental processes and outcomes: Implications for the study of development and psychopathology. *Development and Psychopathology, 12,* 333–356.

Grotberg, E. H. (1999). The international resilience project. In R. Roswith (Ed.), *Psychologists facing the challenge of a global culture with human rights and mental health* (pp. 237–256). Vienna, Austria: Pabst Science Publisher.

Grotberg E. (1995) *A Guide to promoting resilience in children.* The Hague: The Bernardman Leer Foundation.

Grotberg, E. H. (2000). International resilience research project. In A. L. Comunian & U. Gielen (Eds.), *International perspectives in human development* (pp. 379–399). Vienna, Austria: Pabst Science Publishers.

Grotberg, E. H. (2001). *Tapping your inner strength: How to find resilience to deal with anything.* Oakland, CA: New Harbinger Publications, Inc.

Hinojosa Ojeda, R. (2001). *Comprehensive migration policy reform in North America: The key to sustainable and equitable economic integration.* Los Angeles, CA: North American Integration and Development Center, School of Public Policy and Social Research, University of California.

Hispanic Association of Colleges and Universities. (2002, July 18). Teaching advocacy and activism. *Harvard Gazette* [On-line]. Available: http://www.hno.harvard.edu/gazette/2002/07.18/09-civilrights.html.

Infante, F. (1997). *Acciones específicas que los jóvenes y los agentes de salud toman para promover la resiliencia en los primeros: Tesis para optar al grado de licenciada en psicología.* [Specific actions that youth and service providers use to promote resilience in the youth: Thesis to obtain psychologist's license.] Santiago, Chile: Universidad Diego Portales.

Infante, F. (2000). *Strengthening organizational capacity: Document for discussion.* Washington DC: Latin American Youth Center.

Infante, F. (2001). La resiliencia como proceso: Una revisión de la literatura reciente. In A. Melillo & N. Suárez-Ojeda (Eds.), *Resiliencia, descubriendo las propias fortalezas.* [Resilience: Discovering your inner strengths.] Buenos Aires, Argentina: Paidos.

Institute for Mental Health Initiatives. (2002a). *A review of the literature on resilience in Latino youth.* Unpublished paper prepared for the Center for Mental Health Services.

Institute for Mental Health Initiatives. (2002b). *Comparison of resilience in four Latino populations.* Unpublished paper prepared for the Center for Mental Health Services.

Kaplan. H. (1999). Toward an understanding of resilience: A critical review of definitions and models. In M. Glantz & J. Johnson (Eds.), *Resilience and development: Positive life adaptations* (pp. 17–83). New York: Plenum Publishers.

Latinos in school: Some facts and findings. (2001). Retrieved August 2002, from http://www.eric-web.tc.columbia.edu/digests/dig162.html (ERIC Document Reproduction Service No. EDO-UD-01–1).

The longest journey: A survey of migration. (2002, November 2). *The Economist,* 1–16.

Luthar, S. (1999). *Poverty and children's adjustment.* Newbury Park, CA: Sage Publications.

Luthar, S., Cicchetti, D., & Becker, B. (2000). The construct of resilience: A critical evaluation and guidelines for future work. *Child Development, 71,* 543–558.

Luthar, S., & Cuching, G. (1999). Measurement issues in empirical study of resilience: An overview. In M. Glantz & J. Johnson (Eds.), *Resilience and development: Positive life adaptations* (pp. 129–160). New York: Plenum Publishers.

Marin, J. & Marin, A. (1991). Research with Hispanic populations. *Applied social research methods series* (Vol. 23). Newbury Park, CA: Sage Publications.

Masten, A. (1999). Resilience comes of age: Reflections on the past and outlooks for the next generation of researchers. In M. Glantz & J. Johnson (Eds.), *Resilience and development: Positive life adaptations* (pp. 281–296). New York: Plenum Publishers.

National Coalition of Hispanic Health and Human Services Organizations. (1999). *The state of Hispanic girls.* Washington, DC: Author.

National Council of La Raza. (2002a, July 24). NCLR eport reveals the untapped potential of the Latino vote [News release]. Retrieved November 21, 2002, from http://nclr.policy.net/proactive/newsroom /release.vtml?id=21340.

National Council of La Raza. (2002b, July 22). NCLR announces new campaign to empower future generations of Hispanic Americans [News

release]. Retrieved November 21, 2002, from http://www.nclr.policy.net
/proactive/newsroom/release.vtml?id=21320.

National Foundation for Teaching Entrepreneurship. (2002). Retrieved
November 21, 2002, from http://www.nfte.com

National Research Council, Board on Children and Families. (1995).
Immigrant children and their families: Issues for research and policy. *The
Future of Children: Critical Issues for Children and Youth, 5* (2), 72–89.

Rumbaut, R., & Portes, A. (2001). *Ethnicities: Children of immigrants in
America.* Berkeley, CA: University of California Press.

Rutter, M. (1987). Psychosocial resilience and protective mechanisms.
American Journal of Orthopsychiatry, 57 (3).

Rutter, M. (1990). Psychosocial resilience and protective mechanisms. In J.
Rolf, A. Masten, D. Cicchetti, K. Nuechterlein, & S. Weintraub (Eds.) *Risk
and protective factors in the development of psychopathology* (pp. 181–214).
Cambridge, MA: University Press.

Sanchez, G. (2002). Y tú qué? (Y2K): Latino history in the new millennium.
In M. Suárez-Orozco & M. Páez. (Eds.). *Latinos: Remaking America.*
Berkeley, CA: University of California Press.

Suárez-Orozco, C., & Suárez-Orozco, M. (2001). *Children of immigration.*
Cambridge, MA: Harvard University Press.

Suárez-Orozco, M. (2001). Globalization, immigration, and education: The
research agenda. *Harvard Educational Review, 71,* 345–365.

Suárez-Orozco, M., & Páez, M. (2002). *Latinos: Remaking America.* Berkley,
CA: University of California Press.

U.S. Census Bureau. (2000). The Hispanic population in the United States:
March 2000. Washington, DC: U.S. Department of Commerce, Economics
and Statistics Administration.

CHAPTER 8

COMMUNITY RESILIENCE: A
SOCIAL APPROACH

Elbio Nestor Suarez-Ojeda with Lilian Autler

Introduction

In this chapter, we discuss resilience from a social or macrolevel perspective in order to look at how communities confront large-scale disasters and calamities: earthquakes, floods, drought, economic crisis,
state repression, systematic terrorism, etc. As this list indicates, there
are two basic types of collective adversity: natural disasters and those
brought about by humans or society in general. In both cases, poverty
aggravates the severity of the disaster and the number of victims.

Nonetheless, it has been possible to create an overarching framework to characterize the positive factors or pillars of community
resilience, on the one hand, and those conditions that inhibit or
weaken it (antipillars), on the other. The reality of Latin America,
impacted daily by natural or social disasters, has offered a rich forum
for experimentation. Observing the effects of these frequent hardships and the responses of different communities has allowed us to
continuously refine our framework and create a hierarchy of key factors based on these observations.

These observations have been possible thanks to the fact that
numerous institutions (nongovernmental organizations, universities,
government agencies) have incorporated the principles of resilience,
either tacitly or explicitly. For example, many courses and degree
programs in the fields of health care and education currently include
the theme of resilience. It is also worth noting that on July 17 of

2002, the lower chamber of the Argentine legislature approved a resolution recommending that the executive branch include the concept of resilience in teacher training programs throughout the country.

It is generally recognized that this collective or community focus on the notion of resilience has been a Latin American contribution, as discussed in the work of well-known European authors (Cyrulnik, 1996; Vanistendael, 2000).

The Paradigm of Community Resilience

Latin America, due to both its geography and its social conditions, is a continent prone to major natural and social catastrophes, including earthquakes, floods, cyclones, famine, civil wars, guerrilla wars, and senseless repression. We could say, without exaggeration, that every Latin American community has had to confront disasters that tested its resilience, in a collective sense. At the same time, an important legacy of the region's Mayan and Incan traditions is the widespread practice of social solidarity in responding collectively to emergencies.

Therefore, it is not surprising that the Latin American approach to resilience has focused on the collective and is rooted much more in the field of social epidemiology than in classic approaches based on the observation of individual cases.

Social epidemiology analyzes the health care context and the health/illness process as collective situations and seeks their explanations in the surrounding social structures and processes. Disasters that affect large population groups provide the opportunity to analyze collective phenomena in and of themselves and to change the object of study. Rather than individual attributes, we look at the collective ability of human groups or societies to confront adversity and work together to achieve well-being. Throughout the continent, in its frequent and varied succession of catastrophes, we have observed very different ways of responding to such events. How can we explain the fact that, faced by the same type of catastrophe, some societies begin reconstructing the very next day and others remain lethargic for long periods? We believe that the keys to an explanation lie not in individual characteristics, but in the social conditions, in the group relations, and in the cultural and ethical aspects of each society.

From this perspective, the community resilience approach alters the epistemological base of the initial concept, changing not only the object of study, but also the posture of the observer and the criteria used in observing and identifying the phenomenon of resilience when expressed collectively.

Since 1995, when we first proposed some theoretical elements of community resilience, we have analyzed numerous events in different parts of Latin America, using tools from the field of social epidemiology. Using a model similar to that of Wolin and Wolin (1993) for individual resilience, we propose a paradigm that can be applied to the collective and community context. Every disaster suffered by a community causes damage in terms of loss of life and resources, and no one denies how painful this can be. But these events can also be viewed as the kind of *marveilleuse malheur* described by Boris Cyrulnik (1999). Misfortune can serve as a challenge that mobilizes the population's capacity for solidarity and ends up renovating not just the physical infrastructure but also the social fiber of the community. In cases of strong earthquakes (the most common type of natural disaster in Latin America), we have seen communities that very quickly organized themselves and rebuilt the city, improving the urban layout and distribution of services, which, in turn, had positive repercussions on the health of the inhabitants and on their sense of ownership as citizens. It is evident that these communities had some type of protective shield, related to their inherent conditions and values, that allowed them to "metabolize" the negative event and respond constructively.

Based on such observations, we have been able to identify *pillars of community resilience*, similar to those proposed by Wolin and Wolin (1993) in the individual realm. Observing the dynamics in different communities has allowed us to identify certain key conditions, chosen from a longer list in our original heuristic model, that are most frequently present in groups that overcome disaster most quickly and successfully. These fundamental pillars are

> collective self-esteem,
> cultural identity,
> social humor,
> good government, and
> spirituality.

By *collective self-esteem* we mean the feeling of pride in and satisfaction with the place where one lives. This includes awareness of the natural and constructed beauty of the place, identification with the values espoused by that society, and enjoyment of cultural and recreational activities. This attitude can be perceived in the use of regional or local identifications: the way in which someone says "I'm a Californian" or "I'm a New Yorker" shows a lot about the person's satisfaction with that condition. Satisfaction implies recognizing that one is part of a society and sharing the values that motivate that society. It makes sense, then, that those cities or localities where one sees a high level of collective self-esteem are better able to recover from setbacks.

Cultural identity refers to the persistence of a social being in its unity and sameness over the course of changes and diverse circumstances. It is an interactive process that occurs throughout the life cycle and implies the adoption of customs, values, idiomatic expressions, dances, music, etc. that become inherent components of group identity. This process provides the social group with a sense of sameness and continuity that helps it to confront and overcome a wide variety of adverse circumstances. In this era of rampant globalization, the persistence of societies capable of preserving their cultural identity is a source of hope for humanity.

Panez, Silva, and Panez (2000) claim that this recognition of what is distinctive about our own culture encourages a form of group affirmation that fortifies the use of resources to face and resolve difficulties. This helps to explain why populations that respect and celebrate their traditional cultures have shown a greater capacity for repair and rebirth after suffering hardships. For example, some countries have made their indigenous traditions a central column of the national education system.

The defense of cultural identity should certainly not blind us to the undeniable phenomenon of cultural flow and exchange. Media of all types penetrate our communities with influences that are very different from those of our ancestors and that are often assimilated by the population, without necessarily causing any harm. Diverse experiences indicate the need to practice a rational eclecticism when defending anything native. But it is also evident that the more secure and established a group's cultural identity, the better able it is to deal with outside cultural influences without losing the essence of its own collective being.

Humor, in general, is one of the variables related to resilience that has been most studied and considered, especially as it regards individual development. In shifting to a collective perspective we take into account the contributions of Daniel Rodríguez (1997), Stefan Vanistendael (1994), and Giselle Silva (1999), as well as the definitions proposed in the First Regional Training of the Bernard van

Leer Foundation. By *social humor* we mean the ability of some groups to find comedy in the midst of tragedy when faced by a phenomenon that affects them as a group. It is that capacity to express in words, gestures, or body language the comic, incongruous, or hilarious aspects of a given situation, creating a calming or pleasing effect. Some groups are associated with their own peculiar forms of humor, such as "Jewish humor," "Scottish humor," and so on. In the case of Jews, there is a rich literature about how that special sense of humor was helpful in confronting the horrors of the concentration camps. Vanistendael (1994), among others, points out how political jokes have helped entire populations to endure the hardships of dictatorships. Indeed, the oral transmission that mocks and exposes the absurdity and crudeness of dictators has often been the *ultimun moriens* of freedom and also the beginning of liberation. In this sense, humor is an adaptive strategy that facilitates a mature acceptance of the collective hardship and allows a certain distance from the problem, thereby clearing the way for taking decisions to resolve the problem. The act of emphasizing the incongruous or hilarious elements of a situation promotes a kind of divergent thinking that is more likely to lead to original and innovative solutions, even in the midst of crisis.

We will not attempt here to classify the different types of humor, because this has already been done by several of the authors cited. However, it is worth referring to the types of humor that are most closely related to resilience, especially in their collective expressions. We have found that positive effects on resilience are closely associated with the type of intellectual humor based on wordplay and puns, in which one is able to play with the language because of the distance that exists between the words and the things they represent (Rodriguez, 1997). In this context, humor is a metaphor, the intuition that establishes a link between two impossible things. Humor is an infraction, which at the same time allows a reordering of chaos and possibly the means of saving ourselves from it.

What we call *iconoclastic humor* targets generally accepted conventions and questions the myths propagated by false national pride. When a nation or group has a high level of collective self-esteem, humor aimed at symbols, great figures, or myths need not provoke insecurity.

There is much more to be said on this theme, which is so attractive and closely related to the essence of resilience. For the sake of our framework, though, we would just like to emphasize the importance of humor as a fundamental pillar of community resilience and its clear relationship to the ability of populations to overcome catastrophes. Using appropriate strategies, there are many possibilities for cultivating and developing humor as a strategy for resilience.

A fourth component of resilience, of special relevance to Latin America, encompasses what we have called *good government* or *collective honesty*. This refers to decency and transparency in the handling of public affairs, but goes beyond administrative or bureaucratic propriety. It implies the existence of a collective conscience that condemns dishonesty in public officials and in the population in general and values honesty in fulfilling public roles. Administrative perversions are most serious when they affect not just the governing elite, but permeate all levels of society. In terms of the capacity to recover from disasters, the level of honesty is a fundamental factor. No one is willing to offer solidarity or efforts toward reconstruction if he or she does not trust those administering the resources assigned to the task.

A fifth pillar, which has manifested itself more clearly in recently observed cases, is *spirituality*. This does not imply participating in any specific religious practices, but rather the condition of a society that values spiritual expressions that transcend denominational differences. We have seen that when people come together after a cataclysm and are able to pray as a group, even if they subscribe to different beliefs and traditions, recovery gets underway more quickly. As Vanistendael (2000) puts it, spirituality is a realism that seeks a deeper understanding of life and allows us to accept tragedy as a test or a challenge. The spiritual life of a society can encompass believers and nonbelievers by putting solidarity into practice and strengthening people's confidence in their ability to change their difficult circumstances. Such spirituality comes close to the concept of "realistic hope" (Loesel, 1994).

The list of social characteristics that favor community resilience is extensive, but here we have focused on the five pillars that, in light of recent observations, seem to be the most significant. Other important conditions include the ability to generate authentic and participatory leadership, the exercise of effective democracy in day-to-day decision making, and inclusiveness based on a lack of discrimination.

As antitheses to these pillars, we have also detected conditions that reduce community resiliency or, in other words, that inhibit the capacity to respond with solidarity to collective adversity. Some key antipillars include malinchismo,

fatalism,

authoritarianism,

government corruption, and

impunity.

In allusion to the well-known episode in Mexican history, we have used the term *malinchismo* to describe the obsequious admiration of anything foreign, especially that which comes from the developed world or the dominant culture. This attitude contradicts the values of cultural identity and collective self-esteem. Our Latin American communities are prone to take other societies as their group of reference, often a distorted image of that society. In doing so, they renounce their own group identity, thus negating their own human, cultural, and ecological resources and diminishing their capacity to respond to crises. For example, it is a shame to see the prevalence of blond, light-skinned models in our mass media, even in countries that supposedly admire the beauty of their dark-skinned inhabitants.

Another negative factor is *fatalism*, understood as a passive attitude of helplessness when confronted by hardship. Unfortunately, some religious teachings exacerbate this nonresilient attitude, implicit in the acceptance of whatever happens as preordained destiny. Some sects have even opposed vaccinations, because they interpret them as a show of human's arrogance in trying to interfere with divine will. Without venturing into theological terrain, we believe that a reasonable position is to accept the occurrence of tragedy, but to interpret it as an opportunity to demonstrate our capacity for rebirth. As Loesel (1994) points out, religious belief or spirituality is, in general, a protective factor, both at the individual and at the collective level. But its exaggeration to the point of fanaticism transforms it into a negative factor.

Authoritarianism and totalitarian governments have been a widespread ill during the twentieth century. Their negative effects on community and individual resilience have been well documented over the century, repeatedly leading to war. Prolonged periods of dictatorship inhibit the emergence of alternative, spontaneous leadership that is so crucial in situations of collective crisis. Chronic centralism in decision making weakens the ability to innovate and generate new responses to unpredictable situations. Though it is true that at the beginning of the twenty-first century almost all Latin American countries have elected civilian governments, we are still far from the routine exercise of decision making with legitimate social participation. Long decades of dictatorship have left profound scars on daily life, and rigidity and authoritarianism persist to different degrees in a number of realms, from child-care centers to workplaces.

The scourge of *corruption* deserves mention as a significant negative factor. As we already said, no population is willing to provide its labor or donate resources toward reconstruction after a catastrophe if it cannot trust that they will be properly managed. In the reality of Latin America, corruption is the principal inhibiting factor for community resilience. Therefore, we will devote a few paragraphs to the topic.

In general terms, corruption emerges in a society when the private interests of public officials invade and take over the public sphere. Even more serious is when it permeates the entire community, either in the form of tolerance of corrupt officials or as small-scale daily practices. Our experience in Latin America shows us that several countries have reached a state of corruption in which such practices are entrenched in every level of society, in both the public and private sectors.

At times, some of these countries have become true *cleptocracies*, a term used to describe situations where public policies are expressly oriented to providing opportunities for the illicit enrichment of those governing.

Such levels of corruption affect not only resilience, in terms of the capacity to respond to disasters, they also undermine the social capital of the country, reducing its prospects for economic development.

We could not omit from this list the negative effect of *impunity*, as it applies to government leaders and other public officials. Impunity implies the lack of punishment for criminals who, though recognized as such by the society, are out of reach of the judicial system. It is devastating to any sense of collective undertaking to know that those who ruined the economy of a country are enjoying the luxurious life of the jet set. Just as negative for collective self-esteem and community resilience is the image of dictators and torturers who receive de facto impunity, due to the cowardice of civilian governments or the complicity of a legal system that permitted their crimes. Both types of impunity coexist in Latin American countries, often producing a generalized sense of social fragmentation that is difficult to overcome.

The list of negative factors is much longer, but we have highlighted those that appear most frequently and seem to stand out as inhibitors of collective or community resilience.

In summary, each community seems to have a profile of collective resilience that combines both pillars and antipillars. The particular combination suggests a vector that allows us to estimate the resilience of that group, both for the purpose of prognosis and for interventions with the aim of strengthening the community. Furthermore, the surprising expansion of interest in resilience in academic circles offers the opportunity to undertake research and quantitative studies that can undoubtedly shed new light on the determinants of this collective phenomenon and will make possible more accurate interventions in order to reduce the suffering of human beings in situations of extreme adversity.

The process for passing the law in Argentina regarding resilience involved a Camara de Diputados consisting of 250 members. They voted on a bill initiated by a few members who had learned about resilience from Dr. Suarez-Ojeda. Dr. Suarez-Ojeda, director of the International Center for Studies of Resilience (CIER) and a pioneer in this effort to bring resilience into Argentina, held more than 100 seminars, workshops, and conferences during the previous five years concerning the role of resilience in society. The interest led to a resilience curriculum in the schools of medicine, public health, nursing, and social work. And as a minister of health in the Province of San Luis, Dr. Suarez-Ojeda was able to demonstrate the effectiveness of resilience programs, especially for youth. Time is needed to build such interest and coalitions, and results must be persuasive. The value of demonstrating effective results is not often lost on those who are part of making decisions about where a community, in fact, where a country, is going in order to become competent, effective, and resilient.

Resilient Communities in the United States

Contributed by Edith Henderson Grotberg

There are resilient communities in the United States that demonstrate their capacity to deal with adversities. Oklahoma recovered from the bombing; Columbine recovered from the shooting; New Orleans recovered from repeated floods and hurricanes; New York is still recovering from the terrorist attacks of September 11, 2001. These communities demonstrate resilience. Two other communities qualify as resilient: one is a community in northwestern Virginia and is described at some length, the other is a small community of Latinos in New York City and is described more briefly. The interesting fact is that neither of these communities thought of itself as resilient until they were given the word, its meaning, and the reality of their efforts. Then, of course, they saw that they were, indeed, resilient.

The Story of Winchester, Virginia

Winchester, Virginia, lies at the northwest section of the state, within the county of Frederick. The current population of Winchester is 24,141 and of Frederick County, not including the Winchester population, is 61,315. For Clarke County, involved in some programs with Winchester and Frederick Counties, the population is 13,111. As you read the description of this community, you may want to identify the characteristics of a resilient community described by Dr. Suarez-Ojeda.

Winchester has a long history, having been established in 1732, many years before America's independence from England. It survived the War of Independence, the Civil War, changing hands 72 times during that war, and survived the wars of the twentieth century. Its location was highly desirable in terms of agriculture, available water, and extensive lands. It was the oldest city west of the Blue Ridge Mountains and was the edge of the civilized world for many people, becoming a growing center of commerce and political power. The city and surrounding areas were places for Europeans, who received land grants, to settle. The area around Winchester became a major granary for the state and for the eastern seaboard. Mills sprang up along the rivers and tributaries, and with mills and farms, a system of interconnecting roads followed. As the area grew, so did the appeal of the city to businesses and professional service providers.

Steve Bauserman of the Winchester City Council, gave a speech in 2002 in which he summarized the history and growth of Winchester. He identified the many people who provided leadership as the city and county became a community, increasingly concerned about community issues. He reflects the tremendous pride citizens of the city have, even when they move far away from the area, as he did, after graduating from school. Having been born and raised in Winchester, however, he made a quick decision to return after learning that historical property in the city was being destroyed. He wanted to join the forces to stop the destruction and to prevent such future efforts. His pride in his place of birth made him vow that the history of Winchester and Frederick County would not be destroyed, so he participated in successful efforts to protect the historic buildings and stayed on to be part of the community. He is fully aware of the continuing pride that citizens of the city express in all that they do to maintain, improve, and enrich both the city and the county.

He described the role of Winchester in the Revolutionary War and the Civil War; leaders of those events often came from Winchester. George Washington, for example, began all three of his careers in Winchester. First, in his position as a surveyor, he was hired to survey some of the lands of an owner of large plots of land; second, in his role as a colonel in the militia, he was in charge of protecting the citizens of Winchester during a time when the perceived marauding presence of Indians was regarded as a threat. And while serving in that capacity, he positioned himself for winning a local election, thus starting his third career as a politician, which led to his becoming the first president of the United States.

Steve Bauserman then described how the men in the community, who had sufficient funds for free time, provided services to the community. They most frequently made their contributions through the churches, but made some independent of those institutions. That base was enlarged when women were able to contribute to the community beyond the home, and when blacks—African Americans—and Hispanics joined in making contributions to the community. The enlarged base extended beyond the churches, while still including them.

Citizens of Winchester became state legislators, influencing many laws and, especially, a more sophisticated understanding of state funding. Senator Harry F. Byrd, Sr., for example, started his political career on the city council, but soon went on to the state and federal levels. One of his most enduring legacies at the state level was his adoption of the "pay-as-you-go" strategy for state spending. This strategy, and his overall grasp of business principals and sound budgeting, turned the state budget from a deficit when he arrived into a surplus when he left.

During the nineteenth and twentieth centuries, with educational opportunities and economic recovery from wars, prosperity returned to Winchester. And with the growing population, many more opportunities were found for serving the community. The citizens added to the traditional church or local, state, and national governmental service, finding satisfaction on bank boards, civic clubs and societies concerned about agricultural issues and local history, or organizations made up of descendants of every war ever fought by Americans. What were once opportunities open only to a few are now open to all regardless of race, sex, economic status, or even age. Young people are increasingly involved in community activities. The fact is clear: as cities and counties grow and reflect changing views of community involvement, members of the broader community are increasingly represented and involved. Democracy takes over from aristocracy.

A very large part of the United States' voluntary spirit stems from its religious heritage. The lessons are as varied as the religions of the hundreds of groups that came and still come to the United States. The common root of these voluntary activities is the awareness that service beyond self is both an obligation and a joy. It is accepted as the ultimate universal truth. Charity can be a response to an immediate need, or charity can apply to the public at large. Winchester increasingly sees itself as concerned with the public at large; indeed, it is a democratic, participatory community.

A powerful example of the growing interest in viewing the city as a democratic, participatory community is Winchester's Community Consensus Coalition (CCC). According to the coalition's public statements, it was formed in 1999 to create a forum for discussion of issues impacting and challenging the community. The mission statement reads, "The Community Consensus Coalition (CCC) is a consortium of organizations, which seeks to create a collaborative, broadly based vision for dealing with the variety of pressures currently affecting our community, and its potential future viability. Our intent is to build upon the 2020 Vision Project: a joint Winchester-Frederick County visioning effort which was developed from 1989 to 1991."

The fact that more than a decade has passed since translating the vision into action does not detract from the renewed effort; it underscores how innovative ideas grow, have set-backs and grow again. Good ideas resurface as the need for them increases.

The importance of the CCC is that it brought together divergent interests. It consists of 21 organizations and groups and represents 3,300 persons. It was a ready-made body primed for consensus building to address the variety of pressures currently affecting the community and its future viability. It recognized there is a need for broad-based community planning that goes above and beyond political boundaries and interest groups. The CCC indicated its willingness to provide leadership, support, and dedication to accomplish the process in cooperation with local governments. It asked for support in the form of leadership and input on an advisory committee of community leaders. The group was to confirm issues to be addressed and timeliness for action. The intent is to have those actively involved in the services and concerns of the community become involved in decision making that will influence the future, rather than rely on top officials determining the needs and solutions to community issues.

The process identifies issues that fall under some combination of categories including

1. community,
2. economics, and
3. environment.

The process further involves

1. determining the current status and history of a community issue,
2. assessing threats to the current status,
3. assessing opportunities resulting from the current status, and
4. developing a draft vision.

Then the categories are integrated by

1. reviewing and evaluating all potential strategies,
2. selecting priorities,
3. drafting action plans to implement priority strategies, and
4. monitoring the action plans.

The immediate project was to work with the City of Winchester in its community-based planning process. The CCC indicated it was willing to serve as resource base for stakeholders—those affected by decisions—to address that portion of the project examining the issues of concern to the community. Issues would be studied from bottom-up participation and would be a model for future community decision making on issues to be determined. The project would be the first community-based planning initiative to be tested.

The CCC also provided a 10-step procedure for translating the plan into action. Not all communities would adopt each step, but the procedure describes the clear involvement of citizens at each step.

1. The city council authorizes the process.
2. The council president selects two cochairs.
3. The cochairs, president of council, and council liaison select the remaining six to nine members of the committee.
4. Committee members cochair each of the three subcommittees.
5. The city provides demographic data and asks the committee to recommend action as well as a vision for where the city wants to be.

The committee then asks each subcommittee to meet with related stakeholders for input on the vision and actions needed.

6. Stakeholders discuss recommendations with their constituents and report back to subcommittees.

7. Subcommittees then arrange to hold a series of public meetings using fire halls or other neighborhood-based facilities.

8. Subcommittees compile a report of findings and submit a report to the committee. The committee then combines the three subcommittee reports into one report to the council.

9. The council then holds one large public forum, much like subcommittee forums, to give the public one more chance to respond to the comprehensive report.

10. The council then adopts the vision and action plan. Once a year after the adoption, on the anniversary of adoption, the council reports on progress and modifies the action plan as necessary.

Small Communities and the Latino Immigrants from Santo Domingo

The description of Winchester, Virginia, may well be seen as heady stuff. How many communities could even entertain such thinking? The obstacles, the barriers, are surely insurmountable. But, residents in an apartment building can meet and decide what needs to be done to eliminate insect infestations, reduce violence in and around the building, and hire protective services to safeguard the residents. This is being done. Even residents in a single block of homes have organized to take turns monitoring the children, calling police when something seems dangerous or threatening. And families living in a cul-du-sac take turns protecting their children and calling the police whenever a car speeds through. A community can be large or small; it is the sense of belonging and caring about those around one that defines a community. It is identifying common problems and deciding to do something about them that allows a group to become a community. People are not helpless and totally dependent. They are able to organize to deal with adversities themselves. They feel empowered and safe and know when to reach out for help—they are resilient.

A community of immigrants from the Dominican Republic, living in New York City, is an example of such a group demonstrating resilience as it deals with the continuing problems of immigrant status. During the 1980s more than a quarter-million Dominicans entered the United States, settling primarily in New York City. It is not known exactly how many reside there today because many enter through unofficial and often illegal channels. As with other immigrant populations, the primary motivation was in search of better employment and improved living conditions. The first job opportunities were in clothing factories. However, as the clothing industry disappeared, that source of work was closed off, resulting in an increase in unemployment. However, while poverty and unemployment rates sharply increased, a new wave of immigrants from the Dominican Republic came to the United States. This new wave, by contrast, consisted of college graduates and professionals who left because of the lack of opportunity for them in the Republic.

The group as a whole experienced most of the adversities other Latino groups experience; that is, language problems and barriers, discrimination, harassment, problems with the police and other authority figures, bullying and rejection in the schools, and a pervasive vulnerability. The impressive facts are, however, that this group seems to have promoted and drawn on resilience to deal with the many adversities being faced.

Staff of the Institute for Mental Health Initiatives at George Washington University conducted focus groups in Latino communities around the country, one of which was made up of representatives from the Dominican Republic immigrants in New York City. The results of the focus group made clear that these immigrants were particularly resilient in dealing with adversities. One troubling adversity they dealt with was the poor schools.

It is not uncommon for schools located in immigrant communities to be overcrowded and have high dropout and low graduation rates. The Dominican children attended a school that had one of the worst track records in the entire state. In addition to poor academic instruction, the school was not providing the students the benefits of positive Latino role models who looked and sounded like them. And many parents felt the curriculum needed to be adapted so the children could be exposed to their own cultural history, thereby feeling recognized and respected as part the larger society. The parents knew that education was a major avenue to improve their lives, and they knew that giving them a greater voice in decisions concerning education would be important. They took action.

One action was to back a New York Decentralization Law that allowed noncitizen parents who had children in the public school system to vote in school board elections. As a result of that law, more than 10,000 immigrant parents registered as "parent voters" and voted in the school board election. They voted for those candidates who made clear a commitment to improving the schools and building new ones. As a result, construction of new schools was approved. This was a significant victory for the Dominican population. And as another result, a shift occurred in parental involvement. As parental involvement increased, family ties increased, with parents feeling closer to their children and sharing many experiences through school activities. This victory also meant that the time it takes for a new immigrant family to assimilate into the new society decreased. The focus on education encouraged many Dominicans to become trained as educators, seeking employment in education administration and teaching positions in public schools.

The Dominican community is one of the most organized ethnic groups in the United States, leading to the formation of many advocacy organizations. These advocacy groups have been created to help represent and support Dominicans in business, labor, trade, and education. Groups of Dominicans, irrespective of organizational structure, have been able to bring about change by coming together and expressing their views. Dominican taxi drivers, for example, who were excluded from the taxi organization and were therefore unlicensed, came together to speak out against city regulations that inhibited their business. That, in turn, reduced the spread of violent attacks against drivers. Dominicans also came together to form the Dominican Youth Union. This Union is an educational organization addressing the needs of adolescents and has been successful in promoting resilience in youth. It organizes activities that celebrate and honor those high school graduates who have been accepted into Ivy League schools. It has also created a pre-college program that now has over 300 local high school students. These organizations provide leaders who are role models for strengthening the people, increasing their ability to deal with adversities, and to demonstrate resilience. This group of Latinos has engaged in resilience behavior to organize their community into powerful groups that can advocate for important and necessary changes.

At the risk of implying this community has been successful in all its actions, it must be pointed out that one major change tended to affect families negatively, and that was the greater freedom of women to become wage earners. The jobs available were for women more than for men, and the result was that in many families the women worked and the men did not. This not only changed the traditional cultural gender roles, but created a great deal of stress in many families. Domestic violence, alcoholism, and divorce became frequent. Despite the negative aspects of this shift in women's role, positive aspects were seen by women back in the Dominican Republic as they began to seek greater freedom for their lives. Not all outcomes involving resilience are win-win. The path can be bumpy.

Dealing with a Major Adversity

There are times when one adversity dominates a community's concerns and can become the rallying point for increasing community involvement. Again, Winchester is an example of a community dealing with such an adversity, that is, drugs. The initial response to the adversity began with two mothers and grew into a citywide and countywide organization. An article, "A Community Unites to Combat Drugs," written by Teresa Lazazzera (1987) appeared in the *Winchester Star* reporting on the process. She described how the area built a successful coalition that began with the two mothers concerned about the effects on their children of the growing drug problem in Winchester and Frederick County. They cofounded, with Jim Longerbeam, a retired Army colonel, and his wife, Shelda, the organization, Kids Are Our Concern (KAOC) in 1980, with Jim as chair. KAOC spearheaded a community effort to combat drugs, especially involving children and youth. The Longerbeams took the lead in raising money to build buildings and provide resources for the activities of KAOC. The founders emphasized the importance of focusing on children and youth because of their vulnerability and the deep need of parents to protect their children. The community continuously, even today, finds that the common concern for children and youth overcomes conflicts that could destroy the efforts.

Within a few years of organizing KAOC, the results indicated a measured decrease in drug use among students, increased drug and alcohol programs in local schools, and more alcohol-free activities for young people, such as dances, plays, and outings. Students formed a group, Friends Who Care, and sponsored dances and other activities for teens in conjunction with KAOC.

The antidrug coalition forming in the community, consisted of parents, students, social workers, law enforcers, and elected officials. The coalition benefited from a week-long antidrug training workshop, where they addressed the perceived growing epidemic of cocaine use and distribution among children. One of the results was the formation of Project CLEAN (Community Leadership through Education, Advocacy and Networking) in 1986, an agency initiated by police and state officials that brought together groups such as KAOC and Friends

Who Care, groups already fighting the drug problem. Again, Jim
Longerbeam was the first chairman, now of CLEAN, Inc. And again,
he and Shelda raised money, this time to begin a teen center and provide resources for the new organization. Another consistent participant
in the development of KAOC and CLEAN, is J. Michael Foster. He had
been the executive director of a nonprofit group dealing with adolescent substance abuse, prevention, intervention, and residential treatment, so it was easy for him to join in the development of these new
organizations. As executive director of Healthy Families, Northern
Shenandoah Valley, he is part of the vast community coalition to eradicate the drug problems and to enrich the lives of children and youth.

CLEAN soon became incorporated as a nonprofit agency and has a
continuing history that reflects not only how communitywide efforts
deal with drug abuse, but how communitywide efforts enlarge the
scope of concerns, addressing new problems as they emerge. A brief
look at the growth of CLEAN clarifies how a community can be
increasingly involved in dealing with adversities—not only old and
continuing ones, but also with new ones that inevitably emerge.

However, the primary focus of CLEAN, Inc. continues to be to
develop and implement communitywide programs directed at reducing the demand for and availability of alcohol, tobacco, and other
drugs, particularly among youth. CLEAN, Inc. is also that of the
Winchester-Frederick-Clarke Office on Youth and Families, adding a
nearby county of Clarke to the organization. The members of the
CLEAN board of directors represent more than 30 community
organizations and agencies, including law enforcement, education,
youth, parents, business and industry, social services, recreation, substance abuse treatment, mental health, court services, and the faith
community. It offers programs to provide prevention and early intervention services to adolescents and their families through support
groups, education, preassessment, and referral services. To help teens
and their parents, family intervention programs are available, including educating adolescents and their families on communication skills,
anger management skills, substance abuse, the justice system, community resources, laws and values, and shoplifting intervention.

Many of the drug problems had been seen to emerge from families
where teens and parents were in conflict. This broadening of the
focus from drugs to the contextual environment of family, school, and
community is consistent with current thinking about the need to shift
from focus on the problem to solutions that extend beyond the problem. The increasingly guiding focus has been from children to families to community.

Justine Beck Rose, executive director of CLEAN, points out how the organization started with concerned parents who raised money for programs and increasingly became an organization of professionals. Parents, however, continue to be advocates for the programs and participants in activities and fund raising. She sees the goal of CLEAN as that of creating a community that nurtures and supports children and families so they can reach their full potential. She indicated that the organization brought together grassroots activists as well as professional people representing different agencies. When asked what her highest motivation was for doing the extensive work she engages in, she quietly stated, "This is the future of my child." She sees the larger picture of the community and its needs and feels, as a result, more able to deal with the inevitable conflicts that occur. Her concern for the future of her child extends to concern for all children, being fully aware of how many parents are having problems with their teens that are not easily resolved and who need help from the larger community.

The Youth Development Center Campus, which houses CLEAN, also has a youth activities building, built to accommodate games, dances, shows, sports, study areas, TV watching, and eating. It is a favorite after-school hangout and draws large numbers of youth to its activities. Nearly 500 middle school kids attend dances each Friday night. This, of course, requires some management of behavior, so on the bulletin board is this list of regulations:

1. No drugs or alcohol or related paraphernalia.
2. No smoking or tobacco products.
3. No excessive display of affection.
4. No loitering anywhere in the facility's campus.
5. No vandalism, fighting, use of profanity, nor weapon possession is permitted.
6. Upon admission to the activity building, members may not leave an activity and return the same evening.

The list is simple and clear. The youth who participate in activities do not seem to find them offensive. Police are present at the youth activities, as they are present in the schools. This does not seem to dampen activities or upset the children at school. Rather, they seem to feel comfortable with someone there who can respond quickly to a problem or threat. Besides, the teens claim they are not aware of the police; they seem to fit in with the crowd.

Charlie Stansfield, Administrator, Frederick County Commonwealth's Attorney's Office, is involved with CLEAN and a variety of other

programs in an effort to bring about changes in overall community problems, including child abuse, juvenile and domestic violence, traffic viola-
tions, and felonies. However, he sees the role of his agency as going
beyond his own sphere of responsibility and becoming involved in the
prevention work of other agencies. He goes into the schools as a speaker,
and he answers specific questions about what he and the attorney's office
are doing. He refers people to CLEAN and to recreational centers and
acts as liaison for the different groups concerned about alcohol and
drugs. He deals with conflicts that arise when schools resist law enforcement involvement and prefer to resolve the problems within the school.
The inevitable conflict between punishment and loss of education time is
continuously addressed. The need for coordination with other groups
and agencies lead Mr. Stansfield to say, "We go beyond our profession; we
give 110 percent by linking with others and contributing to and benefit-
ing from that linkage."

The picture is big and all involved work together. The scene
changes when parents are also drug users, when it is clear there are
no class differences among users, when health insurance limits services to detoxification or a 28-day limit in a recovery program. The
effort is still geared toward reducing the use and availability of drugs
and alcohol through education as well as through programs to reduce
the desire for drugs. Reduce the desire for drugs—that seems like a
powerful goal. But, there are programs that can accomplish that by
directing the energy and interest of youth into activities that are
challenging, are dissociated from drugs, build strengths and skills,
and empower youth—that is, promote resilience.

Judy McKiernan is the coordinator for the Substance Abuse
Prevention Program in the Winchester Public Schools. She is on the
board of CLEAN and is the link between programs sponsored by
CLEAN and the schools. She sees an important part of her work as
incorporating social-emotional learning into the schools by pointing
out the importance of such learning to academic success. Confidence
in oneself, expressing thoughts and feelings, respecting others, reaching out for help—all are social-emotional skills as well as resilience
factors and contribute to academic success. Academic success is necessary not only to meet the standards of learning tests that pervade
the schools, but also to contribute to one's sense of accomplishment
and well-being. She suggests to teachers where social-emotional concepts can be introduced in their classes, such as in social studies and
science, both within the scope of the standards of learning tests.

When asked how the students felt about her role in the schools, she
humorously responded, "They call me the Drug Lady!" It seems the

students have accepted her. She is a specialist in school social work and conducts support groups and provides counseling to parents and students having some problems with drugs. She becomes part of federal grant applications and is praised, along with others in the community, for coordination of agencies and programs to deal with drug problems. She has freedom, however, to engage in other activities, because her salary comes from the school system. She has been on the board of CLEAN for more than 15 years and assesses CLEAN as a collaborative, family-like organization.

Judy Landes of the Shenandoah University in Winchester is a member of the board of CLEAN and, as such, writes proposals to submit to foundations, as well as to state and federal agencies for financial support of programs in the schools, in the community, and on the university campus. Her work involves linking college students to community organizations and programs that concern youth. It involves infusing into university curricula information on alcohol and drug abuse. It also involves providing community art programs and plays. What she and others have noted are the changes in the community that require new visions, variations of services, and new directions. She cited the increased population that has brought many Hispanics into the community, with accompanying language and job-related problems; the growing number of people who work more than an hour's drive to and from work, leaving children alone for many hours after school; the gradual disappearance of the middle class, becoming a community of families with low incomes and families with high incomes; and the limited growth room for developing new businesses. Many youth now leave the area after college to find jobs, a fact that has challenged the CCC to find new businesses and job opportunities in Winchester. The circle is complete! The community will deal with the new adversities and strengthen its resilience.

References

Cyrulnik, B. (1996). *Un merveilleux malheur.* Paris: Odile Jacob.

Cyrulnik, B. (1999). *Los Patitos Feos: La resiliencia, una infancia infeliz no determina la vida.* [Bad happenings: With resilience, an unhappy child does not need to remain unhappy.] Barcelona, Spain: Gedisa Editorial.

Freud, S. (1967). Una teoria sexual. [A sexual theory.] *Obras completas* [Complete works.] (Vol. 1). Madrid, Spain: Editorial Nueva Madrid.

Garmezy, N. (1991). Resiliency and vulnerability to adverse developmental outcomes associated with poverty. *American Behavioral Scientist, 34,* 4.

Green, R. S., Queiro-Tajalli, I., & Campbell, C. (2002). *Resilience and violence at the macro level.* Washington, DC: NASW Press.

Grondona, M. (1993). La corrupcion. [Corruption.] *Editorial Planeta.*

Grotberg, E. H. (1995). *A guide to promoting resilience in children.* The Hague, The Netherlands: Bernard van Leer Foundation.

Grotberg, E. H. (1996). *Promocion de la resiliencia en los ninos.* [*The promotion of resilience in children.*] Traducido por N. Suarez-Ojeda. The Hague, The Netherlands: Fundacion Bernard van Leer.

Grotberg, E. H. (1999). *Tapping your inner strength.* Oakland, CA: New Harbinger Publications.

Haggerty, M., Rutter, M., & Mrazek, P. (1999). *Stress, risk and resilience.* Washington, DC: National Academy Press.

Kagan, J. (1991). *Temperament and resilience.* Paper presented at the meeting of Fostering Resilience Conference. Institute for Mental Health Initiatives, Washington, DC.

Kliksberg, B. (1993). *Pobreza: Un tema impostergable.*[Poverty: An imperative theme.] Mexico: Fondo de cultura Economica.

Kliksberg, B. (2000). *Diez Falacias sobre los Problemas Sociales de America Latina.* [*Ten errors about the social problems in Latin America.*] Washington, DC: Manuscrito INDES/VID.

Kotliarenco, M. A., Alvarez, C., & Caseres, I. (1995). *Una nueva mirada de la pobreza. En la persona menor de edad como prioridad en la agenda mundial: Que es lo necesario?* [*A new look at poverty. The priority in a world agenda should be the young child. What is needed?*] Puntarenas, Costa Rica.

Kotliarenco, M. A., Alvarez, C., & Caseres, I. (Eds.). (1996). *Resiliencia: Construyendo en adversidad.*[*Resilience: Becoming stronger through adversity.*] Santiago, Chile: CEANIM.

Lazazzera, T. (1987, December 31). A community unites to combat drugs. *Winchester Star.*

Loesel, F. (1994). *La resiliencia en el nino y el adolescente.* [*Resilience in the child and the adolescent.*] Geneva: Editado por BICE.

Panez, R., Silva, G., & Panez, M. (2000). *Resiliencia en el Ande.* [*Resilience in the Andes.*] Lima, Peru: Una Conferencia. Fundacion Bernard van Leer.

Rodrigez, D. (1997). *Humor y resiliencia.* [*Humor and resilience.*] Presentado en el Seminario Internacional Sobre el Concepto de Resiliencia, Lanus, Argentina.

Silva, G. (1999). *Resiliencia y violencia politica en ninos.* [*Resilience and political violence experienced by children.*] Lanus Argentina: Universidad Nacional de Lanus.

Vanistendael, S. (1994). *La resiliencia: Un concepto largo tiempo ignorado.* [Resilience: A concept ignored for too long.] Geneva: BICE.

Vanistendael, S. (2000). *Resilience et spiritualite: Le réalisme de la foi.* [*Resilience and spirituality: The realism of the faith.*] Geneva: BICE.

Wolin, S., & Wolin, S. (1993). *The resilient self: How survivors of troubled families rise above adversity.* Washington, DC: Villard Books.

CHAPTER 9

IN THE WAKE OF DISASTER: BUILDING THE RESILIENCE INITIATIVE OF APA's PUBLIC EDUCATION CAMPAIGN

Russ Newman

Introduction

In 1995—long before the tragedies of September 11, 2001, made the concept of resilience not just a good idea but a vital one—the Practice Directorate of the American Psychological Association (APA) embarked upon a public education campaign designed to educate the public about the ways that psychology could play a positive role in daily life. No one then could have imagined just how important a vehicle the public education campaign would become as a way to encourage and educate the public about resilience in the wake of terror, tragedy, and hardship.

The terrorist attacks of September 11 have had a profound effect on the country and on psychology as a profession. Everyone was touched in some way by these events—some of us lost colleagues, friends, and loved ones; all of us lost some of our innocence.

Fortunately, far from being victims of the attacks, psychologists were able to mobilize rapidly to become a valuable part of the organized response. They made—and continue to make—a significant contribution to public mental health in the aftermath of the terrorist attacks. The extent of the profession's contribution was not just the result of psychologists having been trained to respond to psychological trauma. It was also the outgrowth of many years of effort by the APA Practice Directorate to build an infrastructure that would enable psychologists to reach quickly beyond their offices and deliver timely psychological services out in the communities where it was desperately needed. Though the country may have been psychologically unprepared for what happened, the Practice Directorate and its grassroots network of psychologists immediately sprang into action to assist at the epicenter of the crisis and to conduct widespread community outreach providing information to help the general public cope.

This immediate response was achieved by bringing together two previously independent functions of APA's Practice Directorate: the public education campaign and the Disaster Response Network. Representatives from the two programs worked with Practice Directorate staff members to develop resource materials that enabled APA members to quickly and effectively respond to their communities' reactions to the terrorist attacks. This also helped pave the way for the forthcoming collaboration to educate the public about resilience and ways to build resilience.

In many ways, APA had built a resilient grassroots organization that stood ready to respond in a time of need. Resilience—the process of adapting well in the face of adversity, trauma, tragedy, threats, or even significant sources of stress—strengthened psychologists' ability to aid the nation in a time of crisis. In retrospect we can see that many of the strategies that are now listed in APA's *The Road to Resilience* brochure as 10 ways to build resilience, from making connections to taking decisive actions, were central to building this strong and flexible foundation (American Psychological Association [APA] Practice Directorate, 2002).

The grassroots public education network provided the solid foundation on which to build the necessary public education response. Three other factors were also critical in developing a public education initiative about resilience that would have the interest and relevance needed to reach the public. The first factor was staying connected to the public pulse. In developing earlier campaigns, the APA Practice Directorate made it a point to go straight to the public to determine what was on peoples' minds through polls, surveys, and focus groups. The second factor was a concerted effort to engage APA members—the human face and lifeblood of APA—those who deal with the public one on one and who need tools and materials for putting the campaign into practice. The third factor was a network of cooperating organizations that included a media partner to extend the messages of the initiative and capture a broader audience.

This chapter will describe how APA's public education campaign infrastructure, combined with the implementation of these three factors, provided a powerful force that allowed the Practice Directorate to take resilience from theory and research and put it swiftly into action.

The Start of the Public Education Campaign

In 1995, health maintenance organizations (HMOs) began to eliminate psychologists from their mental health provider panels, replacing them with less-qualified service providers who would accept lower fees. The APA Practice Directorate realized that the lack of public understanding of psychology, combined with the stigma attached to mental health disorders in the minds of many, was linked to an apparent undervaluing of psychologists' services in the health care delivery system.

Although the public needed education about the value of psychological services, APA lacked the resources to communicate this value through a conventional large-scale advertising campaign. This lack forced APA to find a different, more strategic way to bridge the information gap. Turning to its membership, APA engaged hundreds of psychologists across the country in a national conversation about the current challenges to the profession; members consistently voiced their concerns that "the public does not understand what we do." This internal research also showed that members were not certain how to represent their profession to the public in a way that would resonate well.

APA's Practice Directorate turned to public opinion research to assess the problem. In 1995, eight consumer focus groups and a national telephone survey of a random sample of 1,200 households confirmed what APA had already suspected: there was a significant gap between what the public understood about psychology and the realities and practice of psychological services. When asked on an unaided basis to name the types of professionals specializing in the treatment of mental and emotional health issues, only 23 percent mentioned psychologists first (Peterson & Newman, 2000).

Armed with this information, APA's Practice Directorate, working with communications consultant firms Pacific Visions Communications and Porter/Novelli, closely examined the public feedback and developed campaign messages to explain the value of psychological services in relation to everyday issues—job stress, the influence of the mind on bodily health, and difficult family relations—and how psychologists could help address these issues (Porter/Novelli, 1995). APA's Practice

Directorate used these themes to develop messages about psychology and then tested them in focus groups to see if people made the connection between the issues and psychology.

The resulting campaign developed for the APA by the Practice Directorate was entitled Talk to Someone Who Can Help. It sought to increase the public's knowledge of the field of psychology, and then show how working with a psychologist could help in creating total wellness, which in time could lead to improved family life, physical health, and workplaces, and ultimately to improved communities.

APA then focused on two campaign strategies. The first was to treat the campaign as an education campaign instead of a marketing or advertising campaign. This meant that rather than relying primarily on paid advertising, the campaign would emphasize public engagement strategies relying on earned media through brochures, videos, public service announcements, and other educational materials. The second strategy was to enlist the energies and talents of the vast APA membership to transmit the message to local and regional audiences.

The activities were two-tiered. First the APA Practice Directorate worked to create materials for the Talk to Someone Who Can Help campaign. Then it worked to enlist and train the tens of thousands of practicing psychologists to reach out to the public.

The campaign materials included

- a brochure entitled *Talk to Someone Who Can Help* (APA Practice Directorate, 1996);
- an 800 number for the public to call and order a free copy of the brochure;
- a consumer help center Web site (www.helping.apa.org);
- a how-to kit instructing participating psychologists on how to implement campaign activities, including media relations, community outreach, and fundraising; and
- media outreach materials for participants to use, specifically a television advertisement and three radio and newspaper advertisements covering the three major themes of the campaign.

The APA's Practice Directorate remained committed to maintaining open communication with the public education campaign participants through newsletters and held numerous training sessions sponsored by state associations and practice divisions. By 1998, the Practice Directorate had established a nationwide grassroots network of volunteer psychologists who were willing and able to implement the campaign and its messages and activities at their respective local levels. Regional, state, and local affiliates were encouraged to appoint a public education campaign coordinator to organize activities and to encourage member participation. Once campaign coordinators were recruited, the APA Practice Directorate instituted the campaign update newsletter to tell coordinators and state psychological association executives about current and upcoming activities and provide guidelines on implementation.

By the end of 1998, 54 regional, state, and local psychological associations had become involved in community outreach activities such as mental health–screening day activities and lectures. Thirty-four associations had engaged in media relations activities and 11 had placed local advertising with the help of APA's Practice Directorate matching grant program, which subsidizes paid media outreach activities for state psychological associations. Overall, by the end of 1998, the Talk to Someone Who Can Help campaign had generated 1,304,191 hits to its consumer help center Web site; 5,029 APA members had requested how-to kits; 11,070 consumers had called the help line to obtain the brochure or to request a referral to a local psychologist; and the campaign had reached 22,743,252 households through advertising and local media (Peterson & Newman, 2000).

Development of the Disaster Response Network

The public education campaign network was not APA's only way to reach out to the community. In 1992, as the organization's centennial gift to the nation, APA had entered into a Statement of Understanding with the American Red Cross to establish a network of volunteer psychologists who were specially trained and willing to provide pro bono emergency mental health services to disaster victims and relief workers. These trained psychologists would become part of APA's Disaster Response Network (DRN), which continues to aid the Red Cross to this day.

To join the DRN and be eligible to work on site at Red Cross disaster relief operations, mental health professionals must successfully complete Red Cross Disaster Mental Health Services Training and be licensed for independent nonlimited practice. DRN coordinators from individual state psychological associations conduct several of the operational logistics, such as identifying qualified psychologists and calling on them in times of crisis. State DRN coordinators also work to develop connections with local chapters of the Red Cross and other local relief organizations.

The collaboration between APA and the Red Cross has evolved into an efficient system of communication in times of disaster that makes it possible to send timely and accurate information about disaster-response needs to DRN members. This supports the Red Cross's system for efficiently mobilizing trained and experienced responders.

Over time, the DRN has become integral not only to the Red Cross but also to local crisis agencies and organizations. DRN members have forged effective relationships with local police and fire departments, the disaster-preparedness agencies of state and local governments, and community mental-health centers, where volunteer psychologists handle situations that do not involve the Red Cross (e.g., drive-by shootings, school violence, industrial accidents) but that can be traumatic nonetheless. The DRN in and of itself became part of the infrastructure that allowed psychologists to become directly involved with their communities and give help at the time when it is most needed, thus staying connected to the public pulse (Fowler, 2002).

Warning Signs: A Public Education Initiative to Speak to the MTV Generation

To fully understand how the APA Practice Directorate developed The Road to Resilience project, more history of the public education campaign is relevant—specifically, the period after the APA Practice Directorate's Talk to Someone Who Can Help campaign was first launched. The successful development of the grassroots network of psychologists through this campaign paved the way for an expanded role for psychologists in public education activities. Psychologists were mobilized for grassroots outreach, trained to speak about the value of psychology in a new way, and ready to apply these new skills to an issue of national concern. Around the same time, a rash of school shootings across the country provided a natural if unfortunate subject for this outreach. The public was asking why events like this were occurring and what could be done to prevent them.

APA's Practice Directorate realized that in order to have an effective yet far-reaching youth antiviolence initiative, it needed to educate young people and that doing so through a media partner that had credibility with the large school-age audience in this country would enhance the effectiveness of the program. In 1998, the Practice Directorate forged an alliance with Music Television (MTV) to develop a youth antiviolence initiative. MTV executives were particularly impressed that APA already had an established grassroots infrastructure that could help young people nationwide (Peterson & Newman, 2000). Moreover, the Practice Directorate had research underscoring the relevance of educating teens about the warning signs of violence. According to a poll conducted by Penn, Schoen, and Berland Associates for APA in 1999, 71 percent of young people said they *wanted* to learn to be able to recognize the warning signs of violence and 40 percent were concerned about a potentially violent classmate (Penn, Schoen, & Berland, 1999).

The overarching Talk to Someone Who Can Help campaign focused on the value of psychology in general and was aimed at adults, but the Warning Signs initiative was specifically geared toward young teens. The goal of the initiative was to help the nation's youth in identifying signs of distress and anger—such as bullying, fighting, or talk of suicide—that might portend violent behavior and to help them understand that help is available should they see any of these warning signs in themselves or their peers (Peterson & Newman, 2000). With APA's already established grassroots network of psychologists and MTV's reach and influence on young people, this new public education initiative would be able to convey important information to young people and their families identifying the warning signs of violence and, importantly, where to turn for help. In this manner, the APA's Practice Directorate would continue its initiatives for communicating the value of psychology to the public.

The APA—MTV team set about creating materials that would reach out to teenagers in significant ways. A key element to the media partnership was a 30-minute documentary entitled *Warning Signs* that depicted various real-life violent school events and explored the thoughts, feelings, opinions, and fears of the teenagers and young adults involved. Psychologists appeared as experts in the documentary and drew attention to warning signs in youth behavior that could be considered a precursor to violence. A toll-free number was provided during the airing of the program on MTV so viewers could request a free copy of a *Warning Signs* brochure, another important element of the initiative (APA Practice Directorate, 1998).

Developed by APA members with expertise in youth violence and designed by MTV, the brochure outlined themes underscored in the documentary about the warning signs of violence. It also addressed the issue that violent behavior is learned and therefore can be unlearned. The brochure gave young people commonsense examples of warning signs such as losing one's temper on a daily basis, significant vandalism or property damage, increased use of drugs or alcohol, increased risk-taking behavior, enjoyment in hurting animals, frequent physical fights, and threatening to hurt others. The brochure also gave suggestions for identifying and controlling the thoughts and feelings that lead to violence, and most importantly, it encouraged young people who notice these signs in themselves or their peers to talk to a trusted adult and get help.

Another important means of disseminating the Warning Signs messages was using the grassroots network that the APA Practice Directorate developed during the Talk to Someone Who Can Help campaign. The Practice Directorate created special how-to kits for the Warning Signs initiative and distributed them to interested APA members through a toll-free number to help them prepare for outreach activities that could be implemented in their own communities. The kits contained a discussion guide, information on how to conduct a youth forum on violence, a VHS copy of the *Warning Signs* documentary, information on how to contact local media, and information on conducting other grassroots activities. Template letters were provided to help psychologists make connections with potential cooperating groups ranging from scouting organizations to education associations. Recognizing that schools would be a primary location where forums would be held, APA also obtained a letter of endorsement for the campaign from the United States Secretary of Education. By training psychologists, equipping them with the tools they needed, and encouraging them to hold youth forums on the warning signs of violence, the public education initiative could reach out to those most in need—the students.

Two days before the official launch of the Warning Signs project, with all the materials prepared and ready to go, an event occurred that reverberated throughout the country. Two teenagers from Columbine High School in Littleton, Colorado, killed 12 schoolmates and a teacher and wounded dozens more before turning the guns on themselves. This tragic event showed all too clearly the need to teach teens how to recognize the warning signs of imminent violence. Fortunately, APA's grassroots network stood ready with materials in hand to help teens and parents better understand the problem of youth violence, to help communities attempt to curb violence, and to help the nation heal.

The initial Warning Signs goals had been modest: air the documentary at least once, distribute 50,000 *Warning Signs* brochures, and convene at least 50 school and community forums led by local psychologists. But the demand was immense. Between 1999 and 2001, more than 1,300 Warning Signs forums were held across the country.

By the end of 1999, APA had distributed more than 375,000 *Warning Signs* brochures through an 800 number, online orders, forums conducted by psychologists, and special requests from school districts. The documentary aired more than a dozen times on MTV and reached more than 5 million young viewers (Peterson & Newman, 2000). In 2001 the demand was to continue, and APA would pass the 1.5 million mark for disseminating *Warning Signs* brochures.

Even while interest in the Warning Signs initiative was growing, APA's Practice Directorate was looking to the future to identify other issues of national concern that could be addressed through the public education campaign and that would also reinforce the value of psychology. To determine its next steps, APA returned to the tactics that had been critical in developing the Warning Signs initiative: staying connected to the public pulse, engaging APA members, and developing the network of cooperative organizations to support outreach efforts.

On March 9, 2000, APA launched a new component of the Warning Signs initiative: Warning Signs for Parents. This component addressed a primary concern that had emerged from hundreds of youth forums, where teenagers often said that it was difficult to communicate with adults, especially their parents, about their problems and concerns. In addition, many of the parents involved in the youth forums had requested forums of their own. As a result, the Practice Directorate had developed a new planning kit to assist psychologists in setting up and facilitating forums for parents. This parenting component was introduced in Oklahoma at the Statewide Summit on Safe Schools convened by Governor Frank Keating and keynoted by comedian Bill Cosby. Approximately 10,000 people attended the summit (Peterson & Newman, 2000).

The new Warning Signs for Parents kit included a discussion guide for psychologists to use in parent forums, a communication tip sheet for parents, and a list of reading resources for parents. The new kits were sent to the psychologists who had received the Warning Signs kits. Psychologists were encouraged to host parent forums to advise parents on how to talk with their children about violence, how to keep the lines of communication open, how to listen effectively when their children were ready to talk about a difficult issue, and how to spot the warning signs of violence. Many of these issues had been central to the family life theme in the Talk to Someone Who Can Help campaign.

Although no one focused on it at the time, the Warning Signs initiative did more than pinpoint signs and signals. It also sowed the seeds of resilience in the young program participants and their parents by encouraging them to communicate with one another, thus fostering one of the most important of the 10 ways to build resilience—making connections with others. Every element of the initiative—the documentary, brochures, school forums, and the 800 number—was designed to foster open dialogue and teach teenagers that it was okay to take control—to go to a trusted adult when they witnessed the warning signs in others, or talk to someone when they recognized related feelings in themselves.

The Warning Signs initiative served as an enormous stepping-stone for APA's grassroots outreach efforts, bringing the Talk to Someone Who Can Help campaign to a new level in what was possible from organized outreach. It illustrated the longevity that can be attained by an effective grassroots outreach initiative and demonstrated one way psychologists could provide a valuable service to their community. It also showed that spin-offs could be created within an outreach initiative to maximize its reach to the public. The Warning Signs initiative provided a model for future public education initiatives to follow. The proven success of Warning Signs would also make it much easier for the Practice Directorate to engage future partners, because although a dollar figure cannot be placed on the buying power of a grassroots network, its past activities can convey the powerful effect such outreach can have.

Altogether, the numerous achievements gained through the course of the Warning Signs project provide a glimpse into the potential of The Road to Resilience initiative over time. Warning Signs also shows how a public education initiative responding to an immediate public need of national concern—in this case, school shootings and the need to help open lines of communication among teens and their peers, parents, and other adults—could evolve over time to become a valuable resource helpful in daily life long after the incident that sparked the initial need for the public education initiative. Looking back upon this evolution charted the course for The Road to Resilience initiative as well.

Disaster-Response Network Activities in Response to September 11, 2001

As the events of September 11, 2001, unfolded, the APA Practice Directorate was deep in the exploration of its next initiative for the public education campaign. But on that day, the world changed, and the public education campaign was put to a new test to quickly mobilize, tap the community connections made through prior grassroots outreach, and help the public cope with an unimaginable tragedy.

It was fortunate that APA also had a mechanism in place through the DRN to involve psychologists in responding to local or national disasters.

By coincidence, the DRN Advisory Committee had a conference call scheduled for noon on September 11, which enabled it to discuss the incidents and initial response efforts. It was clear that an incident of the magnitude of September 11 would draw on resources beyond the DRN's capacity, so the public education campaign (PEC), whose strength and potential for public influence was now well established, was also mobilized to help.

The DRN and PEC Come Together to Develop September 11 Materials for the Public

Representatives from the two groups came together to develop materials that could be used in community outreach to help the public cope with the terrorist incidents. APA first chose to specifically develop materials for helping adults speak with children about the terrorist attacks. This decision was made for three reasons. First, many requests had already started to come into the state psychological associations and to individual psychologists regarding talking to young people about the events of September 11. Second, many APA members involved in the Warning Signs component of the PEC had already developed relationships with their local schools that would enable them to use the materials quickly. Third, by facilitating discussions about talking with children about terrorism, psychologists could provide a tangible service in their local communities and take some of the burden off local disaster response centers, already responding to a variety of public needs following the terrorist attacks.

The APA Practice Directorate, with input from PEC coordinators and the DRN's advisory committee, created electronically available response materials for use by psychologists. The materials were posted widely on practitioner listservs and on the Practice Directorate's Web site, http://www.apa.org/practice, in less than 36 hours after the terrorist attacks. The materials included a cover memo outlining the purpose of the materials, a discussion guide for use by psychologists about talking with young people about traumatic events, a list of Internet resources with information on coping with traumatic events, suggested steps for reaching out to assist local schools, and a document entitled "Reactions and Guidelines for Children Following Trauma/Disaster" that offered suggestions to parents and teachers. A short time later, APA also developed and posted to the directorate's Web site "Coping with Terrorism," which clearly explained the range of feelings and emotions one can have after a traumatic experience, including tips on helping children cope.

APA members expressed appreciation for making user-friendly, current materials quickly accessible. The materials reached far and wide. A week after they were posted, thanks were received from a psychologist in Iceland who downloaded the materials from the Web site and used them to facilitate discussions with the children of U.S. servicemen and women living there.

APA's consumer Web site, helping.apa.org, provided the press and the public with an identifiable location from which to get concrete advice for dealing with the events and its aftermath. Following the terrorist attacks on September 11, 2001, APA released a national news release through PR Newswire with tips for parents to help them talk with their children about traumatic events. Other national media outlets ran helping.apa.org as a resource for information on coping with the trauma of the terrorist attacks.

In addition, during the initial weeks following the attacks, the APA Practice Directorate worked closely with DRN state coordinators and the state psychological association executive directors in the regions most directly impacted by the terrorist incidents. DRN members and local psychologists in these regions staffed Red Cross disaster operation centers. There they aided the victims' families, supported relief workers, fielded requests for assistance from companies that lost employees, and provided pro bono crisis counseling sessions along with a variety of other support services. Psychological associations hosted open houses to provide a forum for community discussion and support.

In states where the fatal flights had originated or had been scheduled to land, DRN members staffed Red Cross family assistance centers that were set up at the airports to aid families and airline workers. Red Cross operations continued for months in New York City. At a center set up close to Ground Zero and at a family assistance center off site, DRN members offered assistance and visited families of the deceased.

Interest in the DRN program skyrocketed. The Practice Directorate received many requests among its member psychologists for information about the DRN, how to join, how to sign up for Red Cross Disaster Mental Health Services training, and how to become actively involved. Practice Directorate staff sent out information and helped members to connect with their local Red Cross chapters and DRN coordinators.

With its volunteer membership on the front lines of coping with the aftermath of the trauma, APA recognized that the general public was not the only audience in need of support during this difficult period in our country's history. Drawing on what would be identified as another of the 10 ways to build resilience—taking care of yourself—the Practice Directorate together with the Advisory Committee on Colleague Assistance developed a document entitled "Tapping Your Resilience in the Wake of Terrorism: Pointers for Practitioners." This document was posted to the Practice Directorate's Web site (http://www.apa.org/practice/practitionerhelp.html) and offered guidance for practitioners on coping with the challenges of working with clients in the aftermath of the terrorist attacks.

Planting the Seeds of Resilience

Prior to the terrorist attacks of September 11, 2001, the Practice Directorate had been exploring the possibility of a work stress documentary to continue the activities and the central message of the PEC, which is to talk to someone who can help. Although perhaps still relevant in a post–September 11 world, this message now seemed too simple a picture of what was on the minds and in the hearts of the public. So, it was back to the drawing board for a better vehicle to communicate psychology's role, a better way to demonstrate the value of psychological services, and a new approach to help the public understand that their currently expressed need was well within the scope of psychological practice.

APA had surmised that the events of September 11 and subsequent threats of anthrax had created a *new* sense of uncertainty among the public, an assumption that needed to be further explored. As it had done before for its previous campaigns and initiatives, the APA Practice Directorate went to the public and held six focus groups in three very different regions of the country. Focus groups conducted in Indianapolis, Los Angeles, and Baltimore served as sounding boards to discuss uncertainty, stress, and related issues from the September 11 terrorist attacks and to gather feedback on language for a possible public education initiative around uncertainty, resilience, or self-discovery. In fact, focus group participants clearly expressed a desire for self-discovery in the wake of the September 11 terrorist attacks and generally viewed self-discovery as a positive and beneficial process of realizing something about themselves that they didn't know they were capable of doing or of finding strength they didn't know they had.

The attacks and other recent events apparently made it more socially acceptable to talk about stress, anxiety, and other psychological or emotional topics that previously were taboo. In all groups, participants expressed feelings of shock, anger, fear, frustration, anxiety, fatigue, depression, and stress as a result of the attacks. Many participants agreed with the statement, "I feel like I live with chronic stress," and talked about their worries about the economy and the security of their loved ones.

Participants responded positively to messages about resilience. Although all Americans were affected to some extent by the terrorist attacks, there was a resistance to themes and messages that emphasized the overwhelming nature of the attacks and the resulting uncertainty. Even while expressing their horror and the emotional impact of the attacks, participants described a corresponding determination not to surrender to these emotions or to change their way of life in response to the attacks—not to give in or give up. Instead, they wanted to persevere and to continue doing things they have always done, perhaps to demonstrate to terrorists that Americans' spirits are unbroken. Themes of bouncing back from overcoming hardship seemed to connect with Americans' determination to continue living their lives. Almost universally, participants expressed confidence that most people will bounce back from the initial emotional impact of the attacks. This finding was consistent with APA's review of the existing psychological research on recovery from traumatic events, which suggested that most people would return to their normal level of functioning six months after a traumatic event (Pann, 2001).

The Road to Resilience Initiative: Message Development

Surprisingly, the word *coping* had negative associations for many participants in the focus groups. They felt the word implied accepting something that won't change. Others felt that it sounded like not taking action. Similarly, the term *dealing with* had associations of not taking action. *Living with* had the negative association of having a long-term problem, whether or not the individual was doing anything about it. *Living with* sounded chronic and somewhat hopeless. Most participants made positive associations with the word *resilience,* saying it suggested strength and bouncing back.

Notable comments from the focus groups include the following:

- *Coping* sounds like you're talking about a problem. It sounds negative.
- *Coping* is just accepting it. You accept it because it happened and you can't change it.
- *Dealing with* sounds more like business where coping sounds more like feelings.
- *Living with* suggests that you have something in your life, whether or not you're dealing very well with it.
- *Resilience* is recovery; bouncing back. It implies strength. Being tough. You can be pushed down, but you will come up. It acknowledges reality. You have internal strength.
- *Resilience:* Whatever the occasion may be, you rise to it. Depending on the situation you're put in, you don't have a choice. You would be surprised with what you can do if you don't have a choice. (Pacific Visions, 2001a)

Approximately five months after the September 11 terrorist attacks, APA had the opportunity to once again communicate with the public about the continuing impact of the terrorist attacks. A poll conducted in January 2002 by Greenberg Quinlan Rosner Research for APA and *The Infinite Mind* public radio program found there was a high level of public interest in information on how to become more resilient in times of trauma and uncertainty. The poll also found that more than three-quarters of Americans agreed that they had tried to simplify their lives and focus on what really matters. Seventy-one percent of Americans reported having spent more time trying to gain perspective on their lives (*Infinite Mind* & Greenberg Quinlan Rosner, 2002). The research reinforced that, more than ever, people wanted to be resilient and seemed to be open to psychological process, self-examination, and self-discovery. It was clear from the findings that the events of September 11 had had a real impact, but that Americans were trying to work their way back from this tragedy.

Partnering with Discovery Health

After learning from the public that resilience was an important theme for the next initiative and building on the paradigm developed in the Warning Signs campaign, APA's Practice Directorate sought to enter into a joint venture with a national cable television channel capable of reaching millions of people to coproduce a documentary on resilience. The Practice Directorate set its sights on the Discovery Health Channel because of its focus on health and educating consumers, and its appreciation of research and the use of experts. Decision makers at Discovery Health were sold on the potential of the partnership, in large part, because of the expertise APA brought to the subject and because of the strength and proven track record of the national grassroots network, which they believed could help expand their own viewing audience.

The following excerpts, taken from a concept paper that helped cement the relationship with Discovery Health, provide a good articulation of the Practice Directorate's thinking about what needed to be done. They also provide a glimpse of the larger societal issues and context being considered when the television program about resilience was being proposed to Discovery Health.

> The U.S. unemployment rate is now the highest it's been in 21 years, and economists say the 9/11 attacks had a devastating impact on the already weak U.S. economy, and we are now in recession. On the health front, despite new research and medical breakthroughs, one in four Americans will still die from cancer, and millions of families each year cope with children who have a disability or chronic illness. Now there is the prospect of random terrorist attacks. And it's likely everyone will face one or more traumatic events in his or her lifetime.
>
> In recent focus groups conducted by the American Psychological Association (APA) following the 9/11 attacks, men and women of all income levels and ages described life today as "uncertain." It's a feeling that existed but was not articulated before the 9/11 terrorist attacks. This sense that the "other shoe is going to drop" is compounded by the fact, they say, that they were already living with a chronic level of stress daily, resulting from pressures both at work and home.
>
> "It's in the back of my head every day, what's next, when is it coming, I know it's coming," said one woman in a Baltimore focus group, while a man in a Los Angeles focus group said, "It scares me to look into the future."
>
> But Americans are bouncing back from this latest trauma, as they always have. Psychological research shows a majority of people will return to their normal level of functioning before the attacks. In fact, even people who have been impacted directly by a traumatic event generally regain equilibrium in one-half to three years following the event.

Whether it's coping with the loss of a family member, maintaining a positive outlook in the face of a life-threatening illness, dealing with a job loss, or having the wherewithal to carry their family through tough times, many people have a difficult time explaining what gives them their inner strength. In psychology, it's called "resilience" and resilience can be learned, experts say.

Documentary Program Concept

In a one-hour cable television special that would air on the one-year anniversary of the 9/11 terrorist attacks, these and other characteristics of resilience can be explained to the public through the telling of real stories of resilience and expert psychological commentary. They will serve as true demonstrations of inner strength and help viewers to look at their own capacity for resilience.

These real stories bring to life any person's capacity to deal with hardship. National polling and focus groups demonstrate that this information is of interest to Americans, particularly women who make the health care decisions for their families. The one-year anniversary of the terrorist attacks will also help drive interest in the documentary. For nearly everyone, it will be felt to some degree. By highlighting the different ways people cope with the hardship and uncertainty in their daily lives, this program can help viewers with their own self-discovery that can lead to resilience. (Pacific Visions, 2001a)

The APA Practice Directorate's Road to Resilience initiative was designed to provide the public with tools and information to help them develop and build resilience in response not only to September 11 but also to any other traumatic event or hardship they may encounter. This initiative was intended to help the nation build resilience that would carry them well past the events of September 11 and through the rest of their lives, better equipped to face other adversities they may encounter, such as death of a loved one, loss of a job, serious illness, or other major hardship. The overarching messages of the initiative included the following concepts:

1. Resilience can be learned.
2. Resilience is a journey, not a single event or point in time.
3. Each individual's journey is different.

As with each of the earlier initiatives that were projects within the Talk to Someone Who Can Help PEC, the underlying goals of the resilience initiative were demonstrating to the public how psychology could be valuable to them by helping in these uncertain times, while providing members with tools to reach out to the public on a local level.

In developing the issues central to this initiative, the Practice Directorate sought out a panel of APA members who were experts on resilience. The next step was to interview the experts and ask them specific questions around the issue of resilience, such as, "What issues should a public education campaign on building resilience highlight?" and "What should a brochure aimed at the public regarding resilience include?" These interviews helped form the basis of how to promote the idea of resilience to the general public. They also helped the APA Practice Directorate staff further delineate the basic messages:

4. When people are faced with adversity, there are steps they can take.

5. Resilience is a process.

6. Resilience is not exceptional, and the behaviors associated with resilience are ordinary behaviors and can be achieved by ordinary people.

In keeping with the structure of past PECs and initiatives, the Road to Resilience initiative emphasized the value of stepping back to evaluate our psychological well-being in these stressful times—especially with respect to our own health, work, and family relationships.

The documentary, which would become one of the centerpieces of the resilience initiative, directly addressed the concerns of millions of Americans anxious about living in uncertain times. It used September 11 as a springboard rather than an exclusive focus, and it illustrated that resilience can be applied to a wide array of hardships, such as unemployment or the death of a loved one. To do this, it was agreed that the documentary should feature a diverse group of people, of different ages, races and ethnic groups—not only people who directly suffered from September 11, but also others who experienced other hardships and tragedies in their lives. State Street in Brooklyn, New York, became the common thread for the story because it is a diverse neighborhood with residents and workers whose personal experiences demonstrate building resilience through a variety of tragedies and hardships that many Americans might experience in their lifetimes. A fire station that had lost members when the World Trade Centers collapsed is also located on State Street.

In addition to the documentary, the APA–Discovery Health collaboration also produced a brochure that became known as *The Road to Resilience*, now available to the public through APA's consumer Web site (helping.apa.org) and the program's national consumer information toll-free line, 1-800-964-2000. Created with input from the panel of APA experts, the brochure explores the idea of resilience in easy-to-understand terms. It begins with a definition of resilience, emphasizing that it is *not* a trait that people either have or do not have, but rather it is a skill that can be learned. It also emphasizes that a primary factor in resilience is having caring and supportive relationships. The brochure then outlines some important factors that people can develop in themselves that contribute to resilience, including

- the capacity to make realistic plans and take steps to carry them out;
- a positive view of yourself and confidence in your strengths and abilities;
- skills in communication and problem solving; and
- the capacity to manage strong feelings and impulses.

The brochure also emphasizes that developing resilience is a personal journey, unique to the individual, and that people, thus, use varying strategies to help them build resilience. The section of the brochure entitled "Ten Ways to Build Resilience" highlights concrete actions individuals can take to get through difficult times. This section of the brochure has been extracted and used in many publications nationwide. The full text of the brochure *The Road to Resilience* is reprinted at the end of the chapter in appendix 1.

To ensure that central themes and messages about resilience contained in the brochure would resonate with the public, APA turned again to the public for input. A focus group was convened in Los Angeles, during which the brochure was well received. Following a review of the complete brochure content, many participants in the focus group commented that they learned connections with others are an important aspect of resilience. "It could be built through family," one participant said. This feedback provided the reassurance that messages in the brochure had hit their intended mark. As one participant commented, "It is something I have been thinking about but was not able to express."

Beyond the documentary and brochure designed for public use, another key resource developed for The Road to Resilience initiative was a practitioner tool kit provided to psychologists to help them conduct community outreach with messages about resilience. Like the how-to kits designed for the Talk to Someone Who Can Help campaign and the Warning Signs initiative, the Road to Resilience tool kit instructs psychologists on how to implement resilience initiative activities to extend the message of resilience to the public, including media relations, community outreach, and conducting local discussion forums. The tool kit also contains instructions for how psychologists can order brochures to disseminate to the public as well as a copy of the Posttraumatic Growth Inventory, which is an exercise that helps people assess how they may even have grown through their struggle with adversity and points to areas they should focus upon in order to experience further personal growth. Armed with this tool kit, psychologists would be better prepared to engage in outreach efforts, educating the public about resilience.

Implementing Outreach through Existing PEC Infrastructure

The resilience project partnership with Discovery Health was first announced to members during the APA's state leadership conference in March 2002. At that time a call to action was issued for APA members to act as guides on the psychological journey of individuals throughout the nation to find meaning in the events of September 11. Psychologists were encouraged to use their knowledge, research, and clinical skills to engage in efforts to turn personal tragedy into triumph and help turn our predicament into human achievement, as Victor Frankl conveyed in his book *Man's Search for Meaning* (Frankl, 1946).

After months of development, APA introduced The Road to Resilience initiative and the accompanying documentary during APA's convention in August 2002. The Practice Directorate conducted a training session on use of the outreach materials, and participating psychologists were able to sign up to receive the new Road to Resilience tool kits in time to do community outreach and hold discussion forums for the anniversary of September 11 and beyond. Tool kits were also sent immediately to every state psychological association's PEC coordinator and executive director so they could begin to familiarize themselves with how to do outreach with the resilience materials.

Within the first two months after the resilience project was launched, PEC coordinators swiftly moved into action. A total of 10 state psychological associations conducted trainings for members using the resilience materials at their state conventions. Some state psychological associations were able to offer continuing education credit for their resilience training workshops. Psychologists nationwide ordered brochures to place in offices, distribute at community meetings, and hand out at specially called resilience forums. Following are some specific sample highlights of how materials were

quickly put into use within just two months after the resilience project materials were provided to psychologists across the country:

- A special launch of The Road to Resilience project was held at a
  movie theater in Bethesda, Maryland, on September 9 in conjunction with the Maryland Psychological Association, Discovery
  Health, Comcast Cable, and the Mental Health Association of
  Montgomery County. An estimated 150 people attended this event,
  which included a screening of the documentary and a discussion by
  a panel that included a Maryland resident whose husband was one
  of the casualties of the terrorist attack on the Pentagon.

- A psychologist in Nevada reported using the resilience materials
  for a meeting with a health reporter from the local ABC affiliate.
  The reporter produced a story that aired on the anniversary of
  September 11 and referred to both the APA consumer toll-free line
  and the helping.apa.org Web site address.

- A psychologist in California conducted aggressive media outreach
  and was quoted about resilience in three local newspapers—the
  Long Beach Press Telegram, the *San Bernardino County Sun,* and the
  Inland Valley Daily Bulletin—with a total circulation of several hun-
  dred thousand. Beyond informing the public of how to obtain the
  brochure, *The Road to Resilience,* the article also prompted numerous requests from the public for psychologists to facilitate local discussion forums.

- The Pennsylvania Psychological Association distributed the
  brochure on September 11, 2002, at the State Museum of
  Pennsylvania in Harrisburg as part of the Flight 98 Remembered
  exhibit.

- A psychologist in Missouri distributed resilience materials during a
  presentation at a regional safety conference. The psychologist
  noted that the video was very well received, and no brochures were
  left lying on tables after everyone had departed. "I might also mention that while the video and materials do discuss 9/11—there are
  references to other kinds of traumas, stressors and coping strategies contained within the material, so the material is not just a
  rehashing (or) reliving of 9/11 but is broadly helpful to people."

- A psychologist in Iowa distributed 500 of the brochures at the
  Stand Tall America event on September 11, 2002—a commemora-
  tive concert at Sec Taylor Stadium in Des Moines, Iowa.

Once again, the APA Practice Directorate was able to put its
resilience initiative in motion by using the established grassroots
infrastructure that had been created for the Talk to Someone Who

Can Help campaign and further developed during the Warning Signs initiative.

Resilience beyond Terrorism

The resilience initiative activities have extended well beyond a simple reaction to the September 11 terrorist attacks. At this writing, psychologists nationwide continue to conduct discussion groups and forums centered on achieving resilience at senior assisted-living facilities, hospitals, libraries, churches, and other community and professional centers.

- The East Coast sniper attacks in November 2002 sparked the idea for Dr. Denise Walton's resilience presentation to a faculty group at Temple University along with a local police officer in the Washington, D.C., area. The highly publicized attacks made everyone feel uneasy about their personal safety. The title of the presentation, which was chosen by the administration of the university, was "Feeling Safe in an Unsafe World."

  Walton said the police officer provided practical tips on how to keep safe physically, while she focused on "how to keep safe emotionally," discussed the definition of resilience, and shared the 10 ways to build resilience from the resilience brochure as well as the Posttraumatic Growth Inventory (Tedeschi & Calhoun, 1996).

  "The switch to my topic of resilience was difficult for them because their needs to feel safe were predominant," Walton said. "But they saw the value of the information in the end." Dr. Walton's presentation was well regarded and received positive feedback from the university administration.

- In Illinois, psychologists made two resilience presentations to more than 50 journalists at a meeting of the Chicago Headline Club. The resilience presentation was customized to focus on the workplace and learning how to become more resilient in coping with work stress.

"Once we got the group going, they shared very personally," said Dr. Nancy Molitor, one of the leaders of the presentation. "They spoke about how they take their work home with them, how the boundaries are blurred between work and home, and how they tend to go out with other journalists."

Christine Tatum, technology reporter for the *Chicago Tribune*, said she left the workshop with a more hopeful outlook on her work life. "The message of resilience is one that should be in every journalist's toolbox," she said. "Journalists are asked to do superhuman things at times, from meeting extremely tight deadlines to having to be 100 percent accurate and working long hours. We walked away from the session with some hopeful messages, including that it's okay to admit that you're not perfect and that you can say no."

Conclusion

As the Practice Directorate discovered, the tools and activities it had developed in the initial Talk to Someone Who Can Help campaign and fine-tuned with Warning Signs, combined with the trained and experienced cadre of DRN and PEC psychologists, provided a formidable array of tools for creating and delivering The Road to Resilience initiative. Like initiatives before it, The Road to Resilience project shows promising signs of having a widespread national impact and longevity. Within the first two months of the initiative, 20,000 brochures had been distributed and nearly 700 psychologists nationwide had received tool kits. By establishing a foundation of activities with which to create an outreach initiative—first by investigating and taking the public's pulse, next by developing partnerships with like-minded organizations with complementary skills, and, finally, by capturing the imagination of its broad membership base— the APA's Practice Directorate had turned the theory and research on resilience into action. The events of September 11, 2001, had opened a window to self-discovery not only for the public but also for the field of psychology—proving it could really make a difference and help people through troubling times.

Appendix 1: The Road to Resilience

Introduction

How do people deal with difficult events that change their lives? The death of a loved one, loss of a job, serious illness, terrorist attacks, and other traumatic events are all examples of very challenging life experiences. Many people react to such circumstances with a flood of strong emotions and a sense of uncertainty.

Yet people generally adapt well over time to life-changing situations and stressful conditions. What enables them to do so? It involves resilience, an ongoing process that requires time and effort and engages people in taking a number of steps.

This brochure is intended to help readers with taking their own road to resilience. The information within describes resilience and some factors that affect how people deal with hardship. Much of the brochure focuses on building and using a personal strategy for enhancing resilience.

What Is Resilience?

Resilience is the process of adapting well in the face of adversity, trauma, tragedy, threats, or even significant sources of stress—such as family and relationship problems, serious health problems, or workplace and financial stressors. It means bouncing back from difficult circumstances.

Research has shown that resilience is ordinary, not extraordinary. People commonly demonstrate resilience. One example is the response of many Americans to the September 11, 2001, terrorist attacks and individuals' efforts to rebuild their lives.

Being resilient does not mean that a person doesn't experience difficulty or distress. Emotional pain and distress are common in people who have suffered major adversity or trauma in their lives. In fact, the road to resilience is likely to involve considerable emotional distress.

Resilience is not a trait that people either have or do not have. It involves behaviors, thoughts, and actions that can be learned and developed in anyone.

Some Factors in Resilience

A combination of factors contributes to resilience. Many studies show that the primary factor in resilience is having caring and supportive relationships within and outside the family. Relationships that create love and trust, provide role models, and offer encouragement and reassurance help bolster a person's resilience.

Several additional factors are associated with resilience, including

- the capacity to make realistic plans and take steps to carry them out,
- a positive view of oneself and good self-confidence,
- skills in communication and problem solving, and
- the capacity to manage strong feelings and impulses.

All these are factors that people can develop in themselves.

Strategies for Building Resilience

Developing resilience is a personal journey. People do not all react the same way to traumatic and stressful life events. An approach to building resilience that works for one person might not work for another. People use varying strategies.

Some variation may reflect cultural differences. A person's culture might have an impact on how he or she communicates feelings and deals with adversity—for example, whether and how a person connects with significant others, including extended family members and community resources. With growing cultural diversity in the United States, the public has greater access to a number of different approaches to building resilience.

Some or many of the ways to build resilience in the following pages may be appropriate to consider in developing your personal strategy.

Ten Ways to Build Resilience

Make connections. Good relationships with close family members, friends, or others are important. Accepting help and support from those who care about you and will listen to you strengthens resilience. Some people find that being active in civic groups, faith-based organizations, or other local groups provides social support and can help with reclaiming hope. Assisting others in their time of need also can benefit the helper.

Avoid seeing crises as insurmountable problems. You can't change the fact that highly stressful events happen, but you can change how you interpret and respond to these events. Try looking beyond the present to how future circumstances may be a little better. Note any subtle ways in which you might already feel somewhat better as you deal with difficult situations.

Accept that change is a part of living. Certain goals may no longer be attainable as a result of adverse situations. Accepting circumstances that cannot be changed can help you focus on circumstances that you can alter.

Move toward your goals. Develop some realistic goals. Do something regularly—even if it seems like a small accomplishment—that enables you to move toward your goals. Instead of focusing on tasks that seem unachievable, ask yourself, "What's one thing I know I can accomplish today that helps me move in the direction I want to go?"

Take decisive actions. Act on adverse situations as much as you can. Take decisive actions, rather than detaching completely from problems and stresses and wishing they would just go away.

Look for opportunities for self-discovery. People often learn something about themselves and may find that they have grown in some respect as a result of their struggle with loss. Many people who have experienced tragedies and hardship have reported better relationships, greater sense of personal strength even while feeling vulnerable, increased sense of self-worth, a more developed spirituality, and heightened appreciation for life.

Nurture a positive view of yourself. Developing confidence in your ability to solve problems and trusting your instincts helps build resilience.

Keep things in perspective. Even when facing very painful events, try to consider the stressful situation in a broader context and keep a long-term perspective. Avoid blowing the event out of proportion.

Maintain a hopeful outlook. An optimistic outlook enables you to expect that good things will happen in your life. Try visualizing what you want, rather than worrying about what you fear.

Take care of yourself. Pay attention to your own needs and feelings. Engage in activities that you enjoy and find relaxing. Exercise regularly. Taking care of yourself helps to keep your mind and body primed to deal with situations that require resilience.

Additional ways of strengthening resilience may be helpful. For example, some people write about their deepest thoughts and feelings related to trauma or other stressful events in their life. Meditation and spiritual practices help some people build connections and restore hope. The key is to identify ways that are likely to work well for you as part of your own personal strategy for fostering resilience.

Learning from Your Past
Some Questions To Ask Yourself

Focusing on past experiences and sources of personal strength can help you learn about what strategies for building resilience might work for you. By exploring answers to the following questions about yourself and your reactions to challenging life events, you may discover how you can best work through difficult situations in your life. Consider the following:

- What kinds of events have been most stressful for me?
- How have those events typically affected me?
- Have I found it helpful to think of important people in my life when I am distressed?
- To whom have I reached out for support in working through a traumatic or stressful experience?

- What have I learned about myself and my interactions with others during difficult times?
- Has it been helpful for me to assist someone else going through a similar experience?
- Have I been able to overcome obstacles, and if so, how?
- What has helped make me feel more hopeful about the future?

Staying Flexible

Resilience involves maintaining flexibility and balance in your life as you deal with stressful circumstances and traumatic events. This happens in several ways, including

- letting yourself experience strong emotions and also realizing when you may need to avoid experiencing them at times in order to continue functioning;
- stepping forward and taking action to deal with your problems and meet the demands of daily living and also stepping back to rest and reenergize yourself;
- spending time with loved ones to gain support and encouragement and also nurturing yourself; and
- relying on others and also relying on yourself.

Places to Look for Help

Getting help when you need it is crucial in building your resilience. Beyond caring family members and friends, people often find it useful to turn to the following resources.

Self-help and support groups. Such community groups can aid people struggling with hardships such as the death of a loved one. By sharing information, ideas, and emotions, group participants can assist one another and find comfort in knowing that they are not alone in experiencing difficulty.

Books and other publications. These resources written by people who have successfully managed adverse situations such as surviving cancer can be helpful. These stories can motivate someone to find strategies that might work for them personally.

Online resources. Information on the Web can be a helpful source of ideas, though the quality of Web-based material varies among sources. The APA Help Center, online at www.helping.apa.org, is a good site to check.

For many people, using their own resources and the kinds of help listed above may be sufficient for building resilience. At times, however, an individual might get stuck or have difficulty making progress on the road to resilience.

A licensed mental health professional such as a psychologist can assist people in developing an appropriate strategy for moving forward. It is important to get professional help if you feel like you are unable to function or perform basic activities of daily living as a result of a traumatic or other stressful life experience.

Different people tend to be comfortable with somewhat different styles of interaction. A person should feel at ease and have a good rapport with a mental health professional or a support group.

Continuing on Your Journey

To help summarize several of the main points in this brochure, think of resilience as similar to taking a raft trip down a river.

On a river, you may encounter rapids, turns, slow water, and shallows. As in life, the changes you experience affect you differently along the way.

In traveling the river, it helps to have knowledge about it and past experience in dealing with it. Your journey should be guided by a plan, a strategy that you consider likely to work well for you.

Perseverance and trust in your ability to work your way around boulders and other obstacles are important. You can gain courage and insight by successfully navigating your way through white water. Trusted companions who accompany you on the journey can be especially helpful for dealing with rapids, upstream currents, and other difficult stretches of the river.

You can climb out to rest alongside the river. But to get to the end of your journey, you need to get back in the raft and continue.

Information contained in this brochure should not be used as a substitute for professional health and mental health care or consultation. Individuals who believe they may need or benefit from care should consult a psychologist or other licensed health/mental health professional.

The American Psychological Association Practice Directorate gratefully acknowledges the following contributors to this publication:

- Lillian Comas-Diaz, Ph.D., Director, Transcultural Mental Health Institute, Washington, D.C.;

- Suniya S. Luthar, Ph.D., Teachers College, Columbia University, New York City, New York;

- Salvatore R. Maddi, Ph.D., The Hardiness Institute, Inc., University of California, Irvine, Newport Beach, California;
- H. Katherine (Kit) O'Neill, Ph.D., North Dakota State University and Knowlton, O'Neill and Associates, Fargo, North Dakota;
- Karen W. Saakvitne, Ph.D., Traumatic Stress Institute/Center for Adult & Adolescent Psychotherapy, South Windsor, Connecticut;
- Richard Glenn Tedeschi, Ph.D., Department of Psychology, University of North Carolina at Charlotte, North Carolina.

The American Psychological Association (APA), located in Washington, D.C., is the largest scientific and professional organization representing psychology in the United States. Its membership includes more than 155,000 researchers, educators, clinicians, consultants, and students. APA works to advance psychology as a science and profession and as a means of promoting health and human welfare.

Discovery Health Channel takes viewers inside the fascinating and informative world of health and medicine to experience firsthand, compelling, real-life stories of medical breakthroughs and human triumphs. From the people who bring you the Discovery Channel, the most trusted brand on television, Discovery Health Channel is part of a major, multimedia business designed to help consumers lead healthier, more vigorous lives. Discovery Health Channel and Discovery.com/health were formed by Discovery Communications, Inc. (DCI), a privately held, diversified media company headquartered in Bethesda, Maryland.

For additional copies of *The Road to Resilience* brochure call 1-800-964-2000 or go to helping.apa.org.

References

American Psychological Association Practice Directorate. (1996). *Talk to someone who can help.* [Brochure]. Washington, DC: Author.

American Psychological Association Practice Directorate. (1998). *Warning signs.* [Brochure]. Washington, DC: Author.

American Psychological Association Practice Directorate. (2002). *The road to resilience.* [Brochure]. Washington, DC: Author.

Fowler, R. (2002, April). *Responding to school violence: Warning signs.* Keynote address delivered at the Iowa Psychological Association spring conference. Des Moines, Iowa.

Frankl, V. (1946). *Man's search for meaning.* New York: Washington Square Press.

Infinite Mind & Greenberg Quinlan Rosner. (2002). *Poll.* [Unpublished document]. American Psychological Association, Washington, DC.

Pacific Visions Inc. (2001a). *Consumer focus group executive summary.* [Unpublished document]. American Psychological Association, Washington, DC.

Pacific Visions Inc. (2001b). *Resilience documentary concept paper.* [Unpublished document]. American Psychological Association, Washington, DC.

Pacific Visions Inc. (2002). *PVC/APA focus group report.* [Unpublished document]. American Psychological Association, Washington, DC.

Pann, J. (2001). *Managing with uncertainty: Report on the psychological effects of the September 11th attacks on American society.* [Unpublished document]. American Psychological Association, Washington, DC.

Penn, Schoen, & Berland Assocs. (1999, March). *Juvenile violence poll.* [Unpublished document]. American Psychological Association, Washington, DC.

Peterson, J., & Newman, R. (2000). Helping to curb youth violence: The APA–MTV "Warning Signs" initiative. *Professional Psychology: Research and Practice, 31,* 509–514.

Porter/Novelli. (1995). *Public perceptions of psychology and psychologists.* [Unpublished document]. American Psychological Association, Washington, DC.

Tedeschi, R., & Calhoun, L (1996). The posttraumatic growth inventory: Measuring the positive legacy of trauma. *Journal of Traumatic Stress,* July 1996, Vol. *9,* 455–471.

CHAPTER 10

RESILIENCE AND TRAGEDY

Edith Henderson Grotberg

Certainly, you would like to be resilient in everyday events that you perceive as threatening, that make you afraid, that make you feel vulnerable, that challenge your ability to respond with resilience. But there is a special place for resilience and tragedy, particularly when the tragedy contains so much to threaten your basic need—survival.

A small mountain town in the state of Virginia reluctantly allowed a school of law to open its doors and bring in "outsiders." It is not uncommon for people in isolated small towns to be suspicious of outsiders and doubtful of their promise to revive the depressed economies of their towns.

So, when a failing student at the school of law went on a shooting rampage, killing the dean, a professor, and a student, and injuring three others, the life of the school itself was in jeopardy. The town's people had been right. They knew no good would come from letting the school into the community in the first place. Outsiders were nothing but trouble. But that is not what happened. Instead of the school closing, leaving the town to which they had brought such a terrible tragedy, 32 students walked across the stage four months later to receive their degrees, defying the prediction of the death of the school.

Rather than closing the school, the people of the town demonstrated their resilience in powerful ways. Here is what they did.

The man who became dean after the shooting indicated he felt that closing the school would happen only if they let it. What did happen was that major figures in Virginia drove or flew to the town to offer condolences. These leaders were role models for how to deal with tragedy and restored sufficient order and confidence so the school could function. Students then went back to their studies, daily routines were restored, and the administrators made decisions on how to remember the tragedy and how to go on. Instead of the school being rejected as a dangerous place to attend, applications for admission for the next year almost doubled. The strength of the school and community was seen by prospective students as the place to go.

The student who had been injured returned to school within three weeks, even though she was not nearly recovered, only determined. She certainly drew on confidence in the supports around her, her inner strengths, and her skills in dealing with the pains she experienced as she continued her classes. She was not alone in showing resilience. Students demonstrated empathy and compassion as part of their daily lives. While they were finishing the last four months of the school year, they raised thousands of dollars for each of the six children who had lost a parent. Empathy and compassion are probably the greatest expressions of resilience.

One observer commented that people just stated what they were going to do to help and that it was everyone working together that brought a sense of normalcy. Even though there are survivors still suffering with the injuries they sustained and others who are still grieving over the loss of loved ones, the town did not allow the tragedy to destroy their sense of a strong, resilient community. It is often the sense of vulnerability that brings people together and strengthens them as they deal with tragedy.

Members of this community intuitively drew on resilience factors and engaged in resilience behavior to bring the community through this tragedy. It is important to make overt, however, what was done intuitively, because unless you have a vocabulary for what was done, you cannot teach others what they can do to deal with tragedy. Role modeling is fine, but a role model isn't always available nor is being dependent on a role model always desirable. A certain autonomy and independence for responsible, resilient behavior are also desirable. The language of resilience plays a crucial role.

Homelessness

Homelessness is common throughout the United States, but a particularly vulnerable group is homeless teens. Do you know that there are more than a million homeless teens in America? They are labeled *street children*, or, more precisely in the United States, they are usually referred to as runaways. But not all street children are runaways. Many of them are *push-outs*—their parents don't want them. These teens are usually thought of as incorrigible delinquents who want to leave home, that their decisions to run away are impulsive, and that they never want to return. In fact, many of them were seeking freedom from abuse at home, and running away was an act of last resort to protect them from physical, sexual, or emotional abuse. Many wanted reconciliation with their families. When families of these runaways were examined, it was clear that the parents were not warm and supportive of their teens and tended to reject them. Violence and sexual abuse were common to many of the families.

No matter why they run away, these teens have common problems: The need to work or beg rather than continue with school, being harassed and exploited, having no safe place to live, and suffering from bad health. Here is an account of one group of street kids, runaways.

Boys in a Box

"We all live in a box," one of the kids said.

"A what?" I said. [This is a woman from a shelter who wants to help these teens.]

"A box," he said.

"How many of you live in it?" I asked.

"All six of us," he said.

"Six of you, in the same box?" I said.

"Well, yeah," another teen said, a little embarrassed at the thought. "I mean, it's a big box."

"Yeah, lady," still another one said. "It is pretty big."

"It really concerns me that you are outside," I said. "Why aren't you home?" (although I already knew the answer).

"I don't got no home," one of the kids said. "My father . . . my father beats me. I had to run. I was really afraid he was going to kill me."

"Same with me," another one said. "Me, too," the biggest one said.

"My mom and dad beat me, too," the final one said.

The six teens huddled closer together and stared at me, trying not to look too ashamed or embarrassed about how they looked and how they sounded. They were dirty and bedraggled and unkempt, dressed in rags.

"It's really not a bad box," one said. I could tell he felt hurt and desperately needed my approval.

"I'm sure you make it as good as it ever could be," I smiled, and put my hand on his back.

"Yeah, it's a big cement box," another one said. "It has some kind of transformer inside, which is great 'cause it gives off heat and keeps us warm at night. This past winter, that really came in handy."

"Do you think I could see this box?" I asked. "I mean, is that OK?"

They looked at each other, waiting for the oldest one to make the decision. But the youngest one, just turned 13, couldn't wait. "Sure, it's not far from here."

When we got there, the boys scrambled over a chain link fence surrounding a sort of concrete cavern. I didn't try to follow them. The idea of a 55-year-old woman trying to climb a fence was just too ridiculous.

The boys stood in front of their box, beaming with pride.

"It's great," one said. He was obviously the leader. "It's dry and warm and even has a fence for protection. So don't worry about us." The others nodded in agreement.

I wanted to point out to him how quickly he had climbed that fence and how little protection it really was.

"You know," I said, "we've got a great place for you to stay tonight, if you don't want to sleep in this box. We've got warm, clean beds, and good food, and clean clothes, and you can take a hot shower. Would you like to come back to our shelter with me?"

I was trying to act cool, because I didn't want them to see how scared and worried I was for them, because that would only make them more scared and worried.

For their part, they tried to act like they didn't hear me. The moment I invited them in, all eyes dropped to the ground, not ready to trust anyone yet, in a world they already knew could never be trusted.

"Well, thanks, but not now," the leader finally said. "We got it all figured out. We're like a family. We take care of each other."

These teens did not trust any adult, and with good reason. Adults had rejected them, abused them, taken advantage of them. So the very basic resilience factor, the very first building block of resilience is absent. And when trust in adults is absent, the teens look to each other, form their own family, and trust only each other. But not being able to trust adults who are the ones to promote resilience, to provide education and services, to provide trusting love, is to relegate these teens primarily to surviving.

The woman from the shelter knew what their future held as she reflected on her experience with them. She so much wanted to help them but realized what happens when trust in adults is destroyed. Surviving is necessary, but not enough, as she reviewed the experience.

I resisted the temptation to lecture them about their dream world. They probably wouldn't listen . . . and they'll learn soon enough on their own. I just hope they're still alive to learn. I wanted to yell: You call this a family! A family is supposed to protect children and help them prepare for life! Not one of you is over 18. You don't know anything about life yet! But you're going to learn. You're going to learn about pimps and pushers. You're going to learn about pneumonia—and even about worse diseases. You're going to learn about hunger and how quickly you can die. Have you thought about that?

Have you thought about the rest of your lives? Do you really want to live in a cement box forever? And if not, how will you ever get out of here?

I'll tell you how, because there are only three ways: drugs, prostitution . . . or death. That's it, kids. That's your future.

These teens understood enough about living to form a family of their own, with a leader and with trust among its members. What they did not understand was that their acts could only be temporarily successful and that the realities of life as they were living it could only end in disaster and tragedy. Their understandable lack of trust in adults had to be overcome. Here is a true story that demonstrates how to rebuild lost trust and help one teen get out of life on the streets.

Food for Connection

A worker with runaways had food for them every day, serving it on the same spot. She was a steady presence. She could be counted on to be on the same spot every day, and they would come for the free food because they got hungry. The worker would talk to them, and one young man, about 14 years of age, who was a street prostitute, was responding to her a little bit. After she felt he trusted her enough to listen to her, she said to him, "You know, at some point I can get you out of this place and these problems, and I would really like to work with you."

He listened to her, thought about what she promised but said, "No, don't do anything for me; take care of my sister and brother who are still at home in that situation."

She was stunned by his unexpected response, but finally said, "What a wonderful human being you are! Such empathy, such caring for your sister and brother!" She not only had developed a trusting relationship with him, but now she was pointing out what he was demonstrating in terms of resilience.

Well, hearing this stunned him. No one had ever mentioned anything to him that he had done right. Wasn't he seen as a troublemaker doing all those sick things on the streets?

The interaction with the woman changed his life. It was, indeed, a transforming experience. He did accept her help, and he did get out of the situation. He developed skills in computers, got a job, and completed his transformation. She helped at every step and made sure the brother and sister received the help they needed.

Resilience Before and After

There are few people who have no resilience factors. It is more accurate to say that everyone has some resilience factors but that too many do not have enough or do not know how to use the ones they have to deal with adversities. One of the ways to promote resilience in these people is to identify the resilience factors they already have, to build on them and strengthen them, and to promote resilience factors that are weak or nonexistent. Thus, when children, like street children, are brought into programs to help them, it is important to know what resilience is already there, what is missing, and use the program to incorporate this knowledge as the children participate.

I was a member of the Street Children Expert Panel to assess the resilience of street children who were participating in programs to help them get off the streets. It was my responsibility to provide reliable information on resilience so that the resilience of these children could be measured at the time of entry into a program and after completing a program. The children were on the streets in Peru and Brazil, but their experiences and the role of resilience in their lives are universal. Cultural and geographic differences are minimal in relation to resilience (Grotberg, 2000, 2001).

What were the adversities encountered by children living on the street prior to entry into the program? Most of the children, ages 14 and under, were using one or more drugs nearly every day prior to entering the program. Although they were young males, about one-quarter of them said they had sold sex for money, food, or drugs, and about half of those said they seldom used condoms. About three-quarters of the children reported having used a weapon in a fight, and most reported that the police had threatened them at least once or twice. Six out of 10 children indicated they had been beaten at least once or twice by the police, and about one-third said they were beaten by the police every day.

These children tended to be from single-parent homes, had little education, and had either skin or respiratory problems when they entered the program. They had been on the streets from one month to 10 years before entering the program.

How were children recruited for the programs? Most of the children said they entered the programs because they wanted to change their lives and stop using drugs. Many first heard about the programs through program street workers. These street workers approach children in the street cautiously and try to win their trust. The majority of children were referred by these street workers or by other programs.

The programs seek to rehabilitate children from using drugs and remove them from life on the street by building their character, instilling self-confidence, and giving them opportunities to acquire new skills that will enable them to lead productive lives. Some of the program elements include

1. substance abuse detoxification and education,
2. positive reinforcement of desirable behavior and strengthening existing skills,
3. spiritual and emotional development models,
4. cognitive approach through development of reading skills and reintegration into school,
5. therapeutic approach of conducting psychological evaluations and providing personal counseling to children who have problems,
6. health assessment and health care access,
7. life skills and social skill development,
8. sex education,
9. child advocacy with courts, family, getting enrolled in schools, and health care, and
10. family therapy.

The success of the programs tended to be related to how long the children stayed in a program. Furthermore, if the children had been on drugs and came from badly structured families who had given up on them, they tended to leave before they were ready. Another group that left too early tended to be those who had difficulty living with rules, discipline, and authority and who were also attracted by drugs and the freedom of street life.

What are the goals of the programs? The goals of programs set the stage for what will happen to the children during their stay. The goals to be achieved are to help them

1. see themselves as valued individuals who deserve respect,
2. have ethical standards, morals, and respect for others,
3. learn there are adults they can trust,
4. become more educated,

5. build work trades and skills to help them become independent and cope with life,

6. avoid destructive and violent behavior,

7. eliminate drug use,

8. reintegrate each child with family and society, and

9. learn appropriate behavior that will allow them to be integrated with society and become productive citizens.

The underlying philosophy is the belief that change is possible and can be attained through respect and personal development. Program staff recognize that they serve as substitute parents for street children and may be the only adults that the children have learned to trust. They think it is important not to give up on the children, to build their self-esteem, to make them feel special, unique, and valued, and to respect their individuality and confidentiality.

Initially, program staff ensure that the children have a place to sleep and solve basic problems, such as getting them nourishment, clothing, and medical treatment. They use a multidisciplinary approach to child development. Staff psychologists conduct a psychological evaluation and provide individual counseling as needed. In addition to general educational programs offered through local schools, children receive occupational training and participate in artistic workshops. There are workshops where the children can learn computer skills, carpentry, music, art, etc. There are also workshops dealing with substance abuse, sex education, and other life skills. When necessary, program staff serve as advocates with the courts, police, and getting special health care.

The success of the programs was achieved when the children demonstrated

1. self-motivation to stay off drugs and avoid violent behavior,

2. ability to set goals, have patience, and delay gratification,

3. development of individual interests and vocational skills,

4. ability to accept personal responsibility and the consequences of their actions,

5. feelings of self-worth,

6. survival and coping skills, and

7. capacity to be grateful.

When children dropped out it was usually because they had trouble living with rules, discipline, and authority. They were attracted to the freedom of life on the streets and all that entailed, including drugs and sex. Often they displayed no affection and had difficulty bonding with anyone.

The resilience these children demonstrated on entering the program was already impressive. Through focus group sessions with the staff, it was determined that these are the external supports (I HAVE), inner strengths (I AM), and interpersonal and problem-solving skills (I CAN) identified in the children:

1. They recognize that they want something better for themselves (I AM respectful of myself).
2. They create tribal communities with other children; help each other in hunting for food and money; and share with others (I HAVE trusting, loving relationships).
3. They demonstrate boldness/courage; can't show fear (I AM confident and optimistic).
4. They demonstrate perseverance; like challenges (I CAN stay with a task; solve problems).
5. They have energy (I CAN generate new ideas and ways to do things).
6. They have keen powers of observation, very analytical and perceptive (I CAN solve problems).
7. They are manipulative; always testing themselves and staff to see how far they can get (not a resilience factor; needs substitution).
8. They are reluctant to accept new kids; jealousy (not a resilience factor; needs substitution).
9. They show loyalty to those who help them (I HAVE trusting relationships; I AM empathic and caring of others; I CAN reach out for help when I need it).

The length of time in the program determined how much resilience would be developed further. Those who stayed in the program longest were more hopeful about the future, found they had greater faith in God, wanted to help others, liked to joke, and would help or defend their friends. The children had acquired skills and education so that they were not so vulnerable to the actions of others. They usually returned to their families and were able to accept limits to their behavior. In other words, they strengthened the resilience factors they had on entry and added to them while in the program, which prepared them to deal with the adversities of life they would inevitably face.

The wonderful thing about promoting resilience is that some resilience factors are almost always in a person. These can be identified and built upon and other resilience factors can be promoted at the same time. Furthermore, these factors—both the ones already there as well as those being promoted—can be redirected to deal with adversities in more socially acceptable and beneficial ways and settings. Look at each of the resilience factors and think about how they could be redirected. Here are some examples.

They Recognize That They Want Something Better for Themselves

The children are now ready to be receptive to new ideas and suggestions about what will be better for them than the streets. This is an opportunity to have materials and suggestions around and available so that choices can be made. Because many of the street children go to school while in a program, the teachers and counselors have important roles to play.

They Have Solidarity, As Defined by Being Supportive of Each Other and Protecting and Defending Each Other

This ability to stick together, to help each other in hunting for food and money, and to share it, is a kind of family. And it is in a family setting that trust can be developed, that most critical of resilience factors and first building block of life and of resilience. These children, many of whom did not want to go back to their abusive families, did, however, learn how to trust others. Without such trust, they can only function by being in full control of themselves and those around them, a lonely, even dangerous kind of living. Fear of loss of control tends to destroy relationships.

They Have Boldness and Courage and Do Not Show Fear

The ability not to show fear is certainly protective when someone wants to abuse you or take advantage of you. Too many times, showing fear is just what a bully, a predator, wants. You are easier to control if you are afraid. Fear is a real emotion and many situations tap it. Fear needs to be recognized so that you can deal with what is making you afraid. Sharing feelings of fear with those you trust helps you minimize those feelings in deciding what to do. You also can get support and encouragement from the person you trusted enough to share your feelings with.

They Have Perseverance and Like Challenges

Staying with a task, refusing to give up, can be shifted from using that talent to steal, for example, to being determined to master a course in school, to sticking with any problem, any adversity in life, until you find a solution.

They Have Energy

In many ways, energy seems tied to temperament. Those who seem to have a great deal of energy also seem to respond quickly to stimuli. They give the impression they are ready to act at any moment and have plenty of energy to go along with that. However, even those whose temperament is more moderate can corral energy for a task and make a commitment to accomplish something. That street children found energy important is interesting because it suggests their initial moving onto the streets was aided by having a good deal of energy to go and to be able to stay and survive—important to relationships, jobs, a country.

They Have Keen Powers of Observation and Are Very Analytical and Perceptive

This ability suggests intelligence, and the children may well have benefited from such intelligence. To survive they needed to watch what was going on around them, recognize danger, and analyze not only the extent of the danger but find solutions. It may well be that street children need intelligence in order to survive. However, this kind of intelligence is not necessary to becoming resilient. But, just think what an advantage this particular kind of intelligence can be in a family, in a community, in a country. Such intelligence can be applied to becoming a lawyer, a doctor, a mechanic, a writer, a salesman, and many more satisfying occupations.

They Are Manipulative, Always Testing Themselves and Staff

This is not a desirable quality to have. No one likes to be manipulated, thus this skill will need to be translated into negotiation skills where there are some rules of conduct.

They Are Reluctant to Accept New Kids and Are Jealous

This, too, is not a desirable quality to have. Jealousy is a most unpleasant feeling, and while it is real and needs to be acknowledged, it also needs to be dealt with. These children had so little affection, so little attention, they found anyone a threat to the seeming limited amount of affection and attention in the program. Dealing with this emotion might be aided by assigning the jealous person to guide the newcomer and show the newcomer the ropes.

They Are Loyal to Those Who Help Them

Loyalty is a wonderful emotion and creates an atmosphere of confidence, concern, and caring that assures everyone is in a safe, caring environment.

Accidents

Resilience helps in the recovery, readjustment, and even transformation of those who experience the tragedy of being in an accident that dramatically changes their lives.

The Broken Back

A man whose life revolved around skiing broke his back in a skiing accident and, for him, life had ended. He sank to the depths of despair, and when he could tolerate no more pain and suffering, he considered suicide. It was such an easy way to end all of this; just to get out of it. But, as he contemplated suicide, he felt the strong counterpull of survival. He called it a white vision. He decided to live and to find meaning to life again, to find a mission to justify going on. He thought about what that mission should be and finally said to himself, "I'm a social guy. I love to talk to people. I'll become a talk show host on the radio." And so he did. His mission, as he saw it, was to send hope and cheer to anyone who needed it. He was transformed by tragedy as he drew on his resilience. He drew from I HAVE support services to help me. He drew from I AM respectful of myself; empathic and altruistic; responsible for what I do; and optimistic and confident. He drew from the I CAN factors: share thoughts and feelings; find ways to solve problems; manage my behavior when I feel like doing something not right or dangerous; find someone to help me. His resilience helped him build a new, satisfying life of giving, sharing, and helping.

The Car Did It

A woman who liked doing her daily run left the house for that pleasure one day and didn't return home for four months. She had been hit by a car going 40 miles an hour, thrown into the air, then onto the windshield, the hood, and, finally landed on the road. Her life was turned upside down. She had come face to face with death. Her values had been challenged and continued to change as she was recovering. She didn't move gracefully, even though she had been very physical and strong, knowing exactly how she wanted to move and doing so. When she saw videos and photos of herself after the accident, she really got a shock because she had turned into a little girl. Like a little girl, she looked awkward and unsure of herself, very slow and uncoordinated.

She needed someone to help her deal with this tragedy, to find the resilience she already had, and to promote what needed to be added so that she could emerge a stronger person. She got that help and through it was able to triumph over the tragedy.

Here are some of the interactions that identified resilience factors already used and promoted those needing to be developed or strengthened:

Helper: Let's talk about what happened after your accident. You may be familiar with the idea of resilience. Some people are resilient, which means they will cope with a disaster, despite the odds. How did you feel about yourself once you realized what happened?

Victim: From the moment I woke up in the hospital, I thought I was going to be okay.

Helper: You remember having that thought?

Victim: Oh, yeah. I remember having a clear decision to make: You can die here or will yourself to be miserable and take the hard road. I do remember a clear choice: It was I was going the other way, which is I am going to be okay. I was going to fight! Most of the time I thought I was going to be okay. There were hideous days as well. I remember just feeling so desperate, so depressed, scared, and miserable. I felt a mess, a broken mess.

Helper: I want to hear the steps you took after you decided you would be okay.

Victim: At the trauma center, I was in a ward on my own because I was so seriously hurt. Once I was off the serious list, I think that was after about five days or a week, they moved me into a shared ward. I remember lying in bed when my father was visiting, and he said: "I would do anything to trade places with you." He is 78 and still at that age your child is your child, and I remember being heartbroken for him because I actually felt stronger, or so I thought! I wanted to just hug him and say don't worry, I'm fighting, it's awful, but I'll pull through. It broke my heart. I couldn't hug him because I was too damned sore and broken and unable to move. But I remember then deciding about having children. There was a small percentage of me still open to the possibility of having a child. But I decided I wouldn't because I couldn't bear anything to happen to my child. You see, I had returned to being a baby myself, and that was enough. The physical and emotional pain and vulnerability was too great. I couldn't take that risk.

The victim is demonstrating an extraordinary amount of empathy, a powerful I AM resilience factor, in her interaction with her father. She is able to submerge her suffering to show caring about him. And her reluctance to have a child is also related to her sense of empathy for suffering, but now her own suffering.

Helper: How about your fiancé; how has he dealt with your accident?

Victim: He was just extraordinary. In terms of deeply affecting him, he always says he is fine. I think he trusted me, really. I think he always believed I was going to be okay, which is quite surprising. At some stages he was affected by my tears. He would try to have a solution, he would say, "don't cry." I said to him, it's okay, I have to cry. He accepted that eventually and let me cry. He still does this, although I don't cry as much. I think he was afraid. It has brought us really close.

Her ability to share thoughts and feelings with her fiancé helped her use an I CAN resilience factor to enrich the relationship as well as work through her own feelings.

Helper: Did you share a lot of activities together, and now that you are well along in your recovery, are you still sharing activities?

Victim: Yes, we did everything together. But, this year, even when I am still recovering, what I have done is absolutely ridiculous, crazy, considering my lack of mobility, double vision, and a few other problems.

Helper: Tell me what you have done.

Victim: Well, I got out of the hospital one month and we took a vacation the next month. You know I was on crutches, had to wear a brace on my leg, and could barely walk. I hobbled onto the plane, climbed stairs to get from the room to the beach, I got into a boat and got out of the boat. I did it because I knew it would make me better. But my fiancé always encouraged me to do it. He is a very positive person, full of love; he's kind and helped me enormously. Remember, these activities were done very slowly, with lots of stops, and lots of help, but I persevered!

She had outside support from a loving, trusting person, which added to her sense of value, to her confidence that she would overcome this tragedy.

Helper: And what else?

Victim: He also encouraged me back into the swimming pool, in that he was always routine oriented, and eager to see me back in the water. I went from dog paddle to learning to swim again. We walked and walked. I dragged myself back and I would be exhausted. Tiredness would then cause my eyes to falter even further. I could only dog paddle because of weakness in my legs and arms, plus I couldn't move my broken arm very far—forget moving it for freestyle.

Helper: When you say you dog paddled, you were aware that you were a phenomenal swimmer. You had to retrain your muscles.

Victim: I still do. It is not 100 percent. I still can't lift my arm naturally.

Helper: So you are still aware of your limits.

Victim: Yes. I do things that I don't think I can do, like reaching for the towel on the towel rack, trying to get something out of the cupboard. I want to get it because that is what gets my muscles moving. I need to feel independent and on the way to gaining some sort of control again.

Independence, or autonomy, is a resilience factor as is trust in one's body. These resilience factors incorporate a sense of control. The need to feel in control of one's body, of one's life, is deep and persistent. The fear of loss of control accounts for much behavior that is dangerous or destructive, especially when it often leads to trying to control others. The opposite of that is to become dependent on others and let them control. Either extreme is destructive to a person's ability to become resilient and to draw on resilience to deal with the adversities, the tragedies of life.

Helper: You indicated earlier that a book had been closed on your life as a result of this experience. What book closed?

Victim: The book closed on any work-related nonsense and time wasting.

Helper: About simple issues like, Do I have to have notoriety? Do I have to be at the top? All those things? Is that what you mean?

Victim: Yes—generally work/office politics and pettiness.

Helper: In other words, external validation was no longer important.

Victim: Yes.

Helper: For the first time in your life?

Victim: I don't think it's 100 percent yet, but it has certainly moved on. And also, where people seem stuck and/or unaware of how fortunate many of us really are. Actually, I think I was already beginning to step away from old ways. You know, something else that is really profound has come out of it. I am okay. You know, I trust myself more. I think I am really strong. I am vulnerable as well, you know, all those things, but I am trying to find the right word. Strong is a bit obvious, but I trust myself. I think I am okay. I do remember thinking in the hospital that I am equipped for this. I am emotionally and spiritually equipped for it. I know what to do here, and I had a plan. I had quite a plan right away. You know, I had rituals and I knew physically what to do, mentally what to do. Having said this, I also had very, very low times, desperate and very fearful. Days where I felt hopeless.

The resilience factor trust is the most basic in all human relationships and human functioning. As was pointed out with runaways, if there is no trust, and especially if there is no trust on oneself, life is reduced to fear, depression, suspicion, cynicism, and, usually, anger and hostility. The strength derived from trusting oneself provides the confidence and faith that events can be dealt with, overcome, even instructive.

Helper: You remember actually making up your mind?

Victim: Yes, yes, absolutely, definitely, on everything.

Helper: So actually you have also the resilience that is there, I can do it whatever it is. Each day is going to be better than the one before.

Victim: Yes. Most days I think about it. Some days I slip, and some days I don't think so. But even when I am feeling that way, what is running beside it is, "You are going to be all right, you are going to be all right."

Helper: Do you actually remember a point at which you thought, "I can choose?"

Victim: Yes, it was in the hospital. I think it was when I was coming out of a coma. I thought: Do you want to die? Do you want to die of misery? Do you want to die of pain? Do you literally want to die here? Or do you want to get better and have a good life?

Helper: What do you think you need to say to other people so that they can know what this means?

Victim: What happens when an accident happens?

Helper: No, for you personally. I think that what you are really saying is you don't want to continue as before—you want to be at a very rich level of existence now.

Victim: Yes. I don't want to be mediocre, and I don't want this accident to just be shoved under the carpet. At the same time, I don't

want that to be my identity, and I don't want that to define me. It
is vital that I live a life with great passion, purpose, and meaning—
more than ever—and appreciate it properly.

Helper: So what is the difference in what you are going to do now?

Victim: I want to pursue feeling better, you know. I don't think that I
am there. I think it changes all the time, but I certainly feel very
strong within myself and I am very self-contained, a sense of great
calm. So what is it that I am going to do? I would be lying if I said
I have 100 percent come to a conclusion, but it looks something
like: Don't procrastinate, change negative patterns, be aware of
them and change them. Life is precious, movement and sight are
precious—appreciate it, get it back, and love it. Compliment others.
Notice things more, listen more!

Helper: Right, so you are saying that one thing was truth, the second
one is to get rid of negativity, third, you said something about
being really good, something about morality. I wasn't sure what
you said.

Victim: Living life honestly, with integrity, and being kind and good to
one another. I feel like I am on a big dipper because I feel close to
people again, and then I don't, and then I do, and then I don't, and
then I feel I get disconnected, and then I feel like, thank goodness,
it is back to normal again, and then in between all that I feel guilty
and I feel ungrateful and I feel a bit ungracious. It is not terrible, it
is not as though those feelings overcome me, but they are certainly
there. I am just sorting through that now.

Hope, optimism, faith in the future, a sense of morality, integrity,
empathy, altruism—these are all high levels of the quality of life, are
goals for countless people, and are resilience factors from I AM, the
inner strengths. Growth in these resilience factors is often the result
of experiences of tragedy. Resilience can transform a person, as certainly is the case with this victim.

Illness

Tragedy in the home often comes in the form of illness. Suddenly, a
family member is diagnosed with a disease that has limited possibilities
of cure. How do family members deal with that? How does the person
diagnosed deal with that? And what do they do when the illness lingers
on for years? And what do parents do when the victim is a young girl?
Megan had been diagnosed with brain cancer five years earlier and
had undergone surgery, radiation, and gene therapy. She was hoping

to avoid chemotherapy, because she didn't want to lose her hair. After all, she was a teenager! But the tumor was growing again. The specialist went over the options with Megan's parents and cautioned them that the chance of any treatment curing her at this point was diminishing. He said that chemotherapy would help reduce the headaches and fatigue Megan constantly felt, as well as her brief spells of dizziness and double vision. The family had to make the decision; it should not be made for them.

The parents wanted to talk about the options before they involved Megan. But, she saw that her mother had been crying and asked about it; so her mother, feeling Megan deserved an answer, told her the truth. There was no reaction from Megan. Knowing how Megan felt about chemotherapy, the parents tried to ease her past her mental block against chemotherapy, since that was the only option left. They were not able to help her, but a neurologist on the staff did. He explained that one of the hardest things for a cancer patient was to even consider another tough treatment when she was feeling good. She wanted to know if she would lose her hair if she agreed to the treatment he suggested. He said she probably would, but that it would grow back when the treatment stopped. He explained how the chemotherapy would work, and he explained the dangers attached to it.

Megan was a typical teenager and wanted to behave as one—she wanted to be accepted and do what her friends do. She wanted to be at school and be part of the scene there. Her parents and school personnel agreed on a special curriculum for Megan that allowed her to carry only half a schedule. A teacher, who was also Megan's on-campus guardian, worked with Megan and the family to adapt to Megan's changing needs. For example, as she lost her ability to remember things she was learning through hearing, she was taught through visual images.

Megan tried to be as normal as possible and to be accepted. She refused offers of special trips or outings by her parents because she just wanted to be treated as a normal kid. Couldn't they understand that? Her close friend said that Megan was one of the bravest people she had met. Megan shared her feelings with her friend, and when the friend realized something was wrong because Megan seemed especially upset, she took Megan to the counselor. When Megan cried about taking the chemotherapy, her friend said it was okay to be scared. The pediatric cancer specialist talked to her about day-to-day concerns related to chemotherapy and told her to keep up her energy by eating whatever appealed to her. He also talked about ways to deal with her hair if it began to fall out. He suggested a shorter hair style that made use of wigs and scarves. Megan's sister said she would shave off her own hair if Megan's came out, and the younger brother said his was already so short it would be like being bald, too. The entire family had been with her during the chemotherapy sessions.

Megan's teacher, who knew she loved young children and was aware that she could not take difficult subjects, got her into a preschool three days a week to acquire credits in life skills at the high school. The children adored her.

Each summer for four years Megan had attended Camp Fantastic for one week. The children who attend are also ill with some condition, but the camp leaders are used to seeing kids, not diseases. For one, the kids don't have to explain anything to anybody. The goal of the camp is to get the kids who are fighting for their lives to say, "I can do this!"

Let's look at how resilience was promoted and applied in the family as it dealt with the severe health problems Megan faced.

I HAVE Trusting Relationships

The love and trust in the family were always there for each member, and there was never any wavering in its consistency. Megan could trust her parents to be honest with her, and they were. When she asked her mother why she had been crying, the mother did not try to conceal what she had just learned from the doctor. The brother and sister were also supportive and did an especially endearing thing when they talked about what they would do with their own hair, as it became clear Megan would lose hers. The doctors, nurses, and teachers never betrayed or abused the trust the family placed in them.

Teachers changed the curriculum for Megan as her condition worsened, knowing she wanted to stay in school and be with her peers. Her doctor expressed empathy over her fears about losing her hair but he did not attempt to gloss over the fact that she would probably lose it.

I HAVE Access to Services

The family had access to the best services and the resources to pay for them. This is not always the case, but you can see how effective such access is for people facing tragedies. She had a teacher who was willing to be quite flexible about Megan's course of study, not only in the way she could learn (visually, with less focus on hearing) but also in what she could learn (arranging school credits through preschool work). The opportunity to attend Camp Fantastic was especially helpful.

I HAVE a Stable Family

The family was constant in its support of Megan and made changes as her condition required. Megan knew her family was there for her. Her parents offered special trips or outings and allowed Megan the opportunity to decide for herself whether or not she needed those things. The entire family had been with her during the chemotherapy sessions.

I AM a Person Most People Like

Megan had many friends, and even the children she taught liked her. She had a best friend, but was liked by her peer group as well. It did not matter that she was limited in what she could do. She was accepted. Her best friend liked her so much she kept an eye on her emotional state, and when Megan seemed especially upset, she even took her to the school counselor to make sure she'd be okay.

I AM Generally Good-Natured

Megan had the ability to distance herself from some of the more distressing aspects of her increasingly serious health condition. She kept active and attempted to focus on things she could do and let go of the things she could not do. Her strong desire to perform as much school work as she could, even if it meant just half a schedule, is a good example of this.

I CAN Stay with a Task

Megan was persistent in her work, whether it was with the young children or in her assignments. She returned to them as soon as she recovered from therapy, and she stayed with them as long as her health permitted.

I CAN Express Thoughts and Feelings in Communication with Others

Megan had an indirect way of communicating with others—she did much of her communicating through the choices she made. She wanted to be like other teens. She wanted a sense of identity. She insisted on being treated like her peers. She did not want special trips or outings.

Notice that not all the resilience factors were used as Megan, her family, and those around her helped her deal with her adversity, her tragedy. Different resilience factors were used by different people, playing different roles, as a tragedy was faced and dealt with. Each drew from the pool of resilience factors, selecting those most likely to achieve the result: helping Megan deal with the tragedy.

Special Tragedies

Tragedies seem inevitable. You may have experienced a tragedy or may even be in the midst of one; certainly, you know someone who has experienced a tragedy. A tragedy, as you know, is often in the eye of the beholder. However, there are experiences a person, a group, or even a nation has, that are clearly seen as tragedies.

The tragedy of the Vietnam prisoners of war is one such tragedy that no one questions. American pilots were shot down over Vietnam, beginning in 1963, and many stayed prisoners for more than seven years in the most unhealthy and brutal circumstances. Here were American pilots, who were the cream of the crop, as they liked to identify themselves, flying with great confidence and pride, suddenly being downed. Their coming had been known to the Vietnamese soldiers. The capture of these pilots and crews was the beginning of a life in small, dark cells, repeated series of torture, including arms being twisted to separate from sockets, beatings, breaking bones, and lack of food or medical care. They were considered war criminals, and they needed to think about what they would do.

The prisoners report that they had to keep thinking about their situation and resist revealing military secrets under the pressure of brutality. They reported that the American flag stands for freedom, and the enemy can't take that away. When they realized they had to bail out of the planes, for some, their life passed before them as they floated down in parachutes. For some, 100 rifles were aimed at them, and they put up their hands. They realized they were not invincible and were scared. As they were walked to the prison, people stoned them and spit on them, and some children stuck bamboo sticks into their skin.

One man reported that his leg had been thrown out of joint at the knee, and one of the Vietnamese soldiers, after reading hand signals from the prisoner of what he needed, actually pulled the leg back into shape. Not all enemies were monsters. One pilot had a gun with him but decided not to kill himself.

The families back home, learning of the fate of their husbands, fathers, sons, lived from day to day, hoping their loved one wasn't being tortured. They didn't want to believe people would be cruel.

But the cruelty was extreme, and the men reported losing control of bowels, vomiting, to the point they would sell their mother to relieve the agony. They made up stories and gave false information in hopes the torture would stop. As one prisoner said, "Actually, beatings are easy. After so much pain, your body just shuts down. And you would roll back, bounce back. You took torture as long as you could and gave as little information as possible."

The prisoners decided they couldn't break. They would pray, and some would put a rag in their mouth so their screams could not be heard. Or they screamed into a blanket when they thought of the length of time they would have to be prisoners. When one man was told by his fellow prisoner, it would probably be two more years before they got out, he could handle that. But then, two more years went by, and then two more years, and then more, for a total of seven. They also developed a communication system with each other, using tapping codes on walls. Different taps and combinations of taps were developed over time—the prisoners could communicate. Later, they developed visual codes with their hands and, without seeing each other, got to know each other. The guards wanted to prevent communication to prevent the prisoners from getting strength from each other. The guards hurt the leaders badly, but they came back, still the leaders.

When prisoners were put on television, they gave signals that they were being tortured so that America knew what was happening. They did this at great risk, but were determined to communicate.

Health was a critical problem, and one man couldn't sleep because of boils all over his body. He dealt with this pain by squeezing the puss out of the boils and painting a picture on the wall with it. He also decided he would draw what he saw and experienced when he got out, and he did.

When the torture was too great to tolerate and a soldier wrote a confession, he would return to his cell, cry like a baby, because he felt he had let his country down. "You do your best," one prisoner said. "You lie, cheat, steal, but you are not giving anything away. You want to return with honor to America." They looked out for each other: All they had was each other and their reputation.

The changing attitude in America that the war was wrong caused the families of the prisoners to stop talking about their loved ones. And, when the prisoners heard about the protests in America, they were stunned.

Some of the prisoners memorized the names of other prisoners, probably through the tapping system. They repeated these names after they were released so that all prisoners could be accounted for. One prisoner used a singsong for his list, and when asked to slow down, he said he couldn't. They could tape his words and slow down the tape.

Members of families of the prisoners began to organize to protest the way the war was going and to demand that their loved ones receive more humane treatment. It was not until 1969 that policy was changed and international rules became mandatory.

Prisoners had ways to live through each day. One, an engineer by training, built a house in his head, taking care of each step in the process. Others wrote poetry in their head. Some dwelled on their wives and children; others couldn't. One had to move or die, as he indicated, and so he would run in place, do sit-ups and other exercises, and prayed a lot. Every Sunday they signaled each other for prayer; then signaled for the pledge of allegiance. They would set up short-term targets—home for Christmas, home by Thanksgiving. They had an abiding faith that their country was not going to forget them, and that helped sustain them. The prisoners said they did what they could to maintain a quality of life.

When war was over in 1972, the prisoners thought they would be cheering wildly, but, in fact, they were quiet. Those who had been in longest said they would believe peace when they saw it. They were emotionally drained and had been fooled too many times. They had built an emotional shield, and it took time to break that after they were released. It was hard for them to shed tears.

In retrospect, they felt that few people were called on to use everything they had. They felt they were better people as a result of the experience. They noted that they were warmly treated when they returned to America, but that other soldiers did not get the same reception, honor, or care they received. Their dearest friends continued to be cell mates and they refused to become bitter. They felt that bitterness destroys, and their greatest satisfaction was that they were alive. That was better than being listed as being killed in action.

The resilience in these men is clear. They built trusting relationships among themselves and became role models for each other, especially the leaders. They drew on inner strengths of faith, confidence, self-respect, and respect for others, keeping an even temperament and showing empathy and caring for each other. They used interpersonal and problem-solving skills, managed their own feelings and behavior; and reached out to each other for help as they dealt with the extreme adversities they faced each day, each year.

No one questions that the events of September 11, 2001, were a major tragedy to the nation. The tragedy of terrorism is that it destroys not only lives, but, for many, arouses such fear that they cannot function. However, story after story about the way resilient people responded to the acts of terror provide real-life accounts of the value and role of resilience. The resilient people became stronger as they refused to succumb to the tragedies perpetrated by the terrorists. They were transformed as they decided to help others who experienced similar losses. They became, and still are, role models for the power of resilience to deal with tragedies. One family who lost a son in one of the World Trade buildings has set up a music scholarship because he loved music and, as the mother said, "He will be alive one day a year as the person who received the scholarship plays." High school youth, shocked into silence by the event, are looking for careers in human services at new, much higher rates. Schools played important roles in helping children deal with the tragedy, calling parents when that seemed appropriate, organizing group meetings to help those children having trouble dealing with the tragedy, and providing the services of counselors. Some schools distributed the booklet *What Do You Tell the Children?* (Baruch, Stutman, & Grotberg, 1995) or referred to a Web site where the booklet could be printed out. That booklet had been written after the Oklahoma bombing tragedy and had been used effectively by others. Governmental leaders, from mayors to state and national officials, became role models for how to deal with the tragedy. Volunteers, from psychologists and social workers to health providers, from firemen and policemen to groups providing food and even dry socks for the people cleaning up the site, demonstrated the determination to deal with the tragedy as they engaged in resilience behavior.

References

Baruch, R., Stutman, S., & Grotberg, E. H. (1995). *What do you tell the children? How to help children deal with disasters.* Washington, D.C.: Institute for Mental Health Initiatives.

Grotberg, E. H. (2000). International resilience research project. In A. L. Comunian & U. Gielen (Eds.), *International perspectives on human development* (pp. 379–399). Vienna, Austria: Pabst Science Publishers.

Grotberg, E. H. (2001). Resilience programs from children in disaster. *Ambulatory Child Health, 7,* 75–83.

INDEX

About the Series Editor and Advisory Board

CHRIS E. STOUT, Psy.D., MBA, holds a joint governmental and academic appointment in Northwestern University Medical School and serves as Illinois' first chief of psychological services. He served as an NGO special representative to the United Nations, was appointed by the U.S. Department of Commerce as a Baldridge examiner, and served as an advisor to the White House for both political parties. He was appointed to the World Economic Forum's Global Leaders of Tomorrow. He has published and presented more than 300 papers and 29 books. His works have been translated into six languages.

BRUCE E. BONECUTTER, Ph.D., is director of behavioral services at the Elgin Community Mental Health Center, the Illinois Department of Human Services state hospital serving adults in greater Chicago. He is also a clinical assistant professor of psychology at the University of Illinois at Chicago. A clinical psychologist specializing in health, consulting, and forensic psychology, Bonecutter is also a longtime member of the American Psychological Association Taskforce on Children and the Family.

JOSEPH A. FLAHERTY, M.D., is chief of psychiatry at the University of Illinois Hospital, a professor of psychiatry at the University of Illinois College of Medicine, and a professor of community health science at the University of Illinois College of Public Health. He is a founding member of the Society for the Study of Culture and Psychiatry. Dr. Flaherty has been a consultant to the World Health Organization, to the National Institutes of Mental Health, and also the Falk Institute in Jerusalem.

MICHAEL HOROWITZ, Ph.D., is president and professor of clinical psychology at the Chicago School of Professional Psychology, one of the nation's leading not-for-profit graduate schools of psychology. Earlier, he served as dean and professor of the Arizona School of Professional Psychology. A clinical psychologist practicing independently since 1987, his work has focused on psychoanalysis, intensive individual therapy, and couples therapy. He has provided disaster mental health services to the American Red Cross. Dr. Horowitz' special interests include the study of fatherhood.

SHELDON I. MILLER, M.D., is a professor of psychiatry at Northwestern University and director of the Stone Institute of Psychiatry at Northwestern Memorial Hospital. He is also director of the American Board of Psychiatry and Neurology, director of the American Board of Emergency Medicine, and director of the Accreditation Council for Graduate Medical Education. Dr. Miller is also an examiner for the American Board of Psychiatry and Neurology. He is founding editor of the *American Journal of Addictions* and founding chairman of the American Psychiatric Association's Committee on Alcoholism.

DENNIS P. MORRISON, Ph.D., is chief executive officer at the Center for Behavioral Health in Indiana, the first behavioral health company ever to win the JCAHO Codman Award for excellence in the use of outcomes management to achieve health care quality improvement. He is president of the board of directors for the Community Healthcare Foundation in Bloomington and has been a member of the board of directors for the American College of Sports Psychology. He has served as a consultant to agencies including the Ohio Department of Mental Health, Tennessee Association of Mental Health Organizations, Oklahoma Psychological Association, the North Carolina Council of Community Mental Health Centers, and the National Center for Heath Promotion in Michigan.

WILLIAM H. REID, M.D., MPH, is a clinical and forensic psychiatrist and consultant to attorneys and courts throughout the United States. He is clinical professor of psychiatry at the University of Texas Health Science Center. Dr. Miller is also an adjunct professor of psychiatry at Texas A&M College of Medicine and Texas Tech

University School of Medicine, as well as a clinical faculty member at the Austin Psychiatry Residency Program. He is chairman of the Scientific Advisory Board and medical advisor to the Texas Depressive & Manic-Depressive Association, as well as an examiner for the American Board of Psychiatry & Neurology. He has served as president of the American Academy of Psychiatry and the Law, as chairman of the Research Section for an International Conference on the Psychiatric Aspects of Terrorism, and as medical director for the Texas Department of Mental Health and Mental Retardation.

About the Editor
and Contributors

EDITH HENDERSON GROTBERG, Ph.D., is Adjunct Professor at the Institute for Mental Health Initiatives at the George Washington University. She became interested in resilience while the Director of Research for the Administration for Children, Youth and Families in the Department of Health and Human Services, Washington, D.C. Her concern about the ongoing research was that it consisted primarily of what was wrong with people. She found the initial research on resilience when she was asked to review a book on the subject. The research, however, left out how people became resilient; it was limited to identifying the factors of resilience found to help children deal with the adverse situations they were living in. Thus began the International Resilience Research Project which provided evidence that resilience can be promoted and used to deal with situations of adversity experienced in 27 sites in 22 countries around the world. The growing interest in resilience attests to its effectiveness. Dr. Grotberg is President of the International Council of Psychologists.

LILIAN AUTLER, M.A., is a Community Development Planner who works with communities to help them address the many problems communities face as they plan for the future. She engages in research on what effective communities look like and applies that information to communities she works with. She is also a translator, and translated this chapter from Spanish into English.

It seemed important to find resilient communities in the United States and E. H. Grotberg found two which are reported in the chapter.

RHODA BARUCH, Ed.D., established the Institute for Mental Health Initiatives (IMHI), which is now part of the George Washington University School of Public Health and Health Services. Her intent was to bring information about how to promote mental health via the media. This led to a series of conferences attended by writers and producers of radio and television shows who discussed how concepts of mental health could be incorporated into the shows. Parallel to this was a series of publications of *Dialogue,* which presented information on various topics of interest to the media. Resilience became a critical addition to the series as IMHI increasingly saw the role of resilience in dealing with specific problems, such as bullying, mismanaged anger, and depression.

STEPHANIE DELUCA, Ph.D., is a post-Doctoral Fellow in Developmental Psychology at the Civitan International Research Center. She provides therapy for some 60 families who have members with neuromotor impairments. She contributes stories to the chapter from her clinical work.

KAREN ECHOLS, M.D., is a pediatric physician at the Civitan International Research Center. She engages in therapy with children in community-based early intervention programs. Further, she is following 100 children through their developmental stages. She provides information to the chapter about the role of therapy in the promotion of resilience.

FRANCISCA INFANTE, Ed.M., is a Licensed Psychologist who has been involved with resilience since 1996. Her major area of interest is the role of resilience in Latino youth and families as they become immigrants and adapt to a new culture and society. She has evaluated the promotion of resilience programs among indigenous populations in Peru, Bolivia, and Argentina. These programs were supported by the Bernard van Leer Foundation as part of their interest in the promotion of resilience. Ms. Infante is the Specialist for Adolescent Development at the Pan American Health Organization (PAHO) in Washington, D.C. She was a major contributor to the *Manual for the Identification and Promotion of Resilience in Children and Youth,* published by PAHO in 1998.

BETTE KELTNER, Ph.D., R.N., FAAN, is the Dean of the School of Nursing and Health Studies at the Georgetown University, Washington, D.C. She is concerned about the long-term needs of children and youth with special health problems; especially as these needs affect family functioning. Much of her focus, then, is to help the children and youth become increasingly independent, using resilience to deal with their many problems. She goes into the field to gather her information and insights and finds the promotion of resilience a most effective contribution to the welfare of these children and youth and their families.

ALEXANDRA LAMOND, M.A., is a Clinical Social Worker in Brooklyn, New York. She is Program Manager for mental health programs in schools in Brooklyn. Her work has included providing services to populations in Mexico and with Latino immigrants in Washington, D.C. She provides many examples from her clinical work on the role of resilience in dealing with the many adversities immigrant youth face.

SANDRA E.S. NEIL, Ph.D., is Chair of the Satir Centre of Australia for the Family. Her work involves bringing family members together to resolve problems that disrupt family functioning. She draws on techniques developed by Virigina Satir, but has found that promoting resilience is a clear part of the process. She is a pioneer in the blending of resilience with the Satir approach to restoring family functioning. Her work on Human Rights around the world is enhanced as she incorporates the promotion of resilience in her many presentations.

RUSS NEWMAN, Ph.D., J.D., is a clinical psychologist as well as a lawyer who currently serves as Executive Director for Professional Practice for the American Psychological Association (APA). He has provided leadership in bringing resilience to the community through a vast network of local psychologists who were rallied as adversities hit different communities. His increased interest in the role of resilience in dealing with these adversities led to the development of a series of brochures, beginning with The Road to Resilience; followed by a series of brochures on Resilience in a Time of War, including one for those interacting with young children, early school-age children, middle school children, and with youth. There is also a brochure addressed directly to youth. And, most recently, the publications for teachers and others, *Teaching the 4th R: Resilience*, and *Give Yourself a Boost: Bounce-Back Strategies to Help with Life's Everyday Problems*. These publications are widely distributed to help in the promotion and use of resilience in times of great stress. They underline the importance of introducing concepts of resilience early in the lives of people and in already established institutions.

JUDY E. PAPHÁZY, Ph.D., is Director of the Counseling and Assessment Association in Melbourne, Australia. She has become a pioneer in bringing resilience into the schools of Australia, as teachers increasingly face behavior problems that threaten the well-being of children. Her style is to involve the entire school in promoting resilience rather than rely on a specific program or method of dealing with the targeted problems. She works directly with the teachers, providing examples of ways to deal with the problems as well as encouraging the teachers to become engaged in solving the problems and promoting resilience in the process. This is a variation to bringing in outside programs; rather it provides the information needed to promote resilience in real happenings.

SHARON LANDESMAN RAMEY, Ph.D., holds the Susan H. Mayor Professorship for Child and Family Development at the Georgetown Center for Health and Education, Georgetown University in Washington, D.C. Before coming to Washington, D.C., she was Co-Director, with her husband, Craig Ramey, of the Civitan International Research Center, University of Alabama at Birmingham. And it was there that the International Resilience Research Project was developed. The Rameys supported the research from its very beginning. They have also contributed extensively to research and publications concerning the development of children. In addition, Sharon focuses on helping families function with resilience as they provide loving care to their exceptional children.

SUZANNE STUTMAN, M.S., M.S.W., B.C.D., is the Director of the Institute for Mental Health Initiatives (IMHI) at the George Washington University School of Public Health and Health Services. She was the leader in developing the Anger Management books and materials for RETHINK, the acronym for learning how to manage anger. She participated in studies of resilience in Latino youth to determine the role of culture in the promotion of resilience. As a private clinician she continues to have firsthand experience with people who were having problems and found how resilience could help them in resolving their problems. She has joined with Dr. Baruch to provide clear examples of the role of controlled exposure to adversities rather than being protected from adversities.

ELBIO NESTOR SUAREZ-OJEDA, M.D., is Director of the Center for Resilience at the University of Lanus, Argentina. He was the recent Minister of Health for the Argentina Province, San Luis, and was a former official at the Pan American Health Organization, Washington, D.C. He was on the Advisory Committee for the International Resilience Research Project and translated into Spanish one of the publications: *A Guide to Promoting Resilience in Children.* He conducted studies on the status of services for maternal-infant health in seven countries in Latin America. He evaluated projects supported by the Bernard van Leer Foundation and became Director of the International Center to Study Resilience. He is the driving force that led to the recent law passed in Argentina that all training programs for service providers must incorporate the promotion of resilience in the curricula.

LESLIE WALKER, M.D., is Head of the Section, Adolescent Medicine, in the Department of Pediatrics, Georgetown University, Washington, D.C. She is involved with adolescents who are at high risk for behavioral problems, including drugs, abuse, violence, sexual promiscuity. She works with their families and develops prevention programs that are used, especially in middle schools, but also by the families.